T0380693

Lessons from My Father and Mother

The Triune Relationship of God with My Father and Mother

Robert K. Auten Jr.

WESTBOW
PRESS®
A DIVISION OF THOMAS NELSON
& ZONDERVAN

WestBow Press books may be ordered through booksellers or by contacting:

WestBow Press
A Division of Thomas Nelson & Zondervan
1663 Liberty Drive
Bloomington, IN 47403
www.westbowpress.com
844-714-3454

ISBN: 979-8-3850-2929-7 (sc)
ISBN: 979-8-3850-2930-3 (hc)
ISBN: 979-8-3850-2931-0 (e)

Library of Congress Control Number: 2024914300

Print information available on the last page.

WestBow Press rev. date: 10/24/2024

Contents

Part 2: Lessons from My Father

To God, my Heavenly Father, who created
me and chose my parents!
To Jesus, the Christ, my Lord, and my Savior!
To the Holy Spirit, who has shepherded
and directed my paths!
To my parents, Robert Keith Auten and
Alyce Dorothy Owens Auten.
To my siblings, Beverly Ann, Karen
Louise, and Daryl Eugene.
To my precious daughter, Johanna Christine Auten.

Preface

As we listen to the Lord through His Word, the Bible, and pay close attention to what He says. Hearing what is of utmost importance and value to Him is enlightening and wise. Since we were made in His image and are now His image bearers, what is most important to Him must also become most vital to us if we are to live in harmony with Him and dwell within His purpose for creating us.

Our acceptance, conformance, and adaptation to God and His will are how we harmonize with Him and live richly fulfilling lives within His grace and promises. We know that the Lord's exceedingly great desire for each of us is that we first reconcile with Him through Jesus Christ, our Lord and Savior, and then prosper in all things and be in health as our souls prosper (3 John 1:2). Jesus affirms God's desire for us as He spoke openly in John 10:10, saying He came so that we may have life and have it more abundantly. Interestingly, based on His Ten Commandments, God pronounces His desire for us to live long, healthy, and prosperous lives right from our entry into the world. He does it in the fifth commandment of the ten given to Moses on Mount Sinai. In addressing Ephesus's messianic and gentile believers, the apostle Paul emphasizes the magnitude and importance of our obedience to the fifth commandment when he glaringly points out that it is "the first commandment with promise." What the Ephesians, under the power of the Holy Spirit, heard Paul say was

> Children, obey your parents in the Lord, for this is right. "Honor your father and mother" which is the first commandment with promise: "that it may be well with you and you may live long on the earth." (Eph. 6:1–3)

The Ten Commandments were written on two stone tablets by the finger of God Himself (Deut. 9:10). God wrote the commandments in order of priority and significance to Himself, with five on each tablet. The first tablet contains God's commandments or laws regarding man's vertical relationship to Him. In contrast, the second tablet refers to commandments addressing our humanly horizontal relationships to one another here on earth. This commandment ordering gives us a clear picture of God's priority and the significance to Him of each commandment. Therefore, by its placement on the first stone tablet, obedience to and honoring our fathers and mothers is very high on God's priority and commandment list and part of our vertical relationship with Him. It also illuminates Jesus's precise description of the Ten Commandments and work of the prophets when He responded to a lawyer's question to Him.

> Teacher, which is the great commandment in the law? (Matt. 22:36)
>
> Jesus said to him, "You shall love the Lord your God with all your heart, with all your soul, and with all your mind." This is the first and great commandment. And the second is like it: "You shall love your neighbor as yourself." On these two commandments hang all the Law and the Prophets. (Matt. 22:37–40)

From Jesus's concise response to the lawyer's question and His conclusion of "on these two commandments hang all the Law and the Prophets," it's clear that Jesus being God, incarnate, with perfect understanding of the Law, that He Himself gave to Moses. First, combined into one the five vertical commandments of the first tablet, referring to them as "the first and great commandment." Then He similarly grouped the five horizontal commandments of the second stone tablet, referring to them as "the second is like it" in His response to the lawyer. By doing this, the Lord casts a bright and revealing light on the significance and importance He attaches to the honor, respect, and obedience He wants, demands, and commands us to give and show to our parents. That is because the fifth commandment is on the first stone tablet and is the commandment Paul addressed to the Ephesians. The commandment is the following:

> Honor your father and your mother, that your days may be long upon the land which the LORD your God is giving you. (Ex. 20:12)

This commandment is among the four preceding it that refer to honor and reverence due to *God only!* It is included in the Lord's proclamation of "the first and great commandment." When people honor, obey, and respect their parents, God regards it as an honor to Himself.

The ArtScroll Stone Edition of the Chumash,[1] along with Hebrew, contains an English translation of the Torah/Pentateuch (the five books of Moses), accompanied by a verse-by-verse commentary from the highest esteemed Jewish sages. The Chumash declares a triune partnership in every human being's life. That partnership is God with the person's father and mother. The Chumash further expresses that if someone honors their parents, God considers it as if that person has honored Him. But if not, that person has likewise dishonored God. With that understanding, Jesus, without any ambiguity, declared the importance and significance of the fifth commandment when He purposely did not answer a particular question from the scribes and Pharisees. Instead, in what appeared to come from out of the blue, He asked them to explain their blatant disobedience and disregard for the fifth commandment. He asked them directly,

> Why do you also transgress the commandment of God because of your tradition? For God commanded, saying, "Honor your father and your mother"; and, "He who curses father or mother, let him be put to death." (Matt. 15:3–4; Lev. 20:9)

Per my Chumash understanding, the honor that the Lord referenced was comprehensive. It referred to not only obeying our parents but also rendering deeds that raise the status of one's parents. Acts that provide them honor and comfort. Including giving and supplying them with food and drink, dressing them, and escorting them as needed. The honor due to our parents is similar but secondary to the recognition we render to God. That is, in fashion to the first three commandments.

1. We must acknowledge who our parents are and their place and priority in our lives. With our recognition, we are to accept their authority over us.
2. We must appreciate and treat our parents with love, respect, patience, and honor. We are to do nothing to cause them to be disgraced or degraded but rather to serve them unselfishly, providing for them when they are old or needy and not for any inheritance or other ulterior motive.
3. We are not to swear in our parents' names or curse them!

The triune (God, father, and mother) partnership and relationship are built on a deep foundation of love, faith, teaching, and instruction throughout scripture. It starts from God and flows into our fathers and mothers. From our parents, it flows into us, their children. God unveils His triune method as He speaks to and commands fathers and mothers, saying,

> Therefore you shall lay up these words of mine in your heart and in your soul, and bind them as a sign on your hand, and they shall be as frontlets between your eyes. You shall teach them to your children, speaking of them when you sit in your house, when you walk by the way, when you lie down, and when you rise up. (Deut. 11:18–19)

The triune (God, father, and mother) partnership is illustrated in the life of Noah as recorded in his historical "Testament of Noah" obtained from the Qumran Caves' Dead Sea Scrolls.[2] As such, all humanity is here today because of the successful execution of God's triune partnership through the line of Noah as he obeyed and submitted to the teachings of his parents. Remember Noah's father was Lamech, the son of Methuselah, the son of Enoch, who "walked with God; and he was not, for God took him" (Gen. 5:21–29).

In the Testament of Noah. Noah says,

> From my birth, my mother taught me in the ways of righteousness. My whole life, I walked in the truth of the Holy One as He had instructed. I kept away from the paths of deceit which led to eternal darkness. I studied the visions of truth and wisdom, prayed ceaselessly, and avoided the paths of violence. Even after becoming an adult, I continued in righteousness, (and) grew in wisdom.

Because of Noah's mother's teachings, Noah's obedience to her (and his father), and his consistent choice to walk in the ways of God, we are here today by God's grace and mercy. Out of one blood, God made us all (Acts 17:26). That one blood came from Adam, through Seth, through Noah. We are, indeed, of one blood. God made us all through Adam. Noah's life confirms that if you train children in the way they should go when they are old, they will not depart from it (Prov. 22:6).

After reviewing my life as recorded in this book, I readily accept the Jewish sages' precept that there are three partners in every human being's life: God, father, and mother. Through this triune partnership, God established how I was raised, taught, trained, instructed, and corrected throughout my life. The purpose was to bring me to Himself for my edification and the fulfillment of His glory, purpose, and will in creating me. God's triune partnership with my parents brought about my conception, birth, teaching, training, instruction, and correction. All of which have resulted in the man and person I am today.

This book is my firsthand recollection, description, and account of God's triune partnership with my parents. It describes how He worked His unique plan for me through my father and mother and has shepherded and directed my paths all my life. A process He has worked to bring me to obedience and love for Him with all my heart, soul, mind, and strength.

Acknowledgments

First and foremost, I thank God, my Heavenly Father, my Savior and Lord Jesus Christ and the Holy Spirit, who woke me up early one spring morning in 2018 with the thought, impetus, and inspiration to write this book.

I greatly appreciate and thank playwright and producer Jack Lightsy for thoroughly reviewing this book's manuscript of part 1, "Lessons from My Mother," and part 2, vignettes 6 and 7. His review occurred early in the manuscript's development, and his feedback and comments were constructive and very encouraging. They confirmed that I was on the right path and should continue.

I greatly appreciate LaSondra C. Webb for the time and effort she expended as she comprehensively reviewed the entire manuscript. Her complete assessment and examination of every vignette, with her comments on each vignette's readability, message, and value, were highly informative and constructive. In addition, her suggestions for improvement were detailed, treasured, and overwhelmingly implemented.

I thank the Lord for the support and prayers of my best friend, Barron L. Grimmett, who constantly encouraged me weekly as I wrote and edited each vignette of this book. Additionally, his feedback and comments after reviewing part 1, vignettes 13–16 and part 2, vignettes 6 and 7 were highly encouraging and rewarding.

I greatly thank Alexandra Rimmer, PT, DPT for her detailed, open-minded review and comments on part 1, vignettes 13–16. They were quite informative and helpful.

I greatly appreciate Dr. Nikki (Noaquia) Callaha Banks, PhD, African American studies, for her comprehensive review of this book's entire part 2, "Lessons from My Father." Her perspective and accompanying comments and suggestions were advisory, informative, and highly valuable.

My great and special thanks to a pastor and teacher, Omar A. Muhammad, formerly of Faithful Central Bible Church (FCBC), Inglewood, California, for his in-depth review and comments of part 1, vignettes 3–9 and part 2, vignettes 6 and 7. They were comprehensive, enlightening, and very encouraging.

I give special thanks to my great-niece, Tanisha B. Auten, for her valuable contemplative and reflective comments on part 2, vignettes 6 and 7. They were enlightening and gave me excellent feedback on her views as a millennial.

I thank my friend and colleague Akram Baluch for his comments and feedback on part 2, vignettes 6 and 7. He gave me a different perspective on how he viewed vignettes 6 and 7 as a Muslim man and an immigrant and US naturalized citizen from an Islamic country.

I sincerely thank Leandra Drummy of Author Solutions/ WestBow Press for her invaluable content editorial comments and suggestions. Without her help, the publication of this book would not have occurred.

Introduction

This introduction reminds us that no matter how modern our world appears, the world is built and operates under recurring fundamental principles of life given by God. Solomon described this cyclic nature of life when he decried, "There is nothing new under the sun" (Eccl. 1:4–11). Therefore, for our good, it is vitally important that we learn the fundamental lessons of life and how we are to operate within this world. But it is said, "How shall they hear without a preacher?" (Rom. 10:14). However, God Himself provides us the preachers. The preachers are our teachers and trainers. Fundamentally, our initial preachers are our parents and God, as He gives direction to the extent that our parents are open and submissive to Him.

Provided we listen and grasp, we learn and comprehend life's lessons from our parents and through the Lord's shepherding and directing our paths. My reason for writing this book is to document the learning path of my life. While, at the same time, illuminating from a bird's-eye view how God works in all our lives. From the Bible's perspective of teaching, warnings, and the stories and observation of biblical characters, it's clear that submitting to God's process and ways is paramount in selecting productive and everlastingly rewarding roads and life paths.

As you read this book, it will become apparent that the Lord is no respecter of persons as you see the parallels of my life with yours, those of your peers, historical persons, and persons of the Bible. God's direction and interaction with me through my parents was the same method He instructed the Old Testament Israelite parents to use (Deut. 11:19). Namely, my parents taught me life's lessons and God's principles *by teaching, instructing, and talking about them when we sat at home, when we walked or rode in the car together, before we lay down and went to sleep at night, and when we arose from sleep and got up.* They taught me as an aspect of the normal flow of life when an opportunistic situation presented itself. From this book's panoramic view of my life, it is crystal clear that the Lord is, in fact, my Shepherd. He continuously directed my paths through my parents, uncles and aunts, teachers, life experiences, and circumstances. The use of His staff to lead and direct my paths is evident throughout the book, as well as His staff's hook to pull me back when I strayed or rebelled against His direction or needed to be pulled out of the mouth and grips of temptation. His rod, that is, His club, is also evident in several areas of my life as He beat back the lion Satan and his lioness demons as they continuously attacked me.

The book is segmented into two parts, providing visibility into God, our Father's teaching, instruction, and guidance methodology through my parents. The two parts are "Lessons from My Mother," containing teachings from my childhood through college. Then, "Lessons from My Father" incorporates father-to-son training and instruction from childhood through college. Each of the two parts contains vignette lessons and experiences related to the title. Each vignette concludes with a "My Takeaway" summary of the wisdom I gained from the vignette lesson.

A literary vignette is not a formal short story but describes a scene or scenes with a word length typically of 1,000 words or less. There are 36 vignettes within this book written as excerpts or panoramic captures of my life's principal "lessons learned." They vary from 580 words to 5,800 words, with an average word length of 2,500 words. For most adult readers,' the average vignette reading time will be about eight minutes.

The lessons are presented in chronological order of my age and their occurrence within the book's two segments. Chronological order, however, does defer to consistency and completeness, where I received an initial lesson with follow-ons to that lesson occurring later in life. Those interconnected lessons, however, are presented in a sequence of related vignettes. The most prominent vignette grouping came from my mother's teachings on the major weaknesses of men and women when I was eight years old. That grouping occurs in part 1 with the initial lesson described in vignette 3, followed by vignettes 4–9.

The entire book is my story. However, its vignettes of lessons and teachings have broad and universal application to all men and women, singles and parents. All include teenagers, young adults, middle-aged adults, and seniors, including grandpas, grandmas, Christians, and non-Christians. The book is a timely source of wisdom and thought-provoking insight from the first vignette to the last.

Elaborating on that comment, I believe the vignettes of part 1, "Lessons from My Mother," and part 2, "Lessons from My Father," will be an invaluable contribution to men and women planning on having children, currently raising their children, or foster parenting. The insights gained will not only stir the reader to reflect upon their own lives but also stimulate those who are parents to look closely at the individuality of each of their children. Then structure and tailor their teaching and training to each child's unique personality so that they grasp and receive their parental messages loud and clear. In addition, I also expect that the love and wisdom God imparted to my parents will likewise be imparted to all others as they read and contemplate the messages of parts 1 and 2. Additionally, as readers travel and journey through this book, I pray they will be sensitive and see God's involvement in their lives, and reflect on their personal experiences as He has been shepherding and directing them.

Looking back, I perceive all that I received from my parents described in parts 1 and 2 were in preparation for my life in God Himself. As part of the God, father, and mother triune partnership identified by Jewish sages[1], my parents brought me to where God wanted me to be. Just as God brought Moses to Mount Sinai and later Moses brought the children of Israel to God at Mount Sinai, metaphorically, at about the age of 20, my parents brought me to God at Mount Sinai and released me into His hands. God, through Jesus Christ, with my submission and acceptance of my place in Him, from that point on has taken over with His shepherding and directing of my life.

Dad and Mom did their job exceptionally well! As part of my relationship with them, when they metaphorically brought me to Mount Sinai, it was time for me to fully submit to God, my heavenly Father, and start "Thinking and acting like the man God created and ascribed me to be!"

I desire that all who read this book will likewise see the applicability of each vignette's lesson to their own lives. Then pull out all the truth that pertains to them for their betterment and an enhanced understanding of God and how He works in their lives. I hope they better comprehend themselves, others, and life in general, knowing in all certainty that God is no respecter of persons. Just as He shepherded and directed Job, Moses, Deborah, Ruth, Hannah, David, Daniel, Paul, and me, Robert, He is also doing the same to you. Therefore, as you read this book, may you receive all God desires for you to get out of it.

In recognition of what I have written, each vignette describes its background and contents accurately and truthfully as I saw, heard, experienced, and recalled. I have not embellished or exaggerated any scene or aggrandized or belittled myself or anyone else. To the best of my ability, everything written is as I saw, heard, remembered, and understood. Note, however, that without distorting the reality of my observations and experience, I have used pseudonyms and incomplete or modified location descriptions and other particulars, where necessary and appropriate, to preserve an individual's privacy and anonymity.

Part 1

Lessons from My Mother

My son ... do not forsake the law of your mother;
for they will be graceful ornaments on
your head, and chains about your neck.
—Proverbs 1:8–9

Vignette 1

Love Always Seeks Maturity

When I was five years old and ready to go to elementary school, my mom took me to kindergarten on the first day. I was very close to Mom, and I knew something would be different as we went to class. Of course, I didn't know what was going to be changed. But something was not going to be the same. The other kids were already seated when we arrived at the classroom about ten minutes before class started. I don't remember seeing other parents in the room when we came; nor did the other kids seem unsettled. Possibly, most of the parents worked and their kids had already experienced some form of daycare or grandparent/teacher supervision. I had not. Mom was a stay-at-home mom, and I had been with her and my younger siblings all day, every day, for my whole five years of life.

As we walked into the classroom, Mom introduced me to my teacher. My teacher was friendly and very polite. She seemed to know how to handle fearful kids on their first day very well and immediately started joyfully and excitedly welcoming me. My quick impression was that she was very comfortable with kids my age and introducing us to school. However, I knew I would not stay there, so her kindness and demeanor made little difference.

I had decided in my heart and mind that I would not leave my mother or let her go without me. However, as the teacher showed me to my seat, Mom stood in front of the classroom, watching me closely and saying goodbye. From the expression on her face, it was also challenging for her to leave me. As she said goodbye, she could see the fear and anxiety on my face as

I thought, *She's going to leave me.* What she saw on my face made it even harder for her to go because she lingered to leave.

With my eyes glued to Mom, I stood beside my desk and chair on the far side of the room, not having sat down. Finally, my teacher very politely asked me to sit down. As I did, Mom turned and walked out the door. As the door closed shut, I kept staring at it. I never took my eyes off the door. I knew that the classroom was not my home, and I wasn't going to stay there. Suddenly, I jumped up, running up the aisle without warning my teacher. Then I quickly turned to the right at the front of the room and blew past my teacher as she attempted to reach out and grab me as I approached her. I side-stepped to avoid her reach without her even touching me. Then in one motion, as I reached the door, I twisted the door handle and burst through the door, yelling, screaming, and crying out, "Mommy, Mommy," as I ran down the hall. Mom was about halfway down the building's hallway, heading toward its outer door. Suddenly, she heard the classroom door behind her burst open, and then my piercing screams calling out for her. She turned around and saw me running fast, engulfed in panic and fright, straight to her. As I approached her, I frantically cried, begging her repeatedly to please not leave me!

When I got to Mom, I latched on her waist like an octopus, as tight as possible. Mom stopped, stooped, and hugged me with tears in her eyes, her face at eye level with mine. The hug was brief, and then she gently and calmly explained that I had to go back to class and that I would be OK. She clarified that school was where I was supposed to be and assured me she would return to pick me up later. That hug and assurance did the trick. Mom took me by the hand and walked me back to class. I passed by my teacher without saying anything. She had rushed into the hall to catch me and stopped when she saw me run into Mom's arms and cling to her waist. She was now holding the door open as I reentered the class, took my seat, and continued to assimilate. Sometime after this, I heard Mom telling someone, probably one of my aunts, on the phone, "Taking Robert back to that classroom was the hardest thing I ever did!" Although it was hard for Mom to leave me that first day of kindergarten, in her love, she did what was best and necessary for me to grow and mature.

As for me, it's been well over fifty years since that day. As I recall it, I still sense the panic and fright I felt when Mom walked out of that classroom without me. In comparison, I've never had or experienced as empty, fearful, and isolated a set of feelings and emotions as I did during those few moments without my mom. I love my mom and have the same affection for her as when I was five. She and my dad are now with the Lord, and I'm truly thankful to Him for choosing and giving them to me as my parents. I miss my mommy and my daddy *greatly!*

My Takeaway

- **Mom truly loved me and would never take me someplace or leave me with someone who would not look after and protect me as she would.**
- **Mom would never leave or forsake me. She would always come back for me! I would always, no matter what, be her son and her highest priority, along with my siblings.**
- **Although emotionally painful to her, Mom's love for me caused her to do what was best for me to grow and mature.**

Vignette 2

If You Are Great, Your Works Will Follow and Confirm Your Greatness

During my early elementary school years, my mom focused on raising my siblings and me as a stay-at-home mother. I had a one-year-older sister, Beverly, a younger sister, Karen, and the baby of our family, my younger brother, Daryl. When my older sister and I got home from school, our first job was to change our clothes. Then we'd go to the kitchen in the dining area, where Mom would always have a small meal for us.

One day, when I was in the first or second grade, I finished my snack, and as was my postmeal custom, I followed Mom around the kitchen, talking to her. Mom was at the sink, washing greens or some other vegetable on this particular day, and I was continually yapping my head off, telling her how great and smart I was.

I remember how attentive Mom listened to me and her patience as she continued her vegetable washing. She didn't interrupt me, but nonverbally, she told me she was hearing. Mom kept doing what she was doing until I finished conversing. When I finished talking, or more accurately, I paused from my self-acclamation to take a breath, she calmly said, "Robert, if you are as great and smart as you say you are, you don't need to talk about how great you are. Or boast about yourself or what you did or what you have accomplished. Your deeds and works will show others how great you are."

Her calm, nonjudgmental words stopped my mouth from saying anything else and grabbed my mind, full attention, and sanity. I thought, *Wow! That's right! My works, deeds, and accomplishments will show if I'm great. They will follow me.*

Although Mom didn't specifically say it, I also received the message "If I don't have any great works or deeds, then I'm not that great after all. My works will testify to how good and great I am. Not my words!" Without saying another word, I went away and pondered what Mom said and started focusing on my output instead of my mouth and how great I believed I was. In those few minutes, it became crystal clear that if I didn't have deeds and works to back up my words, I would look like a fool to others and maybe be a fool to myself. From that day on, I was ingrained to be an "accomplisher" and a "doer." Not a talker!

I took my mom's words to heart and started shadowing my dad. I took on my father's discipline, work ethic, and work quality standards as I grew. I started learning to be a "doer" and get things done right the first time. Dad's scrupulous training by repetition, chastisement, and do-it-again-and-again-until-you-get-it-right process hammered excellence into me. Dad's process embedded Mom's message of having works to attest to what I said, what I did, and what I believed. With Mom and Dad's tandem training and discipline, I steadily became an achiever rather than a talker. I learned to value work and do everything to the best of my ability and knowledge and within the time constraints placed on me to accomplish my tasks.

My Takeaway

- **My deeds and works shall undoubtedly speak louder than my words!**
- **If I project boastful words of my greatness and superiority and don't have deeds commensurate with those words, I will soon be ignored and possibly regarded as a "fool!"**

Vignette 3

The Weakness of Men and the Weakness of Women

When I was eight years old, one weekend evening, we went to San Francisco (SF), California, as a family. At the time, we lived in Richmond, north-east, across the bay from San Francisco. Before heading west onto what's now the I-80 freeway, we stopped to get gas at a Chevron service station. My dad exited the car and started helping service the car and talking to the attendant. At that time, a service station attendant always pumped your gas. My mom was sitting in the front seat on the passenger side, and I was on the gas pump side behind my dad. My siblings were also in the back seat to the right of me.

A car pulled in next to us on the other side of the gas pump with a highly flashy couple in dress and appearance. They also had a distinctive vibe to them. I don't know why. But the woman caught my attention, and I focused on her, never taking my eyes off her. The woman was beautiful and possessed a distinct difference that I discerned and found very attractive but didn't know what it was. I was too young to understand my interest in her and had no idea what I was thinking. However, I must have been staring very intently at her. My mother sensed something, turned her head, and looked back at me. Then she said, "Robert, not all men, but most men, again not all men, but most men can be led wherever a woman wants by the middle part of her anatomy." After a short pause, Mom continued. "Most attractive women know they have that power over men. Many of them know how to use it to get what they desire from men. A woman can lead and manipulate a man to get what she wants. Again, not all men, but the desire for the middle part of a woman's anatomy is the biggest weakness for most men. The weakness of men is the middle of a woman's anatomy."

Mom continued. "On the other hand, men can lead, not all women, but most women wherever they want if they have enough money or are rich. Again, not all women, but most women, are attracted to men or can be enticed by rich men with just a little wooing and attention given to them. Rich men know this and use it greatly to get the women they want and manipulate women to get what they want from them. Robert, the weakness of the woman is money."

Mom didn't go into any details or further elaboration, but at the end of her dialogue, I had an idea and understanding of the messages she conveyed to me. I had been exposed to enough TV, movies, and comments about *Playboy* magazine. That Mom's remarks regarding the impact pretty women had on men and the effect rich men had on women, especially if the man was also famous, didn't stifle me. It was played out on TV and in movies over and over. Although not with the sexual innuendos Mom referred to. In cinema, it was always the pretty woman who was the treasure of affection and the rich, powerful, famous, or hero man who got the beautiful woman. I had also listened with interest when I heard grown-ups discussing the new *Playboy* magazine and its "Center Page" in a hush-hush and discrete manner. Additionally, I had seen what newspaper movie sections and gossip columns reported about beautiful women and their connections with rich and famous men. Therefore, neither Mom's comments regarding the power of pretty women over men nor the ability of wealthy men to lure women bewildered me.

Nor was I surprised or fazed by the implications that women use their attractiveness to lure men into their web to get what they want, and men of wealth allure women in a vice versa manner to get what they want. Those female-male and male-female power moves didn't disturb me because I had already been innocently alerted.

I had also overheard my mom and aunts discussing men and who they found desirable and undesirable. Occasionally, I heard them call some famous men "dogs" or say, "He's a dog!" At the time, I assumed what they meant was. "The dog man," as they described him, was incredibly selfish, concerned only about what he could get from a woman, not her. So it wasn't a big step for me to think that some women were like that also, although I never heard my dad, uncles, or any other man describe a woman as such.

Therefore, with my simple reasoning and my TV and movie experience, I was not mystified, stymied, surprised, or shocked by Mom's lessons. However, I had no idea why Mom said what she said to me or her purpose and motive for pointing out what she had. Additionally, I didn't know what she saw or heard that stimulated her to say what she spoke to me. Or why Mom thought giving me the lessons at that time was essential. Also, I didn't know how to use the information she gave me or its importance and relevance. As I said, I was only eight years old and not anywhere as mature as the people I saw in the movies or those discussed in the newspapers or who I heard about in *Playboy* magazine. They were all adults.

When Mom spoke to me, I listened to her carefully but never took my eyes off the woman. However, I didn't ask Mom anything about what she said, nor did Mom ask for my response. It was a simple set of passive lessons on the weakness of men and the weakness of women. I received Mom's teaching and tutorial as something I would need some time in the future, but not then. Nevertheless, as we drove off, continuing to SF, I pondered and mulled over what Mom said. The following thought stayed with me: *When I grow up, I'd better be mindful. Mom tells me that I have a weakness I must guard against carefully. She has alerted me that women can use their beauty and the middle part of their anatomy to control and get what they desire from me and get me to do what they want me to do.* As we traveled, the prominence of that thought took root, and it became clear that Mom had indeed informed me of a weakness I was born with but never to let rule or control me. I gleaned her instruction for me was to be one of the *"not all men"* she distinctly and repeatedly referenced.

Thus, after believing I understood what Mom said and why she said it, I accepted Mom's informative message as essential, one that I should not forget. Therefore, like I had heard some grown-ups say, I consciously placed the information and warnings she gave me on my memory shelf to take down later when I needed them. Once I did that, my mind was at rest, and I enjoyed the remainder of our family outing without thinking of it anymore.

Confirming Message: A Lesson from My Uncle Fred

We visited my mom's sister and brother-in-law, my aunt Carrie and uncle Fred, a few months later in Los Angeles, California. I was in the den alone with Uncle Fred, and for some reason, just like my mother did at the Chevron gas station, out of the blue, Uncle Fred started teaching me a lesson. He said, "Robert, the foolish woman goes after your money. She goes after your pocketbook. But ah-ha! Ah-ha! The wise woman, the wise woman, goes after your heart. She knows that once she gets your heart, she also gets your money and pocketbook."

I knew I didn't have the complete picture, but I did realize the importance of what Uncle Fred told me. However, just like with Mom, I didn't ask him why he told me what he told me or what his purpose for telling me was. I just thought, *This is kind of what Mom told me about the weakness of women. It is similar. Therefore, it must be important since I've received the same message twice from two people. I've got to remember this and not forget it! I must store it in my mind so I won't forget it!*

My Takeaway

- **The weakness of men, most men, but not all men, is the middle part of the woman's anatomy. However, this is *not* to be my weakness.**
- **The weakness of most women is money (i.e., financial security). Men can woo and lead women, but not all women, wherever they want to go if they have enough money.**

Vignette 4

The Weakness of Men and the Weakness of Women

Sequel 1: The Weakness of Men Is the Middle of the Woman's Anatomy

From time to time, as I grew up from adolescence through puberty, I recalled the men's and women's weakness lessons I received from my mom and my uncle Fred. Even though I wasn't interested in girls, I learned that someday I would be from one of my much older male cousins. He had voluntarily taken it upon himself to share some things long before I should have known them. Some years later, without any descriptive details, I also heard from my dad, older men, and older teenage boys that a time was coming when I would be interested in girls. Thus, as I approached puberty, I accepted that at some point, I would like girls, and they would like me, too. Therefore, per Mom and Uncle Fred's message of how money attracted women, I reasoned that women would come after me left and right if I was successful and had financial resources. I thought, *My older cousin has girlfriends, and from what he told me, he liked what they have. He undoubtedly is also not afraid of their "cooties."* Thus, from what he said and how he and some of my older female cousins favorably teased me about girls, I accepted that girls would want me someday, and I would also want one, two, three, or four of them.

However, the good thing was Mom's message regarding my inherent weakness for what a girl has and what she could give me was now etched in me. I knew any feelings and desires that arose in me for any girl, and her asset was never to rule or control me. Nor was I to let a woman manipulate or sway me with her smooth, enticing, and alluring words. Instead, I was to stay conscious of my mental and physical inclination toward the "choice fruit." Its accompanying passion was never to supersede my wisdom, knowledge, proper restraint, and common sense. Nor was I to allow girls to use me, through my inherent weakness, to get what they wanted from me or cause me to be a follower. Nor to do things that I shouldn't do, that I didn't want to do, or to go places where I shouldn't go or where I knew better than to go. My overriding sense was that Mom had given me a valuable lesson when I was younger, which I didn't fully understand. Nor did I need it at that time. But now, based on what I was starting to sense within myself, I had arrived at the time to use the information with my dad's repeated message of self-discipline and proper judgment in every area of my life.

As I entered puberty, indeed, girls started looking different to me. My juvenile mind continued to think, *With enough money and popularity, I can have who I want and when I want her.* Based on the way I was now viewing movies, I thought, *Wow, she looks amazing, and it's the rich, powerful, or hero man who always gets her. What's wrong with that?* I need to be like him. My thoughts, however, regarding getting what I wanted, although very desirable, were challenged and countered by my knowledge that "the weakness of the man is the middle portion of the woman's anatomy." That precept, now permanently etched into my psyche, kept me under control, not allowing my mind to wantonly stray. It was of much higher consideration and priority than my growing desires.

Girls increasingly looked attractive to me during middle school: sixth, seventh, and eighth grade. It appeared that some girls I had grown up with from elementary school changed overnight. From one day to the next, I would see them and think, *From where did you come? I've known you since third grade, and now you're different. You are gorgeous. You are not only attractive, but you have breasts too.* They now had some magnetic eyesight allurement that forced me to gaze upon them. I additionally wanted their attention and an opportunity to talk to them. I never wanted to before, but now I wanted to be around them. I additionally wanted to do something great and out of the ordinary when I was in their presence. I desired to impress them and be noticed by them above all the other boys.

Soon after, I wanted more than a girl's attention. As Mom had warned me, I now wanted what they had. Namely, the unique fruit in the middle of a girl's body became a central focus. It initiated a "tug-of-war" between what my body and mind wanted and what my mom said was never to rule me. The battle increased in intensity as I heard some of the older boys describe their "incredible sexual experiences," which I later learned were lies and distortions. However, as I heard them, I wanted what they were getting and to do it with who they were doing it with. I also started thinking like them. *Man, I wonder what it would be like to do it with her. I have to get myself some of that! Wow! She sure is fine. Wouldn't it be good to get some of what she has?*

Metaphorically, my focus was now on the "tree of life" in the middle of a girl's garden. Mom's message was now inherently clear and tangible to me by experience. It was no longer Mom's message; it was now my message. I now owned it! It was my responsibility to control myself.

Mom said most men's weakness was "the middle part of a woman's anatomy." As all of you know, its anatomical name is the vagina. My former wife's family called it the "Molly." Like King Lemuel's mother knew, as recorded in the book of Proverbs, like my mother knew, as my former wife knew, and like I believe most women know, a woman's beauty and sex appeal through her "Molly" has incredible power over men. Her sexual assets can draw and attract men to put down their boyish ways and enter a lifelong committed marriage and family relationship, with joy unspeakable. The "Molly's" allure additionally has potentially destructive power over men that women can use to lure and manipulate them if they choose to use their assets in that manner. Women of virtue and wisdom know that the gift given by God for good can be and is easily perverted to do evil. Just as the devil spoke to Eve in the garden, he also whispers thoughts into the hearts and minds of men and women to stir up our desires and "lust of the flesh" to think and act contrary to God's Word and our benefit. As such, in her wisdom and choice of words, Mom warned me about the power of the "Molly." Similarly, in her own words, three thousand years earlier, King Lemuel's mother warned him about the "Molly." Her words were these:

> What, my son? And what, son of my womb? And what, son of my vows? Do not give your strength to women, nor your ways to that which destroys kings. (Prov. 31:2–3)

As I matured, I added to my understanding of what Mom and other women meant when they called men "dogs." An uncanny number of men have not taken control of themselves. Instead, they have given in and over to their sexual impulses and desires. Their "lower heads" control them rather than their "upper head and minds." On more than one occasion, my former wife, when she heard of a man of reputation or influential position "fall" because of his sexual escapades or dalliances, her response was "The powerful Molly strikes again!" As a man, it is abysmally sad, disappointing, and frustrating to see and hear of so many men, including men of the cloth (ministers and priests), year after year falling to the "powerful Molly." Or far worse fall to their perverse sexual desires and lust, committing horrendous sexual acts against women, girls, boys, and even against men and with other men. They have no control or restraint over themselves, and from the evidence of their continuous actions and behavior, they have refused to bring themselves under control. Or as taken from scripture, they refuse to crucify their "flesh with its passions and desires" (Gal. 5:24).

For me, the call of the "Molly" grew increasingly louder through my high school sophomore, junior, and senior years. Before starting my junior year, I had taken a substantial amount of etiquette training and had eliminated my crude and coarse "locker room" thoughts and talk. My thoughts and talk had matured substantially. However, not my desire. I no longer thought of girls as merely sex objects to "do it with," pondering phrases like "I have to get me some of that!" I now thought of them as a choice of delectable fruit to be plucked and slowly enjoyed.

I'm glad my mother and aunts are not here to read this. If they were, I don't believe I would have another birthday! However, in keeping with the truth, I'll continue.

My thoughts, plans, and talk matured into wanting to woo girls romantically and gently lead them into a hot, romantic state where they wanted me. Then I read their body language invitation to me, knowing that I had won the challenge and earned their affection. My well-thought-out approach was not the raw locker room stuff I heard from older boys when I was younger but a sophisticated, cultured approach. It came from training as a recruited member of a socially sophisticated teenage boys club, the "Sophisticates," including the gentleman persona of "Paladin" from a once-popular TV series. All combined with what I gleaned from reading some books and being very impressed with the romantic poetic wit and prose of French swordsman and soldier Cyrano de Bergerac.

Additionally, I added what I garnered from sneaking and reading some *Playboy* magazines and Hugh Hefner's gentleman philosophy and perspective on love and sex when I visited the house of one of my aunts who subscribed to the magazine. Then after seeing Sean Connery in cinema as James Bond, Agent 007, go about his job, I confidently finalized my romantically alluring approach. In my mind, I rehearsed my methods, strategy, and philosophy so that when the time came, I could do my job patiently, smoothly, romantically, and suavely.

When that time did come, in the form of my hormones driving me to pursue the enormous treasure I now wanted and what I saw James Bond routinely get, my values, conscience, and sense of guilt never fully allowed me to execute my plan. In support, I believe by God's forethought all my thinking and strategizing was accompanied by a series of unconscious, involuntary nighttime wet dreams that released my sexual tension and desire when it rose above a certain level. Thank the Lord for this! I assume it was part of His plan. The night dream mechanism worked similarly to maintenance people turning cranks to give off steam or release water to relieve the pressure on pipes or dams that had built up and exceeded a certain level. The involuntary release was a big help. A huge help! It relieved me and kept me from ruining some young lady's life and my own. I certainly wasn't going to do self-stimulating and self-manipulating as my friends told me they were doing. I didn't slam or openly judge them for doing what they did. But I did ask one of my friends, "Why would you ever do that?" What they were doing was incredibly gross, unmanly, weak, and immature to me. I looked at them as being undisciplined and out of control. It seemed to decry my father's lifelong teachings of being strong-minded, self-disciplined, doing what was right at all times, and not following the crowd or doing anything against my will. However, the most prominent picture exposed to me as I listened to my friends was "This is just what Mom implied when she told me, 'not all men.'" I perceived my friends as yielding to their desire and lust, allowing it to control them. I was determined not to let my desire for sex or its allurement rule, control, or overpower me. I was determined to control myself and not be like other men. That included not self-stimulating or doing other artificial stuff to relieve myself. Years later into my adulthood, it hit me that Mom's message to me at eight years old was very similar to the message God gave Cain when He told him, "Sin is crouching at your door; it desires to have you, but you must master it" (Gen. 4:17).

However, in confession, sexual desire certainly wasn't easy for me to master. If I were to describe what I was sexually sensing at that time, it probably is best depicted in the 1986 movie *Little Shop of Horrors* with Rick Moranis. The part of the movie that best demonstrates the desire for sex I experienced was when Audrey II, the outer space alien plant, was strongly lusting not for sex but for blood. Although the object of my desire was different from Audrey II's, the intense passion or lust for what I wanted and was interested in was the same as depicted and audibled by Audrey II in the musical scene "Feed Me Seymour."[1]

I don't know whether Mom had Dad talk to me because she thought it was time or if Dad knew what I was going through and decided to speak to me. In either case, one day, Pop bluntly told me, "If you get a girl pregnant, your mother and I will not care for your baby. That is your responsibility. You will get a job! And if necessary, you will leave school and work full time doing whatever you need to support your baby. You will also marry the girl, and if she doesn't want to marry you, you will still go by her house every weekend to see that she and your child are cared for and doing well or if they need anything!"

Dad's message was very sobering and injected the fear of adult responsibility into me. It also brought to my attention the reality that I would have to pay for my actions and the consequences. What frightened and got to me most was Dad's comment about me leaving school and working. That thought was repugnant and loathsome to me. It meant going to work doing what I didn't want to do. It meant stopping my sports involvement and education and being stuck in Fresno for the rest of my life. We had moved to Fresno early in my eighth-grade year because my brother, for medical reasons, needed a dryer climate. Fresno was an agreeable and pleasant town, and I learned and prospered in sports and other life skills. However, having grown up in the San Francisco Bay area, vacationed and spent holidays in Los Angeles, and traveled west to the East Coast by car, seeing much of what our nation offers. Imagining living or getting stuck in Fresno for the rest of my life was a deeply depressing thought.

Dad's scenario was so detestable that I started and stopped short of going all the way on three occasions in high school as the thought of my father's stern conversation, warnings, and possible consequences of my actions came to mind. The three occasions occurred when I was in my junior and senior years. Unfortunately, my lust and desire and my excellent planning, polite, well-mannered, and romantic passion got the best of the girls I was with and me. It occurred once in the back seat of our family car while I was on a date. Then twice in my bedroom, I completely obliterated my parents' trust while they and my siblings were out of town visiting my grandmother and aunts in Los Angeles.

On those three occasions, I stopped short at the point of entry because my father's words returned to me as loudly exploding bombs in my mind. The fear of the potential consequences he warned me of far exceeded the excitement, desire, and pleasure my body was pushing me to experience. That fear also drowned out the devil's voice, encouraging me to continue. As I suddenly stopped and withheld myself from entry, one girl was quite upset and very angry with me and never wanted anything to do with me after that day.

Although desiring me and having fallen under my suave, debonair James Bond approach, two other girls, both virgins, were very grateful that I did stop. Interestingly, the sexual allurement between those two girls and me immediately disappeared when I halted. As it did, we redressed and continued enjoying our time together, remaining friends and going out on other enjoyable, nonsexual subsequent dates.

Although I needed help from my dad's stern warning, I did not allow the middle of a girl's anatomy to rule or control me in keeping with my mother's edict.

My Takeaway

- **What I wanted from girls and what girls wanted and desired of me did not come at the proper time in our lives, nor were our desires worth the risks and potential consequences of our actions**
- **My selfishness, greed, desire, and lust, no matter how strong, should have never exceeded my parents' trust in me as it did when they went out of town and left our home in my hands.**
- **Unfortunately, in high school, I saw firsthand the germination of sexual desire and lust that led to what my mom, my aunts, and other women meant when they said, "He's a dog."**
  - **Thank God I stopped when I did on all three intimate occasions and opportunities that I had and did not consummate my relationship and damage a young girl's life or my own.**

Vignette 5

The Weakness of Men and the Weakness of Women

Sequel 2: Experiencing and Confronting My Weakness

When I was twenty years of age and a junior in college, I shattered my left elbow in baseball practice, a life-changing event that ended my baseball and sports career. Since I was a child and first played baseball, it was the first time I didn't have a participatory sport as my primary physical outlet. My grandmother had told me, "An idle mind is the devil's workshop." Unfortunately, I inherited an idle mind from loneliness over losing baseball, my "real girlfriend and love." The devil's key to opening the workshop was the emotional emptiness from losing my life's passion and goal.

Although I was an electrical engineering (EE) major and very much liked mathematics and physics, my desire for engineering in no way, shape, form, or fashion came anywhere near my passion and love for baseball. With the loss of my emotional zeal for life and physical activity, I started experiencing a magnitude of sexual need and desire I had no idea I had. What I felt was well beyond anything I understood my mother described to me at the Chevron gas station when I was eight years old. During that lesson, Mom emphasized the lure a woman could have on men, specifically on me when I matured. The pull I was experiencing was not an allurement coming from seeing a woman's sexual beauty or hearing her romantic words. Quite the contrary, this was a sexual beast within me, of a size and weight I had no measurement of. Nor did I have any knowledge of its ravenous appetite. It started injecting sexual thoughts and desires into my mind with increasing frequency and magnitude to levels reaching far beyond anything I experienced in high school.

In truth, the sexual tensions I sensed and worked through in high school were no comparison to what I was now feeling. I believe it was my body's programmed but fallen nature's desire to procreate and to procreate *now!* My emotional void and lack of exercise unlocked the beast's shackles and opened its cage. Now it was out, extremely hungry and on the hunt.

The "beast" in me arose like a voracious sexual fire of passion. My dad had never told me about anything like this. However, the seriousness of Mom warning me, at eight years old, that I had this weakness came fully to my mind. I knew with certainty that I was not to be like other men. I was to control my passion for the middle portion of the female anatomy and not allow myself to be ruled or governed by my desires. The differences between what Mom told me and the drive I was experiencing were threefold. First, what I felt was internally initiated without the promptings of a female. Second was its enormous power to grab and hold my attention; third was its urgency for fulfillment. What I experienced was indeed horrible. Downright horrible! I had always had control of my thoughts and desires. Now I was overwhelmed. What I was now sensing was nothing like anything I had ever experienced in my mind or body. The pressure was incredibly forceful. The "beast" was saying, "I'm in control now! I'm fully grown and unyielding! I want my *cookie,* and I want it *now!* Not tomorrow, not next week. I want it *now!"*

Thank God I still had the last say. The "beast" had no power to override my choice, and Mom had instilled in me what choice to make. I executed the option to not be like other men. My sexual passions and desires would not rule me!

Apparently, I went through this stage of life much later than my friends did. I reasoned that they were going through this in high school when I internally criticized them and had no tolerance for the self-stimulating things they were doing. I now believe I was under the same pressure they were under then. However, I was not going to self-stimulate or make a habit of going to X-rated movies or reading pornographic material like I knew some young men did. However, late in my junior year, after turning twenty-one, I did see an XXX-rated film that several of my engineering friends highly recommended to me, some having seen the movie multiple times. I don't remember the film's title, but I do recall that the movie was well-written and artistic in quality. Its over twenty-one years of age, XXX rating was due to its vivid picturesque scenes of real, nonsimulated boyfriend-girlfriend tender lovemaking and romantic sex. I confess that I liked the film a lot, an awful lot. I learned some intimate things about sex and lovemaking that I had not known. I also saw and learned how to be pleasant, soft, gentle, kind, cultured, and romantic in ways I hadn't known before. I also received some enhanced knowledge of what I thought I knew.

However, watching the movie, I quickly sensed the large luminous caution sign with Mom's teaching in front of the screen. The poster spoke loudly. It informed me that indulging in the type of film I was viewing was not in my best interest mentally, emotionally, or behaviorally because of the joyful sexual stimulation, interest, and consciousness it was arousing in me and feeding to the "beast." Therefore, either during the movie or right after it, I decided not to see the film again or any other XXX-rated video.

From what I sensed and felt from the movie's audio and visuals, the film exposed firsthand the desire and potential weakness in me that Mom said most men had. It was now crystal clear that I also had the passion and propensity for that weakness. But I would not feed it or let that weakness strengthen and control me. Nor was I going to circumvent my sexual pressure and discomfort by self-stimulation or tracking down and dating girls known to do the "thang." The desire for sex was loudly, wonderfully, and continuously calling to me as the Sirens' song called to Ulysses (Odysseus) in Homer's *Odyssey*. Yet just like Ulysses did, per Mom's warning, I behaviorally and as mentally as I could tied myself down to my ship's mast of discipline and self-restraint. I didn't deny that the power and strength of my desire for sex were like roaring, white-hot flames inside me, but I was not going to add fuel to those flames and empower them to control, overtake, and manipulate me.

In addition to the consciousness of my mother's message, I noticed a much greater moral consciousness of God than I had in high school or that I ever had before. In high school, my parents' words were the restraints that kept me within bounds. Now that I was a junior in college, I sensed that I was growing much more God conscious and sensitive to His Word and presence than I had ever been before. My development toward the "age of accountability" apparently hit me around twenty, not the traditional age of twelve spoken by some Bible ministers. This thought of my slow rate of "maturity" came to me more than once. I became increasingly convinced that the intense sexual pressure I was now experiencing was the same as my friends contended with when we were in high school.

As I look back, my sexual maturity rate may have been slow compared to other boys. However, as scripture depicts, my consciousness of God and sense of accountability to Him may have been quite normal. From scripture, males twenty years old and above is the age the Lord held those that came out of Egypt accountable (Ex. 30:14; Num. 14:29).

Growing up Baptist, we attended church regularly but weren't the every-Sunday-church type of family. However, over time, my dad, siblings, and I responded to an altar call, joined the church, and were baptized. Mom had grown up Baptist from her youth in Texas and was on our church's Usher Board.

From attending church and hearing God's Word, I knew God's command prohibiting premarital sex or fornication with certainty. Over the months, as my consciousness of God and sense of accountability to Him grew, it became imperative for me not to have sex outside marriage and not even go as far as the heavy petting I did in high school with the three girls from vignette 4. My decision, however, didn't ease the intense sexual pressure I had. It kept building up and up. Unfortunately, I didn't have a strong relationship with God or know His Word well enough to depend on Him entirely and cast all my "care upon Him" (1 Pet. 5:7). Thus, as the pressure significantly mounted, I went to my university's counseling center to speak to and get help from a staff psychologist rather than to the Lord directly. I attended the University of Santa Clara, now Santa Clara University (SCU), a Catholic Jesuit university. From the experienced psychologist, I expected to get some sage Christian counseling with a biblical process that would end the pressure I was going through or help me cope.

However, much to my dismay, I didn't get the feel from the psychologist that he was a solid, knowledgeable, committed Catholic or Protestant Christian. Or that he had any sage advice or suggestions for me. After explaining my reasons for being there, he gave me no answers or advice regarding my dilemma. But instead, he asked me to lie down for what I called a couch session. Then among other questions, he asked me the ubiquitous but, in my case, absurd and irrational question "How long have you hated your mother?" After the first session, he scheduled me for one or two other couch sessions and a couple of additional sessions where I took some written tests. After viewing my written tests, the psychologist completed his formal examination and evaluation. He concluded that I was mentally and emotionally healthy and stable. Which I already knew before coming to see him. I wanted and came to him for a healthy, non-artificial, non-self-stimulating set of advice and mental methods or procedures to ease the sexual tension and pressure I was going through.

I know my thinking wasn't realistically rational, but I wanted to return and feel benign about sex again, as I did when I was ten. I assumed that since the Lord didn't want me to have sex outside marriage, He must also have a way, a method, or a procedure that would allow me to continue with my life and my studies in peace, without all the pressure I was experiencing. What I was experiencing was miserable! It was making my life miserable! I wanted it over, gone, and done with forever! The pressure inside me was an angry tyrant! It hindered me from focusing and doing what I was supposed to do.

The psychologist, however, did not have any good answers for me. First, he initiated the suggestion of me self-stimulating to release the pressure, which for me, was an absolute no! And violation of what I told him the first hour we spoke that I wanted no part of. Then he suggested I get married, which I agreed to discuss briefly per his request. The thought of me getting married was horrendous, and I told him why. My response was "Why in the world would I get married and take on a lifelong obligation with a mate, a family, and financial commitment for the primary purpose of satisfying my sexual urge and desire?" In my mind, marrying a woman for that reason was illogical, insane, and as foolish and thoughtless a decision as I could make and unfair to the woman. It would be like jumping out of a frying pan into the fire without even considering jumping onto the pan's handle and then leaping to safety. His suggestion was about as primitive and noncognitive an answer as he could have given me.

His next suggestion violated scripture. Namely, he didn't have any qualms about advising me to go ahead and have sex. I was healthy and of age, and though intense, what I was experiencing was normal. Having sex was the normal and natural way to grow socially through dating and relieve my pressure. He added that I act responsibly and take normal pregnancy and disease prevention precautions. I stayed composed when I heard that but found it shocking because artificial birth control was anathema to the Catholic Church. I then again stressed my desire to remain within God's bounds. His final suggestion was to take hormone shots to reduce some and possibly all the sexual pressure I sensed. He also said he would refer me to a medical doctor he knew if I wanted to take that path. You talk about a thoughtless comment—no way I would do that to my body. I ended my sessions with the doctor of psychology being no better off than when I first entered his office. I received no sage biblical advice or acceptable standard practice to get relief from my sexual pressure. Nor did the psychologist help me in my moral dilemma to live in conformance and obedience to God and His Word without the sex pressure I was experiencing.

As life would have it, I didn't recall until years later, as an adult, a book written in the 1930s that I got from my dad or someone else when I was an early teenager. The book was about male puberty. The author explicitly said that the way to manage and control the sex drive and pressure a boy sensed through puberty was to rechannel his energy through vigorous physical exercise and intensive brain use through study and reading. I don't know how, but in high school and college, I had wholly forgotten what I had read when I was thirteen. Wow! That was God's way of escape for me, and I had forgotten it. Even worse, however, was that the doctor of psychology at a Catholic university didn't even know of it; if he had, he would have mentioned it to me. With the amount of reading and studying I was doing, if the psychologist had recommended that I run six miles a day or swim a mile a day, my sexual tension would have been extinguished, and I would have been fine.

As a result of receiving no help from the psychologist, my sexual battle raged on without mitigation or attenuation. Finally, some weeks after my final visit, I gave in to the pressure and compromised, taking the psychologist's third suggestion to date and have sex with protection. I had a couple of sexually romantic encounters with a girl I dated and enjoyed spending time with. Then some months later, I had a girlfriend I enjoyed being with and grew to like very much. We grew increasingly close and started making love on the weekends. I never looked at us just having sex, nor do I believe she did. She was not an object; she was much more important and precious to me than that. Mom and Dad's training and upbringing highly elevated my consideration for her. I saw her as a person, not a sex object. I appreciated and respected her as a person with cultivated social skills, valuable gifts and talents, and the fantastic fruit blossoming in the middle of her body. I treated her with the utmost kindness, respect, and consideration, entering our relationship with the expressed intent not to take advantage of her.

However, disobedience to God is still disobedience when you know and accept His will. It's not innocence or ignorance. It's a sin and separates you from Him. Thus, despite all my efforts to abstain from sex, I didn't get any "brownie points" from the Lord that neutralized my sin. Instead, I sensed I got further away from the Lord whenever my girlfriend and I came together. I can't explain it, but with His presence and voice, the Lord appeared to be gradually moving away from me, little by little, every time we came together. Years later, as I grew in the Lord, I realized it was me moving away from Him. I never talked to my girlfriend about what I felt. However, in my fear and concern of losing the Lord and not hearing His voice, I purposely limited the times we came together. As I sensed my drifting away, I also asked the Lord to forgive me and be merciful. I also asked Him to help me not hurt my girlfriend or take advantage of her.

I explain the details of our eventual split below. However, not until a few seconds ago, when I wrote down the gist of what I prayed, did I ever associate our breakup's initiation with my prayer. As I said, I prayed to the Lord for His help in not letting me hurt my girlfriend or take advantage of her. The Lord heard and answered me. As I now remember, our relationship started its closure shortly after I prayed that prayer.

My girlfriend was Chinese, and I am Afro American. Shortly after I prayed that prayer one weekend, my girlfriend went home to visit her parents; as she was talking to her father, she casually asked him a question to satisfy an innocent but expected nonissue of curiosity she had. Additionally, her question was a sounding out and an early warning signal to her father that she was starting to think seriously about someone. She had increasingly growing feelings for me, which supported her strong liking and interest in me. Thus, she asked her father, "How would you feel about me marrying a Black man?" To her horror, he replied seriously, "If you do, I will no longer have a daughter!" In addition to being horrified at her father's response, she was stunned, shocked, and emotionally traumatized!

When she returned to school that Sunday afternoon, she quickly informed me she was back in town. We met on the grass in front of the Engineering Building, and she filled me in on her weekend's pleasant activities and experiences. She then told me what she had asked her father and why. It was very apparent how profoundly cutting his response to her was. Its surprise, shock, and hurt, as well as her sadness and disappointment in her father, were also clearly apparent. As I listened, she explained that her father's response was not how he and her mother raised her and her older sister. Or the way they had ever looked at people. As she spoke to me, it was clear that what she heard from her father was still affecting her deeply. As she talked, large, crocodile-shaped tears from her flooded eyes began to trickle slowly and gracefully, winding down her cheeks. I intently listened to her tell me the question she had asked her father and his immediate response. As I considered, I began to see our growing relationship's potential seriousness and danger. Also, when I heard the question she asked her father, it surprised me that she thought as she did. She was far ahead of me in her thinking regarding our relationship maturity than I was.

I thoroughly enjoyed conversing, talking, being with her, and enjoying her good looks and physical attributes. I additionally enjoyed her wit, cleverness, charming personality, mental brightness, and acuity. However, the thought of marriage had never entered my mind. Nor did I have the desire to get married. Although my baseball aspirations were gone, my ambitions were still fresh and intact, full of self-interest and self-centeredness. My immediate plans culminated in my interest in traveling the world alone for the next year or two after I graduated or as soon as I accumulated enough money. After I obtained a better understanding of myself, life, and what life had to offer, I would decide what I wanted to commit myself to as a career and who to commit myself to in a marriage relationship. However, seeing her tears, I immediately started garnering thoughts about the potential consequences of continuing our love and affection for one another and proceeded on to marry.

In real time, I started thinking, *I cannot promise her anything. I cannot promise that if we marry, I'll always make her happy, she will always want me, or we will never divorce. If we divorce after her father disowned her, what family will she have? She will be alone, and I cannot allow that to happen!* Thus, as she spoke with tears continuously slowly running down her cheeks, I decided right on the spot I had no right to pull her away from her father and family. My on-the-spot, quick, and simplistic reasoning was, *I'm not the only man in the world. If I were, it would be different. However, because I'm not the only man available to her, she still has options to choose from to marry.*

I continued reasoning that her father was wrong for rejecting me solely based on my skin color. However, it still was not suitable for me to pull her away from her father. He has demonstrated his simplicity of thought and foolishness by denying me without knowing me, my values, my character, my upbringing, me as a man, or whether I'm compatible with his daughter. But she is his daughter. I further thought, *As we have children, I won't place our kids in a situation where they would be unwanted, rejected, looked down upon, ignored, or unwelcomed by their grandparents.* My reasoning culminated in thinking, *I must avoid a situation like that at all costs. Because if we married and her father denigrated our children in any way, it would not be a pleasant encounter between him and me in any way.*

Thus, I decided to gradually pull away from her and let our relationship fade out and end pleasantly. As I thought about it, I wanted to let our relationship die without hurting or traumatizing my girlfriend. I thought that was the best plan since I was graduating in the next few months anyway, and she was still an undergraduate student. Even though I was starting to have strong feelings for my girlfriend, it was now clear that I should not change my plans to move from our school location in northern California to Los Angeles four hundred miles to the south after I graduated. My strategy was to live with my parents, who had moved to LA, until I saved enough money to start my around-the-world travel adventure. Thus, right there on the spot, I decided not to change those plans, regardless of my feelings or my girlfriend's request.

Therefore, after I graduated, I moved to LA and temporarily in with my parents. As planned, I gradually allowed our relationship to fade. I started calling her less and less and did not return to

SCU on weekends to see her. I did, however, ask her to spend a weekend with my parents and me and paid for her airfare. My parents had a spare bedroom, and I desired to see her. I enjoyed seeing her and spending that weekend with her and my parents. From my standpoint, we had a great time, and my parents were fond of her. Also, from everything she said and her body language, she liked my parents and felt comfortable in their presence.

On the Saturday afternoon of her weekend visit, my parents were not home, and she and I were in the living room. A beautiful romantic song came on the radio that we both knew. We slow danced to it on the carpeted living room floor without shoes. It was very pleasant and romantic as we held each other and danced. Midway through the song and dance, she looked up at me, right into my eyes. I'll never forget her look and what she said as we held each other warmly, and she gently turned her head up. Just as I previously saw them in front of our school's Engineering Building, her eyes flooded, and those large, crocodile-shaped tears slowly streamed down her cheeks. Looking into my eyes, she said, "Please take me with you!" referring to my planned world travel. There is no denying it. She got to my heart as I looked into her eyes, saw her tears, and heard the sincere, sweet, innocent, childlike softness and plea of her voice and words. However, my mind knew what was best. I would not hurt or jeopardize her relationship with her father. Therefore, I continued my plan. When that weekend ended, I allowed our relationship to fade away and die with the distance between us, our now different lives, and the gradual reduction in our communication. My plan was completed.

In moving ahead one year, at twenty-three years old, through God's leading and grace, I went to a full Gospel church, was explained God's plan of salvation, and accepted Jesus as my Lord and Savior. Once I did, the twenty-four/seven, constant sexual tension I held was significantly reduced. Helping maintain my peace was my change in priorities to stay in the spiritual atmosphere of my church, mature believers, and attend prayer meetings and Bible study.

Through it all, I unquestionably missed God's abstinence mark until I was married. However, through His grace and love, I received His forgiveness. It is also by His grace that, in good conscience, albeit excruciatingly uncomfortable, I did control and restrain myself, not allowing the middle part of a woman's anatomy to master me. As a result, I met my mom's desire for me to be one of the *"not all men"* she referred to. In keeping with what she and Dad taught me, I maintained my honor, respect, and proper consideration for girls and women throughout my growth into puberty and manhood.

My Takeaway

- I greatly thank the Lord for Mom alerting me to my inherent sexual weakness early in life.
- I missed God's mark of sexual abstinence until I was married. However, God has forgiven me.
- Although it was a major battle in my flesh and mind, with God's help, I prevailed and didn't let my desire for the middle part of a woman's anatomy to be my master or rule and control me.
- I made the right decision, for the right reasons, in allowing my relationship with my college girlfriend to fade away for her benefit.

Vignette 6

The Weakness of Men and the Weakness of Women

Sequel 3: The Weakness of Men Is Not to Be Taken for Granted

Embedded in my mother's warning of men's weakness was that sexual temptation and the desire and lust that precede it know no limits. If you give in to it, it will surely take you over. Speaking as someone who has gone through the allurement and surfaced on the other side, I can honestly say one must determine, within oneself, to resist sinful sexual temptation, and any sin for that matter, utilizing the grace and power of God "to the shedding of great drops of blood if necessary." The same as Jesus did when He resisted the temptation to do His will rather than God, the Father's will on the Mount of Olives before He was arrested, tried, and crucified (Luke 22:44).

What Jesus showed us, in deferring to God's will, and I certainly can attest to, is that sin, in some form of desire, namely, a lust of our flesh, our eyes, or the pride of life, will attempt to take over our lives. For many men, but not all, their weakness is the desire for the fruit in the middle of a woman's anatomy. It's a prominent weakness that has been a challenge to nearly all men and conquered an innumerable number, from peasants and great warriors to ministers, politicians, and kings. The sexual beast of desire is demanding, manifesting itself subtly or aggressively, with no consideration and respect for God or His moral standards and boundaries or for what is right or wrong. Nor does the beast have regard for any man, irrespective of who he is, as described below.

After a Sunday service altar call at West Adams Foursquare Church (WAFC) in Los Angeles, I received the Lord as my

Savior. Soon after, I joined the church and felt like I was "home" and where I belonged. I grew quickly and tremendously in my knowledge and understanding of the Lord. My copastors, husband and wife Marvin and Juanita Smith, had a very close relationship with Dr. Benjamin Reed, a highly committed, anointed man of God. He was an incredibly gifted teacher, orator, and pastor of the First Church of God in Los Angeles. Our pastors invited him on more than one occasion to be the Sunday guest speaker at our church.

One day, it popped into my mind to visit his church during the upcoming Sunday service. So I did and was rewarded by hearing a highly enlightening testimonial message. His testimony, with its unmistakable communique, metamessages, and subliminal messages, made a massive and lasting impact on me. The following is my recall of Dr. Reed's testimonial sermon and message.

Dr. Reed said he accepted an invitation to speak at a conference in the Midwest. Unfortunately, I don't recall precisely where. He mentioned completing a successful series of teaching and preaching lessons the night before and disclosed that he slept well and was well-rested. He accomplished his purpose and goals and sat in his luxury hotel's restaurant, relaxed and satisfied with the conference and what the Lord had accomplished. He had hours before his departure back to LA, so he was relaxing after eating, enjoying a cup of coffee, and reading the paper. Suddenly, Dr. Reed smelled this incredible fragrance. It was the most pleasant and pleasing aromatic smell he had ever breathed. His body immediately responded, very pleasingly awakening to the idyllic aroma. He slowly and gradually removed his eyes from the paper and looked up to see where that incredible scent was coming from. As his head turned and his eyes gradually looked up, he saw a woman's beautifully proportioned and shapely legs walking toward him. He said, "I smelled her before I saw her." He repeated, "I smelled her before I saw her." As she approached, walking in the aisle closest to his table, his head and eyes rose to see her entirely. He viewed her legs, magnificent figure, gorgeous face, and lovely hairstyle as she came near. He mentioned again, "I smelled her before I saw her."

He expected her to walk by and meet her husband, boyfriend, or friend as she approached his table. However, she sat down next to him and gracefully introduced herself. Then looking him in the face, she began to proposition him, inviting him to herself pleasantly. She was a classy call girl in words, personality, aura, appearance, and dress! As she propositioned him with her extraordinary charm and elegance, he thought, *I'm thousands of miles from home, and no one knows me here. No one who knows me or who I am sees me right now! There is nothing to stop me!*

I interpreted what Dr. Reed was thinking as the following. With his quick mental speed and vivid imagination, he seriously pondered her request. Contemplating the incredible sight of her nakedness, the delightful foreplay, and the crescendo consummation with her, he cognitively and sensually recognized the tremendous opportunity she presented to him.

As he finished pondering her request, just before he gave his reply, Dr. Reed said, in his inner ear, he suddenly heard the loud, attention-getting, unmistakably clear, and distinct voice of the Lord say, "Benjamin, I see you!" He reported that he immediately felt very sick in his stomach upon hearing God's voice. The Lord said nothing else. He then looked at the woman in her face, eye-to-eye, and said, "You are beautiful! Any man would want you, and I certainly do. However, I fear God, and I cannot!" Without saying anything, Dr. Reed said, the woman looked back at him eye-to-eye, focusing silently and very intently on him for a few seconds. Then after her intense examination, she said, "I believe you." Then she got up and walked away.

After hearing Dr. Reed, I reasoned that the woman, very experienced in her profession, had great confidence and skill in reading men. From all accounts, she was well-versed in determining whether men were telling the truth or using words to cover up their true desires, feelings, and convictions. Therefore, as I pondered the sequence of what Dr. Reed reported, I believe that during the woman's silent examination, she read Dr. Reed through and through, from inside to outside. The professional sex worker seriously considered whether Dr. Reed spoke his true convictions and was unquestionably committed to his statement. After her probe, per her words and actions, she accepted that Dr. Reed told the truth and did fear God above his desire for her.

For me, Dr. Reed's testimony didn't stop there. The lady respected Dr. Reed for the deep love and fear she saw he had for the Lord. Her deferring to his commitment to God injected a strong sense of care, concern, and emotion in me for the young lady. Internally, I started praying fervently with love and passion for the Lord to save her. I prayed, "Lord, that woman has probably never met a man who didn't want something from her. Please, Lord, save her. Let what she saw in Dr. Reed never leave her. Let her reflect and think. There is a man. I met a man. There are some men who have not bowed to 'Baal.' Bowed to the 'powerful Molly.' Lord, she respected You! Father, please respect her like you respected the prostitute Rahab! Lord, I beg You, please have compassion and bring her to You!"

As I completed praying, my imagination immediately took over. Inside me was an incredible thought. It was that one day in heaven, Dr. Reed would hear his name loudly called by that transformed and glorified woman, who would run and jump into his arms with unspeakable joy, thanks, and gratitude to him for illuminating her way to the Lord and into His righteousness. Then Dr. Reed would receive a real kiss!

One of the many lessons I received from Dr. Reed's testimony was that Dr. Reed was as candid with the lady as he was with himself. He never denied the effect she had on him. He repeatedly said, "I smelled her before I saw her," and time after time, commented on her incredible beauty. Listening to Dr. Reed, I recalled what Mom had told me years before about the man's weakness. Dr. Reed's testimony illustrated Mom's lesson and its validation. As Dr. Reed seriously thought about the lady's proposition, his weakness and desire for her enraptured him, capturing his full attention and taking him over completely. He was heading toward putting aside and casting away his integrity, marriage, ministry, livelihood, and everything else for one hour of pleasure with that young lady. Per his testimony, that was his direction until the Lord intervened and returned him to his sanity. Oh my! The "powerful Molly's" sway over men is unreal!

I received a multitude of knowledge and wisdom from Dr. Reed's testimony. However, the three lessons that meant the most to me and I personalized and walked away with were the following:

1. God is always present and sees and hears everything. He will never leave me or forsake me. He can and will keep me to Himself and all else I commit to Him as long as I genuinely "do" want to be kept (Heb. 13:5 and 2 Tim. 1:12). So in the end, it's always, always, my choice to be saved or not! Or resist temptation or not!

To me, this was readily apparent from Dr. Reed's testimony. The Lord came to Dr. Reed's aid when his defenses were down, compromised by the woman's scent (smell), beauty (sight), and words (hearing) were his wisdom and common sense. She conquered three of his five senses to whip him beyond character and moral recognition. Her womanly sex appeal and grace took him "out of his mind" and locked him in his weakness. He was about to be slain, fricasseed, and eaten until the Lord stepped in. In my analytical mind, a thought has occurred to me. What if she had captured all five senses by touching his hands, arms, or face (sense of feel) and then leaning over and kissing him to allow him to taste her lips (sense of taste)? Oh my! What would have happened? It's clear from what he said what would have happened. He was already a mushy, soft pulp of resistance in her hands. God's timing was impeccable! By His grace, she didn't get that far. Jude was right when he told us that our Lord could keep us from falling and present us before His glorious presence without fault and with great joy (Jude 1:24 NIV).

2. The second lesson I got from Dr. Reed's testimony was the following: He knew no one would see him if he accepted and indulged in what the beautiful young lady offered him. He wanted her! He was thousands of miles from home and reasoned in his mind that he could go ahead and indulge in the pleasures he so much desired with the young lady. Then because no one but him would know it, he could go back home and about his life in complete anonymity. After meditating on all Dr. Reed said, I focused on the high-density x-ray picture the lady left on his table in her wake. The young lady exposed a strong, smoldering, hidden, fleshly desire in the "x-ray." The picture revealed a lust for the "Molly" embedded in Dr. Reed's heart. It was not the healthy, insatiable hunger and thirst for his wife *only* that we men are to have. Instead, it was a desire and lust stimulated within him by the lady's glorious scent, captivating beauty, and

enormous sex appeal. Personally, Dr. Reed's testimony and experience were a lesson of immense caution to me. A warning that cast a beacon light on how allowing a forbidden desire or lust to live within me can have dire consequences. Considering Pastor Reed's predicament caused the Lord's bell of Proverbs 15 to ring clear and loud in my ears. The bell bellowed,

> Drink water from your own cistern, and running water from your own well. Should your fountains be dispersed abroad, streams of water in the streets? Let them be only your own, and not for strangers with you. Let your fountain be blessed, and rejoice with the wife of your youth. As a loving deer and a graceful doe, let her breasts satisfy you at all times; and always be enraptured with her love. For why should you, my son, be enraptured by an immoral woman, and be embraced in the arms of a seductress?. (Prov. 5:15–20)

The comprehensive message I got from Pastor Reed's testimonial sermon and these verses was this: "Robert, you must seriously and immediately search your heart and mind for any desire of the 'world.' Surface and rid yourself of every want and desire you know to be against the will of God." I had just heard from Dr. Reed that having hidden, ungodly desires was extremely dangerous. Whether single as I currently was or if I was married, sooner or later, any sinful desire or attitude lurking in me would pop up and out. Like with Dr. Reed, it was most likely going to occur at a time and place of the devil's choosing, a time and place when I'm least expecting it, a time and place when my guard is down. Or from what I learned from Pastor Juanita Smith. At a time when I'm weak spiritually from a lack of the Word or prayer. Or when I'm mentally or emotionally vulnerable from a lack of knowledge, sadness, loneliness, depression, or despair. Or when I'm weakened physically from a lack of nutrition, sleep, or exercise. Therefore, in wisdom, I said to myself, "Robert, if you're holding onto any ungodly desire or contending with the Lord for something you want, let it go now! Immediately crucify it and cast it out now! Don't wait, and don't procrastinate!"

Dr. Reed's testimony was sobering and frightened the mess out of me. It was a loud bullhorn with accompanying flashing red lights. All I could see in my mind was the bright neon-lit warning "Be sure your sin(s) will find you out" (Num. 32:23). I knew I would not have been able to stand under what that woman put on Dr. Reed. She would have had me and whatever amount of money she wanted for her services, plus my following ten future dates, pinned in indelible ink, scheduled in her appointment book. His testimony exposed his weakness and revealed a multitude of my vulnerabilities as well.

In addition, Dr. Reed's testimonial sermon confirmed my mother's message of the weakness of men and the unmatched allurement and seduction power of the "Molly" to draw men to itself. His message was a robust motivational wind that forced me to fast and pray earnestly to crucify all my fleshly desires, goals, and ambitions. It also alerted me that some temptations were too strong to contend with, and as scripture instructed me, I was to flee. To put it another way, taking a theme from the movie *Forrest Gump,* I should run if placed in a situation like Dr. Reed's. The audience of my inner man should loudly shout to me in urgency, "Run, Robert! Run! Run!"

1. The third message I received from Dr. Reed's testimony was that he was attending to his own business at the time of temptation. He was not doing anything wrong, nor was he thinking sensual, lustful, passionate, or inappropriate thoughts but thinking on things of a good report. Dr. Reed was feasting on what the Lord did for the people at the conference through him. However, the Lord warned us to be sober and vigilant; our adversary, the devil, walks about like a roaring lion, seeking whom he may devour (1 Pet. 5:8). Dr. Reed got caught innocently in the devil's eye. Satan sent a perfect temptation to bring him down and strike down his ministry and all other aspects of his life. As scripture says, thank God, He knows how to deliver us out of temptation (2 Pet. 2:9), just like He delivered Dr. Reed.

The clear message from Dr. Reed's experience was "Robert, life is not fair, and the devil doesn't play fair. He plays to destroy you in any way he can and destroy those you influence." I thought,

> Compared to Dr. Reed, I'm just a small pebble in God's pond. The devil, however, is looking to destroy me, like he attempted to destroy Dr. Reed. So don't let it happen! Stay in the Word and constant prayer! Forgive everyone who has done something bad to you or has done you wrong! Don't become resentful and hold grudges against anyone! Forgive them so that you don't "give place" to the devil and that God doesn't turn you over to the tormentors for your unforgiveness. It's not worth it!

My Takeaway

- **Get rid of every evil desire, sin, and attitude. If you don't, sooner or later, any lurking ungodliness is going to pop out.**
  - ○ **The pop out will most likely occur at a time and place of the devil's choosing, when you are least expecting it.**
- **Resist temptation even to "shedding great drops of blood" if need be. That is, with all your effort and might!**
- **Love God and fear God above all else. God will keep you from falling, provided you want to be kept!**

Vignette 7

The Weakness of Men and the Weakness of Women

Sequel 4: My Mother Was Correct: The Weakness of Men Is Undeniable

It's incredible how my mom's message of the weakness of men being the "middle of a woman's anatomy" is universal in truth and independent of the time and age we live. The study of history and human behavior substantially amplifies the importance of Mom's implied direction to me "to *not* be like most men," as the following illustrates.

As spiritual a man as King David was. A man after God's own heart (1 Sam. 13:14), a man who wrote nearly half of the 150 psalms in scripture. The man who single-handedly killed a lion, a bear, and then the giant, Goliath. The same man the women spoke of as they danced and sang their praises. "Saul has slain his thousands, and David his ten thousands" (1 Sam. 18:7). The same David, who entered the city of Jerusalem with the Ark of the Covenant and himself danced before the Lord (2 Sam. 6:14–22). And the man, some have said, loved God more than anyone born except Jesus. Still, being all he was, that man, David, king of Israel, quickly fell prey to the unique middle part of a woman's anatomy.

The "powerful Molly" took David down and took him down hard. His sexual desire for Bathsheba blocked all Torah commandments from his mind. It additionally wiped his memory clean of the hours and days of sweet communion and worship he had with God. The "powerful Molly" essentially overrode his love for God. It blocked out all his thankfulness and gratitude to God for raising him from the sheep pasture to a mighty warrior and king of His people. It blocked out any song of praise to

God that he had written, played, or sung to the Lord. Strangely enough, it blocked out his fear of God and embedded wisdom. As scripture says, "The fear of the LORD is the beginning of wisdom" (Prov. 9:10). Thus, the "powerful Molly," after overriding his fear of God, obliterated his wisdom and took his sanity. The "powerful Molly" took him over completely. Upon seeing Bathsheba's nakedness, he allowed his "outer man," his flesh's insatiable and ravenous appetite for the middle part of Bathsheba's anatomy, to take him over completely.

It was not the unexpected circumstance of seeing Bathsheba bathing on the rooftop that got him. Unpredictable things do happen. Once seeing Bathsheba, David should have been a man with decency enough to preserve her modesty. He should have quickly walked away from the sight of Bathsheba, refusing to allow his mind to dwell on what he had seen. But without question, David was mentally engaged and became satiated with Bathsheba's beauty. Thus, in his mind, David was delighted with what he saw. Like Eve, David stared at the "good fruit" of the forbidden tree. He stared at what was pleasant to his eyes and "good to eat," so to speak, but forbidden. Then his desires erupted. His outer man expressed his euphoric thoughts and desires. "I want some of that! I want all of that!"

King David then gladly acted assertively on his inclination and brought forth his sin of adultery. He allowed his desires and corresponding actions to consummate and bring forth the birth of covetousness, adultery, disrespect, disloyalty, and the murder of one of his most loyal chief commanders, a member of his mighty thirty-seven warriors, Uriah the Hittite, Bathsheba's husband. As James says, "But each one is tempted when he is drawn away by his own desires and enticed. Then when desire has conceived, it gives birth to sin; and sin, when it is full-grown, brings forth death" (James 1:14–15). Ironically, Goliath couldn't even wound or intimidate David with all his might, battle experience, and warrior prowess. But the "powerful Molly" conquered and slew him very swiftly, probably within a matter of hours.

Oh Lord! Who is going to deliver me from my body of sin? Only Jesus (Rom. 7:24–25)!

David had Uriah killed and married Bathsheba after he found out she was pregnant. All in an attempt to cover up his mess. Please forgive me, but I've always wondered if David was so holy, why did God need to send Nathan to him with a parable to get him down on his knees and ask for God's forgiveness (2 Sam. 12:1–13)? He certainly knew right from wrong. As king, David was required to have written down the Law and continuously read the Torah (Deut. 17:14–20). Although he didn't have the Holy Spirit living in him, I'm sure he was still under conviction with a heavy load of guilt for what he did.

Additionally, in Psalm 51:4, David, speaking to God, says, "Against You, You only, have I sinned, And done this evil in Your sight." How does David express no guilt or remorse for what he did to Bathsheba, Uriah, Bathsheba's father, Eliam, also a member of David's mighty thirty-seven, and her paternal grandfather, Ahithophel, David's highly revered counselor? Jesus tells us in Matthew 5:23–24,

> Therefore if you bring your gift to the altar, and there remember that your brother has something against you, leave your gift there before the altar, and go your way. First be reconciled to your brother, and then come and offer your gift. (Matt. 5:23–24)

Thus, if a person has something against us (i.e., we've wronged or hurt someone), we must attempt to reconcile before continuing our relationship with God. After receiving God's forgiveness, should not David, in earnest, have peacefully repaired his relationship with all those still alive he offended? Jesus Christ, God, "is the same yesterday, today, and forever" (Mal. 3:6, Heb. 13:8). Thus, the directive presented in the book of Matthew holds irrespective of the era. I've never understood how David could say to God, "Against You, You only, have I sinned, And done this evil in Your sight." And after forgiving David, the Lord not levy on him the directive to get Bathsheba's forgiveness for what he did to her and her husband and additionally ask for forgiveness and seek reconciliation with her father and grandfather? It appears David was allowed to walk away without considering his sin's impact on Bathsheba, Eliam, and Ahithophel.

As I said, I've never understood this, especially when, in all appearances, David's sin led to Ahithophel's bitterness, unforgiveness, and hatred for him for what he did to his family. That is, to his granddaughter, Bathsheba, and grandson-in-law, Uriah. In all probability, this led to Ahithophel joining David's son Absalom in his rebellion against his father and Ahithophel intensely wanting to kill the king. Then after Absalom did not execute Ahithophel's plan to track down David immediately after the king and his men fled Jerusalem. Ahithophel, apparently giving up on life, went home, set his household in order, and hanged himself (2 Sam. 11:1–12:25; 2 Sam. 15:1–17:23).[2]

Concerning David, the king, and his sin with Bathsheba, my question is this: had David gotten too dependent on himself? Too self-assured with all his victories, too rich in luxury, too many wives (which was against the law according to Deut. 17:17)? Or too idle and drifted into pride, arrogance, and self-confidence? Scripture clearly says, "Pride goes before destruction, and a haughty spirit before a fall" (Prov. 16:18).

David also was under the Law. Why didn't God send Nathan with a death warrant, rather than a parable, to David for his deliberate self-initiated adultery and premeditated murder (2 Sam. 12:1–10)? Per the Law of Moses (Lev. 20:10 and Ex. 21:12), David's actions required him to be put to death. The Torah does not provide a mercy criterion for adultery or clemency for murder. Nor is God a respecter of persons, and He has made it clear to us that to whom much is given, much is required. Therefore, as the nation's leader, the king of Israel, David was also the premier example to the people. He should have been put to death for his crimes, yet he was not. I've never understood this. David lived under the Law, and, per the Law, he should have been killed!

Lord, please don't spank me for saying this or making the comparison. But there is a common saying in the practice of America's justice system that it is better to be "guilty and rich than to be innocent and poor." When I look at David, it appears that it is better to be guilty with a fervent loving relationship with God than to be innocent with a cold relationship with God.

The above appears to be so because, reviewing David's life and his faith in God as a shepherd, warrior, escapee of King Saul and king of Israel, the Word says of David that he was a man after God's own heart (1 Sam. 13:14; Acts 13:22). In another place, it says, "For David had done what was right in the eyes of the LORD and had not failed to keep any of the LORD's commands all the days of his life—except in the case of Uriah the Hittite" (1 Kings 15:5 NIV), for which he should have died. Compared to the pardon of David, a boy who shunned the Sabbath was killed per God's specific word to Moses for picking up sticks on the Sabbath (Num. 15:32–36). God ordered his death by stoning from all the congregation, the same method of death as required by the law for a stubborn and rebellious son (Deut. 21:18–21). Thus, with great presupposition, I assume, per God's judgment, the boy's picking up sticks on the Sabbath was another act of his stubborn and rebellious life. Therefore, God ordered his death to use him as an example to others tempted to follow the defiant and disobedient path. The Torah's explanation of the death penalty for that crime explicitly states the reason as being so that "all Israel shall hear and fear." David was king. Indeed, killing David for adultery and murder would be a far more outstanding and impactful example to the people than killing a boy for insubordination in regard to sending a message to the people that they were to follow God's laws and decrees wholly.

Therefore, from all I understand comes my belief that it is "better to be guilty with a fervent relationship with God" like David had "than to be innocent with a cold or no relationship with God," as it appears the boy was.

As for David, I've come up with two possible answers for God pardoning him. They are the following:

1. "Mercy triumphs over judgment" (James 2:13). The Lord Himself illustrated this with His mercy and nonjudgment of the woman caught in adultery (John 8:4–11). Per the law, she should have also been put to death.
2. God is sovereign and gives mercy to whomever He wills. Paul elaborates on God's divine sovereignty and prerogative by explaining His election of Jacob over Esau and His dealings with Pharaoh during Israel's Exodus (Rom. 9:13–18).

James's and Paul's illustrations make it very clear that God is Sovereign! He has the final word, period! From this, I assume that the Lord's specific message regarding David is "Robert, you are to love Me with all your heart, mind, soul, and strength. Additionally, seek first My kingdom and all its righteousness. If you fall, by My grace, love, and mercy through Jesus Christ, My Son, and your Savior and Redeemer, I will find a way to pick you up. Even as I told you, 'For though a righteous man falls seven times, he rises again'" (Prov. 24:16 NIV).

Thank You, Father. I recognize my whole duty is to fear, obey, and keep Your commandments. I accept Your sovereignty and rule without questioning any further. I gratefully thank You for the grace You have bestowed upon me and the added grace You will provide me in my time of future need.

A man's refusal to control and crucify his fleshly desire/lust for the fruit in the midst of a woman's bodily garden sins against his own body (1 Cor. 6:18). If not quickly halted, his sin of immorality will lead him into rebellion against God, which is like the sin of witchcraft (1 Sam. 15:23). David's son, King Solomon, epitomizes this. Solomon possessed a ravenous appetite, desire, and love for the "fruit of the woman." Although Solomon was the wisest and richest man in all the world, he did not bring his desire and love for the "Molly" under the control of God's Word and Will as described in the following.

But King Solomon loved many foreign women, as well as the daughter of Pharaoh: women of the Moabites, Ammonites, Edomites, Sidonians, and Hittites—from the nations of whom the Lord had said to the children of Israel, "You shall not intermarry with them, nor they with you. For surely they will turn away your hearts after their gods." Solomon clung to these in love. And he had seven hundred wives, princesses, and three hundred concubines; and his wives turned away his heart. For it was so, when Solomon was old, that his wives turned his heart after other gods; and his heart was not loyal to the LORD his God, as was the heart of his father David. For Solomon went after Ashtoreth the goddess of the Sidonians, and after Milcom the abomination of the Ammonites. Solomon did evil in the sight of the LORD, and did not fully follow the LORD, as did his father David. Then Solomon built a high place for Chemosh the abomination of Moab, on the hill that is east of Jerusalem, and for Molech the abomination of the people of Ammon. And he did likewise for all his foreign wives, who burned incense and sacrificed to their gods. So the LORD became angry with Solomon, because his heart had turned from the LORD God of Israel, who had appeared to him twice, and had commanded him concerning this thing, that he should not go after other gods; but he did not keep what the LORD had commanded. Therefore the LORD said to Solomon, "Because you have done this, and have not kept My covenant and My statutes, which I have commanded you, I will surely tear the kingdom away from you and give it to your servant" (1 Kings 11:1–11).

As it turned out for all the world to see, *Solomon clung to his foreign wives in love.* Toward the end of his life, Solomon loved the "powerful Molly" much more than he loved God. The Lord is the same yesterday, today, and forever. Thus, what Jesus said to His disciple Judas (not Iscariot, the traitor) in the Gospel of John unfortunately describes Solomon. Jesus said,

If anyone loves Me, he will keep My word; and My Father will love him, and We will come to him and make Our home with him. He who does not love Me does not keep My words; and the word which you hear is not Mine but the Father's who sent Me. (John 14:23–24)

Solomon abandoned God's Word in preference to clinging and holding on to women "in love," whom God had forbidden, even after God chastised him. His actions let us know who and what Solomon loved "infinitely" more than God. In his defiance, he showed no appreciation of the favor God gave him, being a child borne out of a union that should never have been. A child of God's amazing grace chosen above his brothers.

I believe it was because of David's sincere repentance of adultery and murder, coupled with God's total forgiveness, that as a matter of illuminating His complete forgiveness of David. He chose to bestow abundant grace upon David through Bathsheba, with whom he sinned. Thus, the Lord chose Solomon, out of all his brothers, to succeed their father as king. After being crowned king, God's blessings and grace continued to overflow onto Solomon as He additionally bestowed on him wisdom, riches, and peace within his kingdom during his reign. Yet as a sad commentary to us men, like his father. Despite God's abundant blessings, Solomon still allowed his fleshly desire to rebel against God, preferring the central part of many women's anatomies to God. As stated above, he had seven hundred wives and three hundred concubines (1 Kings 11:3).

Solomon fell so much in his later years that God divided his kingdom because of his disobedience and sins. No biblical record exists that Solomon ever repented and asked God to forgive him. Therefore, whether Solomon was "saved" is unknown to us. Solomon's life and actions warn us men that we have and were born with an inherent weakness for the middle of a woman's anatomy that we must bring under control, or it will control and destroy us!

I genuinely thank the Lord my God for my mother warning me about my inherent weakness for women and the "powerful Molly" God has graciously given them. She warned me very early, several years before I experienced or felt any desire or attraction for sex. Her message was indeed a "Godsend." It prevented me from being taken over by my lust and desires. From what I've learned from scripture, I believe that the woman is unequivocally the most beautiful and desirable creature God made. I've concluded that because of what Genesis 6:1–2, Jude 1:6, and 2 Peter 2:4 tell us. Those verses convey to us that angels did not keep their positions of authority but abandoned and left their proper places for the beauty of women, and they paid for it with their eternal lives.

Elaborating, once angels or "sons of God" left their heavenly, God-appointed positions to pursue women, they allowed the "lust of their eyes," their thoughts, and their desires to take them over when they saw and gazed upon the beauty of women. I don't know how a heavenly creature could fall for an earthly being like that, but it happened. The beauty of women enraptured them, as explained below.

> Now it came to pass, when men began to multiply on the face of the earth, and daughters were born to them, that the sons of God saw the daughters of men, that they were beautiful; and they took wives for themselves of all whom they chose. (Gen. 6:1–2)

And the angels who did not keep their proper domain, but left their own habitation, He has reserved in everlasting chains under darkness for the judgment of the great day. (Jude 1:6)

For if God did not spare the angels who sinned, but cast them down to hell and delivered them into chains of darkness, to be reserved for judgment. (2 Pet. 2:4)

The "sons of God" of Genesis 6:2 are the angels referenced by Jude and Peter. The book of Job explicitly confirms in three places that the "sons of God" refer to angels (Job 1:6–7; Job 2:1; Job 38:4–7). Although the biblical book of Job is the reference, it is consistent to note that early church fathers from the first century also believed the "sons of God were angels.[3]

Note: Many Jewish commentators believe in the "Sethite View." They think that "the sons of God" "are the God-fearing descendants of Seth." Hence, the third son of Adam and Eve, whom Noah and we have descended from. They additionally believe that "the daughters of men" were the descendants of Cain.[4] However, I know of no scriptural evidence substantiating this theory.

Men's uncontrolled desire for sex and the fruit from the "tree of life" amid the woman's garden has ruined their lives and wreaked havoc, misery, fear, degradation, and destruction on countless millions of families, girls, and women. It has also carried over perversely, ruining boys and other men as they have preyed on them, in their insanity, as substitutes for women to satisfy their lust. Throughout history, men of high and low social standing have fallen and been brought down because they never controlled the sexual beast within them and their desire and lust for sex. The irony of this attraction is that it is systematic, or should I say Adamic. Man-after-man, ethnicity-after-ethnicity, nation-after-nation, and empire-after-empire, era-after-era. Men have fallen to the "powerful Molly." Biblically, besides David and Solomon, Samson is another example of man's foolishness, folly, and weakness for sex (Judg. 14–16).

Modern-day evidence of man's sexual desire for "the middle part of the woman's anatomy" is replete. Our daily news, in unpleasant prevalence, reports in all its media genres, in highly publicized headlines, the same story repeated. Namely, sexual assault and abuse charges, sexual misconduct, rape, sexual harassment, and other sexual allegations levied against men of all social, ethnic, economic, and intelligence statuses.

Below is a short list of contemporary famous and influential men publicly accused of sexual assault, sexual misconduct, rape, etc.

- Donald Trump (former US president)
- Roy Moore (former judge)
- Jeffery Epstein (deceased, money manager/financier)
- Harvey Weinstein (entertainment)
- Bill Cosby (entertainment)
- Matt Lauer (media)
- Charlie Rose (media)
- Bill O'Reilly (media)
- R. Kelly (music)
- Andrew Cuomo (former governor of NY)
- Sean John (P. Diddy, Puff Daddy, Diddy) Combs (rapper, record producer, executive, and 3-time Grammy Award winner)
- A multitude of Catholic priests and Protestant clergy

The publicly reported list of names indicates that many men are not controlling themselves, irrespective of who they are and their position in government, entertainment, news, or corporate leadership. Instead, they allow their lust to drive them to damaging outcomes. For example, in the now-infamous *Access Hollywood* video clip,[5] Donald Trump unabashedly talks about reaching out and grabbing a woman's privates in what sounds like a voice of glee. This video illustrates how primal, base, and carnal men can be if we don't control our desires for the "Molly," or worse, when we don't even see the need to control our desires or respect another person's modesty and private parts.

Again, I am so grateful for what my mom taught me at that Chevron gas station in vignette 3 when I was eight. Her message started me on a path to discipline myself against an iniquity, a crookedness, and bentness embedded in me that came with my birth. After David repented of his adultery with Bathsheba and his murder of her husband, Uriah, the Hittite, he identified his inherent iniquity (i.e., his crookedness, his bentness) in Psalm 51. In the psalm, he points to this intrinsic iniquity that caused him to commit his sin. It is this same iniquity that every man, including me, has. As I've said, my mother identified it to me early in my life with her direction for me to master and maintain control over it. Every mother and father should teach their sons early in life what my mom taught me and King Lemuel's mother taught him (Prov. 31:2–3) and what King David's life and Psalm 51 teach us.

At an early age, parents should teach their boys the ways of God and that His grace can and will successfully help them conquer all challenges, obstacles, and temptations in life if they call on God and genuinely do want to walk in His ways. Then with their age and maturity progression. Notify and warn their sons of their "inherent sexual weakness" and their responsibility to discipline and control themselves. Parents should give them the knowledge and tools to do so before they are unwittingly exposed to internet porn, sexual entertainment from TV, commercials, or cinema. And before exposure to what public schools teach regarding sex, sexual orientations, and our society's progressively loose morals and rampant sexual promiscuity.

My Takeaway

- **As illustrated by David's life, it makes no difference how spiritual or close to God you are. Sin still lies at your door, waiting for you. You must rule it! You must make a choice! The right choice!**
- **Solomon, the wisest human being in the world, chose the love of women and sex over God. His sin cost him and Israel greatly.**
- **Earthly knowledge and wisdom will not save you or keep you saved, nor will it lead you to God and His righteousness.**
  - **Only your earnest desire to seek God and obey His Word with the help and power of God's Holy Spirit will.**
- **As demonstrated by Solomon, salvation and being kept out of sin come by our choice. God has called us and is infinitely willing to save us and keep us if we are sincerely desirous to be saved and kept.**

- o **Like Solomon's sin broke Israel apart, any person's sin affects not only the sinner but also others. Including the righteous under their influence, care, and protection.**
- o **No one knows whether Solomon was saved. There is no record of him repenting.**
- **Too many men have ruined their lives, their children's lives, and the lives of others because they have not been taught nor have they taken it upon themselves to control their sexual desires, appetites, and behavior.**
- **Boys should be schooled and trained in the ways and grace of God. Then informed of their inherent sexual weaknesses and how to control themselves. Before they are indoctrinated (brainwashed) by society and mature into puberty.**

Vignette 8

The Weakness of Men and the Weakness of Women

Sequel 5: The Weakness of Men Quantified

"For where your treasure is, there your heart will be also" (Matt. 6:21 NIV). In October 2012, the press widely reported that an Australian documentary filmmaker organized a male ask/bid auction to sleep with a female virgin.[6] The female virgin receiving the highest bid was a twenty-year-old Brazilian college student. The winning bid was $780,000 for an hour, or $994,220 in December 2022, inflation-adjusted dollars.[7] A middle-aged Japanese millionaire submitted the winning bid. He fended off stiff competition from two American bidders and an Indian bidder.

Suppose we analyze the winning bid's value for access to the young lady in the light of where the Lord said your heart would be. Men place a very high value on the middle part of the woman's anatomy. It's a much higher value than anything else I know. To put the inflation-adjusted $994,220 winning bid in perspective, I converted it to its equivalent gold (Au) amount. Using gold provides a universal standard to compare how much men value the "powerful Molly." Gold is a precious metal measured in troy ounces. Troy ounces are heavier than avoirdupois ounces. 14.583 troy ounces equal one pound instead of sixteen avoirdupois ounces. On December 31, 2022, the spot gold value was $1,823.91/troy ounce (per Goldprice.org). Thus, the gold equivalent of the winning bid was 545.10 troy ounces or 37.4 pounds of gold.

One hour of "Molly" is worth 37.4 pounds of gold.

The Australian filmmaker also included a female ask/bid auction to sleep with a male virgin. To put men's lust for the "Molly" in perspective, the female winning the bid paid $3,000 or $3,824 in inflation-adjusted December 2022 dollars for the privilege. The gold equivalent of the woman's winning bid was 2.1 troy ounces or 0.14 pounds of gold.

Speaking loud and clear for all to hear, this price does not represent me. I know I'm worth more than a little over a tenth of a pound of gold.

However, in seriousness, to put these numbers in perspective, men will pay 260 times more for the "powerful Molly" than women for access to the corresponding part of the man's anatomy.

On a much larger scale, the 2015 Havocscope Global Black Market Information, "Prostitution Revenue Worldwide" report [8] reported that the annual global or worldwide prostitution (legal and illegal, including sex trafficking) revenue was $186 billion. Note, however, that the number is conservative in that it is not inclusive of prostitution in all countries; for example, it doesn't include Russia. Adjusting the dollar amount only for inflation, not revenue growth, the equivalent 2015 annual value in 2022 dollars was $230 billion. With a tiny exception, all the revenue was from male-female sex. Table 1 below inserts, for comparison, the adjusted 2022 prostitution revenue into a list of *Fortune* magazine's "Global 500" list of the top five hundred corporations worldwide as measured by their 2022 revenue. This data was obtained online from Wikipedia, which lists the data sources.[9] Table 1 lists explicitly the twenty largest companies in top-down order by revenue from *Fortune's* "Top 500" list with global prostitution inserted. Conservatively, international prostitution ranks number 20 in the top-down list sequence. It is within the top 4 percent of the world's five hundred largest revenue-producing companies. In this discussion, prostitution is the service of a woman selling herself to a man for pay, granting him access to her most private parts. Given the massive annual revenue, it's incredible to see how much sex means to men and how much they will pay for it compared to all other human needs. My mother was right. The lure and desire for sex are men's biggest weaknesses—not all men, but most men. The fact that the "powerful Molly" is within the top 4 percent of worldwide revenue producers testify to it.

Table 1. Reported 2022 Global Prostitution in Comparison to the World's Largest Companies by Revenue

Rank	Name	Industry	Revenue (Billion)	Employees
1	Walmart	Retail	$573	2,300,000
2	Amazon.com Inc.	Retail	$470	1,608,000
3	State Grid Corp. of China	Electricity	$461	871,145
4	China National Petroleum Corp.	Oil and Gas	$412	1,090,345
5	China Petrochemical Corp.	Oil and Gas	$401	542,286
6	Saudi Aramco	Oil and Gas	$400	68,493
7	Apple	Electronics	$366	154,000
8	Volkswagen	Automotive	$296	662,575
9	China State Construction	Construction	$294	368,327
10	CVS Health	Healthcare	$292	258,500
11	United Health	Healthcare	$288	350,000
12	ExxonMobil	Oil and Gas	$286	63,000
13	Toyota	Automotive	$279	372,817
14	Berkshire Hathaway	Financials	$276	372,000
15	Shell plc	Oil and Gas	$273	82,000
16	McKesson	Healthcare	$264	66,500
17	Alphabet Inc.	Inform. Tech.	$258	156,500
18	Samsung Electronics	Electronics	$244	266,673
19	Trafigura	Commodities	$231	9,031
20	Global Prostitution	Sex Industry	$230*	13,828,700**
21	Foxconn	Electronics	$215	826,608

*Inflation-adjusted 2015 ($186 billion) dollars to 2022 dollars.
** 2015 employees. Largest nations: China: 5 Million (M); India: 3M; USA: 1M; Philippines: 0.8M; Mexico: 0.5M.

Examining the amount of money the virgin auctioned herself off for. Along with the combined global prostitution revenue that Havocscope reported and where that value compares with the world's largest income revenue companies. I don't think it is a stretch to say that men value nothing on earth more than the middle portion of a woman's anatomy, that is, the "powerful Molly." David acknowledged his and all men's weakness in his prayer of repentance to God for his sin with Bathsheba when he said,

> Surely I was sinful at birth, sinful from the time my mother conceived me (Ps. 51:5 NIV)

My mother knew what sinful weakness I inherited at birth and quickly made me aware of it. She then let me know that I was to dominate and control it; it was not to control and dominate me.

Once the façade is removed, and we know what men value, it's easy to see the following whys:

- why sex is used to sell products as glaringly displayed in advertising
  - commercial after commercial
  - billboard after billboard
  - movie after movie
  - TV program after program
- why many marriages fail because of low sex frequency, poor sex quality, and other associated physical intimacy issues and problems
- why numerous brutal and lustful males poach upon so many young girls, teenage girls, and women
  - Sex poachers, like pathological beasts, have no concern for the physical, emotional, and mental mutilation they leave their innocent human prey in.

- o Sex poachers violently, seductively, and in many cases masquerade as professionals, unethically violating a female's trust and dignity by handling them inappropriately, thrusting themselves on them, and worse, into them.
- o Sex poachers steal their victim's self-value, self-esteem, and the most intimate aspects of their being and well-being.
- o Sex poachers do all this and more and then move on as if nothing happened.
- why so many girls and young women are wooed, grabbed, and kidnapped for sex slaves and trafficking, per Havocscope (Sex trafficking represents more than 25 percent of the annual global prostitution market.)
- why the prostitution sex industry, although primarily illegal, thrives and thrives globally with conservatively estimated revenues of $230 billion annually

In addition to men paying for prostitution, in a 2017 article entitled "How Big Is the Porn Industry?" [10] the porn industry's net worth was estimated to be as high as $97 billion ($116 billion in 2022). Men's desire and demand to see attractive, seductive women were so lofty that women earned upward of seven times what men made per male/female porn movie scene.

It's staggering when you look at how much men pay for sex through prostitution and pornography. Biblical scripture warns us in 1 Timothy 6:10, "For the love of money is a root of all kinds of evil." Money in and of itself is not "a root" of evil. Instead, the "excessive" or "unrestrained" love or affection for money is the root that leads to all kinds of evil. Therefore, in paraphrase, 1 Timothy 6:10 can be spoken as "the *inordinate* love of money is a root of all kinds of evil" or "the *inordinate affection* of money is a root of all kinds of evil."

Men's demand for sex and willingness to pay the hefty price they pay for it has opened a wide door for those wooed by and possessing an "inordinate affection" for money to step through it. This pool of riches has resulted in the ruthless seduction, pursuit, grabbing, and kidnapping of many girls and young women for sex slavery and trafficking, as well as young boys, as we are now being told. Havocscope estimated that 25 percent of global prostitution, or just under $60 billion annually, came from sex trafficking and enslaved females.

Once we return to the "Garden of Eden" and expand our view of the forbidden tree "of the knowledge of good and evil" (Gen. 2:9), we recognize that the forbidden tree has countless roots of all kinds of evil. Those roots all stem from not loving God with all our heart, with all our soul, with all our strength (effort and might), with all our mind, and our neighbor as ourselves (paraphrase of Luke 10:27). Thus, in further clarification, 1 Timothy 6:10 applies to all roots emanating from the tree Eve and Adam ate from. As such, it applies to having an inordinate affection, desire, or ambition for anything, including ungodly sex and its crossovers of sadism-masochism, homosexuality, lesbianism, and bestiality.

Like money, sex in and of itself is not a root of evil. For within the confines of man-woman marriage, sex is a beautiful, highly pleasurable gift and blessing from God (Heb. 13:4). Therefore, in a parallel application to money, we can adapt 1 Timothy 6:10's paraphrase to become "For the 'inordinate affection' of sex is a root of all kinds of evil" or in keeping with the lesson I received from my mother, "For the inordinate affection of the 'powerful Molly' is a root of all kinds of evil."

The truth that the inordinate affection for "the powerful Molly" is a root of all kinds of evil is clearly evident and openly displayed globally. It's shown in the nearly $350 billion in global prostitution

($230 billion) and pornography ($116 billion) revenue men annually pay to satisfy their inordinate sexual affections. It's incredibly heart-wrenching, however, that that humongous amount of money has nothing to do with the most horrific cost of men's inordinate affection for sex. It doesn't cover the hurt, emotional and psychological trauma, and detriment of self-worth levied on so many women, girls, daughters, sons, and young boys resulting from countless sexual assaults, rape, incest, sexual abuse/murder, and sexual harassment offenses annually levied on them.

Men impose these offenses on girls, women, and young boys because they have not controlled or put their sinful fleshly natures to death. Their sexual predatoriness has destroyed the countless lives of others, stripping those they have preyed on of their self-worth, value, and humanity. Some victims become so altered psychologically or pathologically that the trauma beats them down to seeing themselves in the darkest light of self-esteem and worth, which opens the door to Satan, giving him a horrendous advantage to influence them. As such, some yield to their "beat down" in acceptance of their treatment and predicament. And in agreement with Satan's poisonous solicitations, suggestions, and temptations, submit to suicide, bitterness, hate, murder, revenge, and retribution. Some, as a result, become monsters.

One such female was Aileen Carol Wuornos, whose father was a pedophile and was sent to prison before her birth. As a child early in her life, her teenage mother abandoned her. She lived with her grandparents, where her grandfather, unchecked and unrestrained, repeatedly sexually abused her. In addition to her grandfather's abuse, before becoming a teenager, she was exposed to other sexual activity and exchanged sex for things she wanted. Per her report, at fourteen, she was raped by her brother, who their mother had also abandoned, and she became pregnant and the mother of his incestuous child. Her grandparents later threw her out of their home, which forced her to lend herself to prostitution to survive. Later, she migrated to becoming a thief and murderer of men. Many believe Aileen was America's first female serial killer. Killing seven men and sentenced to death in Florida, dying by lethal injection in 2002.[11] May God have mercy on her soul. Aileen never had a chance in life. Charlize Theron played the role of Aileen in the movie *Monster.*

God has made our weakness clear to our parents and us men. He speaks to us through what King Lemuel's mother said to him.

> O my son, O son of my womb, O son of my vows, do not spend your strength on women, your vigor on those who ruin kings (Prov. 31:2–3 NIV).

King Lemuel's mother told him plainly about his weakness and what it did to other kings. My mom told me similarly. However, Mom was more direct, saying, "The weakness of the man is the middle part of the woman's anatomy." She pinpointed my biggest problem and from where it would come. I'm very appreciative that Mom got to me at an early age so that I could also avoid the same ruin described by King Lemuel's mother. I listened carefully to Mom. Her message, which has never left my mind, was for me to master all my desires and actions.

In summary, Mom planted in me that I was not to be weak-willed, weak-minded, or weak emotionally. Nor was I to be driven by my senses or desires, no matter how natural they appeared to be. Sex and my passion for it was not to master nor control me. Nor was a woman and her enticing words, no matter how beautiful and desirable she was. Although more graphic, Mom's words to me were the same as King Lemuel's mother said to him.

My Takeaway

- Mom told me, "Not all men, but for most men, their desire for the middle part of a woman's anatomy (her 'Molly') is their biggest weakness." What she told me has been quantitatively proven by the amount of money men spend to gratify their sexual appetites.
  - For where their treasure is, is where their hearts are also (my paraphrase of Matt. 6:21).
- Astonishingly, some men with means will pay nearly a million dollars for an hour of sexual indulgence.
- Global prostitution, including sex trafficking, is within the top 4 percent of all worldwide revenue generators.
- Every year, far too many men's sexual perversion wreaks havoc on an innumerable number of girls, women, and boys.
- If a man doesn't control his sexual desires and drive, his whole life will come crashing down at some point upon him. Unfortunately, he will have likely left many traumatized, abused, and assaulted in his path.

Vignette 9

The Weakness of Men and the Weakness of Women

Sequel 6: The Weakness of the Woman Is Money

Returning to the female side of the lesson my mother gave me in vignette 3, she said, "Robert, men can lead, not all women, but most women wherever they want, if they have enough money, if they are rich enough. But again, not all women, but most women, are attracted to men or can be enticed by rich men with just a little wooing and attention given to them. Rich men know this and use it greatly to get the women they want and manipulate women to get what they want from them. Robert, the weakness of the woman is money."

Watching TV, movies, magazines, and commercials taught me much about the world. Those genres made it clear that beautiful women and heroine women were attracted to men of means. It was even more apparent when the man was rich and good-looking, with power, authority, and fame. The rich, the prosperous, and the powerful always got the girl as part of the storyline. Although I never said it to anyone, I never wanted to be poor. From my observation, the poor, the ugly, and the societal outsider never got the woman or anything else.

As with Mom's description of the man's weakness, I didn't comment or ask Mom to elaborate on what she told me regarding the woman's weakness. However, as I grew into puberty, I started changing the tenor of Mom's message from a general lesson on life to a knowledge of women I could use to my advantage. I started liking the idea that I could get whatever girl and woman I wanted if I had enough money, power, and prestige. When I thought those thoughts and allowed my imagination to run with them, I never considered the girl's or woman's character or background, just that she was pretty, shapely, bright, and articulate.

I put aside those selfish thoughts as I continued my growth, maturity, and day-to-day observations of life and people. The Lord gave me an analytical mind, and I used my mind and critical thinking to add some sense to what Mom said about the woman's weakness. I observed how women approached and valued certain things differently from my dad and other men. It was interesting to see how women attached their emotions to material things quite differently from men. I remember Mom once said to one of my aunts or a female friend on the telephone, "Bob (my dad) would be happy with clothes on his back, food on the table, all the bills paid, and enough money in his pocket for a cup of coffee." Mom was not at all that financially simplistic. She needed much more than the bare necessities of life to be happy. From my surveillance of the women around me, it became evident that women generally required the following to be satisfied, as weighted by their preferences:

- an adequate amount of money to fully cover their needs and necessities
- living in a "good house and neighborhood" with good schools
- having an array or plethora of clothes
- having a multitude of shoes ("thousands upon thousands" of shoes)
- being able to schedule regular hair and grooming appointments
  - with money to buy what they view as necessary grooming products
- having a reliable car at their disposal
- having a stable and dependable husband with a good-paying job and benefits

I observed from married family members and some other adult couples that if the wife didn't get what she needed or wanted, then at some time, she was not going to be a happy camper. No matter how hard the man was trying or satisfied with his job and social position, if his wife's needs and desires were not met, there would be friction between them. I'm very grateful that money never seemed to be a significant or overriding problem in our family. However, on a few occasions, my parents unknowingly but poignantly notified me that money was "tight." At those times, I learned how a lack of money negatively impacted my mom. My bedroom was next to my parents' bedroom when I was a teenager. On a couple of separate occasions during the night, when my parents thought my siblings and I were asleep, I heard them having a heated conversation about the lack of money we were then experiencing. Money was the primary thing I remember my parents arguing about. These arguments were extremely painful and tearful for me to hear, and I was glad my siblings were asleep. It sounded to me that Mom was the aggressor and instigator of the confrontation. Also, from what I heard, she exhibited significantly more concern, fear, and anger than my dad regarding our financial situation. It seemed like the accusatory verbal darts that Mom released toward Dad were as if Dad was at fault. He was clearly on the defensive. I never talked to Mom and Dad about their heated financial discussions. However, I did use the information I had heard to drop or delay some of my financial requests to them.

Additionally, I discretely asked my siblings to drop or delay some of their requests to help relieve the financial pressure on our parents. The executable lesson or principle that I got out of what I learned was "Robert, when you get married, you must be financially fit with a good, high-paying job. Do not marry until you are! No matter how much you love her and how much she says she loves you. Don't marry until you are financially well off and are able! If she says that money is not important, don't fall for it! Don't believe it! Don't marry until you are financially well-fit! Or you'll hear it again and again, and you will pay dearly for it!"

Years later, after I had been married for a while, the colloquial proof of that principle was confirmed in a message by Dr. Frederick (Fred) K. C. Price, pastor of Crenshaw Christian Center (CCC) in Los Angeles. During his discourse one Sunday morning, Pastor Price said that early in his marriage to his wife, Betty, finances were tight and had been for a while. As a result, tensions regarding family finances rose between him and Betty. He didn't go into the details. But what I heard him say sounded similar to what I heard in my bedroom when Mom and Dad had their heated financial discussions. Pastor Price summed up one particular conversation he and Betty had. He told her, "I'm doing the best I can!" He said Betty had an equally brief response to him. Her response was "Your best is not good enough!"

It wasn't until years later that I better understood this phenomenon of women. It came after reading chapter 6 of TD Jakes's book *Woman Thou Art Loosed.*[12] After reading that chapter and seriously pondering the sequence in which God created Eve, with respect to everything He made, including Adam. In an aha moment, just as scripture says and Bishop Jakes brought to my attention, I suddenly became conscious that *God created Eve, the woman, absolutely last.* He made her after Adam, out of Adam's rib, after wisdom (Prov. 3:19), after the moral laws that govern us, the natural laws by which the universe operates, the creation of the heavenly bodies, the earth, and all plant and animal life. The "after Adam" is what caught my attention. Before Eve, God had given Adam his home and occupation. His home was Eden, and he was the first and by far the most expert biologist, zoologist, botanist, farmer, etc. who has ever lived. God gave him his job and occupation. He named the animals by their type and tended the Garden of Eden. God provided abundant water to water the garden. From the description of Genesis, it appears that God made and provided a perfect home for Adam, including Eden's environment and weather.

At Eve's creation, her husband, home, food, water, and pleasant environment were there for her. God had provided all of Eve's needs before her first breath and sight of her husband. Her purpose of being a helpmate to her husband, Adam, was known to her at her consciousness. If one didn't know any better, that is, if one didn't know that Eve was not an original creation but rather taken from Adam, bone of his bone and flesh of his flesh. You would think she was the absolute crowning glory of God's creation, the last and most precious of His products, separate from Adam.

After reading Bishop Jakes's book and listening to some of his TV messages on *Woman Thou Art Loosed,* I understood why women start feeling uncomfortable, unprotected, uncared for, get emotional, and go a bit "looney" when their physical body, home, and shelter needs go unmet. Namely, utility bills slip month-to-month, when their mortgage or apartment rent payments are late or unpaid. And when there is little or no money to buy food or provide adequate and safe transportation for her and her children and other necessities of life.

For example, I once felt my former wife's piercing anger, followed by her direct verbal assault on me when I missed paying a utility bill. She had come from a low-income family and upbringing and was very sensitive to the pains of poverty and lack. One day during the first two years of our marriage, she came home to our apartment and surprisingly found our electricity turned off. I had procrastinated in paying the bill and then forgot to pay it due to my involvement with work. My lack of action in not meeting my obligation as provider triggered my wife's fear and anger when she returned to our darkened home without electricity. When I arrived home from work, she greeted me with a furious and fiery verbal assault, followed by an attempted coup to take over our bills and family finances. Neither her assault nor her attempted coup, which I immediately put down, were pleasant. I thought, *Why are you so angry?* as she went off. *This issue is no big thing. Why are you going ballistic? We can use candles tonight, and I'll pay the bill before going to work in the morning.* I'm glad I had the restraint not to engage her or say what I was thinking and wanting to say regarding her angry verbal assault and attempted coup. I think it would have exacerbated the issue.

I assume, internally and intuitively, that women know or sense that the lack of being without the necessities for their person, home, and life is not God's purpose or will for them. That is not the environment they were created in and brought into life. Therefore, their needs that are not adequately met do something mentally and emotionally to them. I perceive that a woman who suffers lack sufficiently to affect her emotionally gets "rocked to her core." She then becomes very conscious and aware of the potential danger to her. Namely, the threat of losing her sustenance, home, protection, lifestyle, and whatever else she deems valuable and necessary for her healthy, protected, and prosperous life. When her rug of provision, comfort, and security gets yanked from under her, it unsettles her whole being.

Mom said, "The weakness of the woman is money." She said, "Not all women, but men can lead most women wherever they want if they have enough money." From what I have heard in my generation, if a man is rich enough and has the resources to provide and fill his woman's material needs and wants, in many cases, she will give up much in exchange for that security. As we have all unfortunately heard, some have seen, and others have experienced, some women will take a lot! Suffer a lot! Accept and put up with a lot of lack in other areas of her life (including possibly mental, emotional, and physical abuse or adultery) to receive and keep her physical and material security.

Thus expanding the definition of money, Mom's statement "The weakness of the woman is money" can be rephrased accurately to say, "The woman's weakness is her need for physical and material security." In truth, it doesn't make a difference whether her finances come from a man, a family inheritance, a prosperous business, or a lucrative job position. So long as her physical and material security needs are fulfilled.

My Takeaway

- **Not all women, but most women can be led wherever a man wants to go if he has enough money, prestige, and power.**
- **As a man, don't get married until you are financially fit with a good, high-paying job or profitable business.**
- **If you're not financially fit, do not let a woman talk you into getting married. Do not be swayed by any argument she makes.**
- **Per my mother, the weakness of the woman is her need for money (physical and material security).**

Vignette 10

A Bad Woman Is Worse than a Bad Man

As I recorded in vignette 3, some months after my family's Friday evening trip from Richmond to San Francisco, similarly, our family headed to SF on another Friday evening. Dad, driving, per his custom, again stopped for gas at the same Chevron service station before getting onto the I-80 freeway to SF. As usual, Pop got out to help service our car and talk to the attendant as the attendant pumped the gas. Mom, per usual, was sitting in the front passenger seat with me sitting on the door in the back seat behind my dad. My siblings were also in the back seat to the right of me.

A motorcycle came in with a man driving and a woman behind him dressed in tight, black, exotic motorcycle gear. I don't know why, but the woman caught my attention, and I focused intently on her. I have no idea what I was thinking. But just like in vignette 3, I must have been staring intensely at the lady. In her sixth sense, my mother sensed the woman's grip on me and looked back and said, "Robert, a bad woman is worse than a bad man." She didn't say anything else, and I never took my eyes off the woman or said anything back to Mom. However, I wondered why Mom said that to me. What was "bad" about the woman? What did Mom see that I didn't see or understand? I saw a stunning, intriguing, beautiful woman in tight, black, leather clothing. I was captivated by her looks. She looked fascinating, adventurous, and fun to be around.

Per my modus operandi at the age of eight or nine, I didn't ask Mom to explain what she said, nor did I understand why she said it. Thus, I tucked her statement away on my memory shelf like I did others until I needed to recall it. However, I can say that whatever I saw in that "bad woman," I liked. She intrigued me, and I desired to spend time and be around her. After all these years, I have a much better memory of that "bad woman" than the glamorous lady I described in vignette 3.

As with many of Mom's and Dad's lessons, I kept this lesson in my mind until I grew and matured. As I did, Mom's simple comment would again return to me whenever an older female's attractiveness, lure, and charm caught my attention. The caution would come as a question of whether the woman was "bad" or not. "Bad" in my mind meant the woman could lead me on a path I should not tread on or didn't want to go on. The early warning Mom gave me was motherly and instinctive on her part. It alerted me that everything that looked good might not be suitable for me. It might be OK for someone else, but not for me.

Looking back, Mom knew something about me that I didn't realize until I was much older. It was how gullible and easily led I could be in the hands of a beautiful, bright, "let us conquer the world together" older girl. For some reason, I liked older, pretty, exciting females. As I noticed this about myself, I assumed that was one reason my dad strictly forbade me to date and become too friendly with girls much older than me. He seemed to know my mental and emotional strengths and weaknesses. For example, when there was talk of skipping me up a grade in elementary school, he replied that I might be above my age group mentally, but I wasn't emotionally. Therefore, I was to stay with my age group.

Three or four years after Mom's lesson, I liked a girl three or four years older than me. She was the older sister of my sister Beverly's friend. Oh my, she was pretty! She was gorgeous! She used to come by our home sometimes with her sister to visit Beverly and occasionally alone. However, she would give me some attention each time she came, talking and teasing me about boy-girl things I didn't understand, but I thoroughly enjoyed listening to her. Her discussions were not salacious but about relationships, dating, and having fun together. She got my attention because she was the first girl to tell me I was attractive. She would often remark on how pretty my eyes were. Except for one of my sister Beverly's friends when I was much younger, no girl had ever talked to me like she did or given me the attention she did in the moments we spoke. She could have been talking and teasing me to satisfy her communication and emotional needs to pontificate with a trusted boy as if I were her younger brother. She didn't have a brother. She had three younger sisters. However, being in the period of life where I was starting "to smell myself," as I heard older ladies call it, I could have easily mistaken her pontificating as interest in me, and that is what I did. I started thinking, *She likes me, and I sure do like her; she can see me as her boyfriend.* Then my puberty-enriched mind took over. I started imagining what it would be like to kiss her and the Shangri-la of that kiss.

My dad put a sudden stop to that kind of thinking. He must have sensed something because although dating was still at least four years in my future, that was the first time he levied the prohibition of dating older girls on me. He reinforced his ban by telling me they could "ruin" me. I didn't say it to Dad when he gave me the commandment, but I did think it, even daydreaming in school, *Let her have me, let her ruin me; she is so pretty. There cannot be a better way to go!* I didn't convey my thoughts to Dad or anyone else, but I sure did think it!

In keeping with my dad's prohibition, I never dated an older girl throughout my dating period. Furthermore, in personal preference and caution to my mother's "bad girl" comment, I neither dated nor was interested in a dominating or controlling girl. Or a girl with no ambitions/goals, self-direction, couldn't hold her tongue, was mouthy, or what people called "had a mouth on her." I interpreted those characteristics as attributes of the "bad girl" or a "bad girl" in the making. In short, the persona I had of a "bad girl/woman" was never an attraction to me.

However, I better understood what Mom told me when I became an adult. At that time, I learned that the person Mom called the "bad woman" could possess far worse attributes than those I ascribed to women when I dated. I never saw women or a woman's nature in the light Mom could have been enlightening me on. But as I grasped more and more of life's reality, it was a startling reckoning and warning to me that some women can be incredibly mean and vicious. Like serial murderers Countess Elizabeth Bathory, FBI Public Enemy Number One Ma Barker, and Nazi Irma Ida Ilse Grese, to name just three. I repeat: growing up, I never imagined a woman could have that kind of nature.

During one of my morning commutes to work in the late eighties, I listened to the *Ken and Bob* show on KABC talk radio in Los Angeles.[13] Their guest that morning was a man who had written a book on terrorists. After gaining their trust, he lived with some of them, learning about their indoctrination and training processes. One thing he said intensely piqued my interest and went years back to Mom, telling me that "a bad woman is worse than a bad man." The book author commented that it was much more challenging to get a woman to turn into a terrorist than a man. However, once she turned, she was much more of a terrorist than her male counterparts. She was more committed and vicious than the men. He also commented that bringing her back to normal once she turned was much more challenging than it was for a man.

After hearing this, I can sincerely say, "Mom, thanks for the warning!"

Lord, thank You for protecting me and never allowing me to cross the path or come in contact with a "bad woman!"

My Takeaway

- **Be perceptive and leave the "bad woman" alone.**
- **Leave the older girl alone until you have adequately matured to match her maturity.**

Vignette 11

Societal Challenges for a "Poor Little Black Boy"

One summer evening, while I was in my middle years of elementary school, my mom and I were outdoors on our front porch doing something I don't remember. Mom suddenly said to me calmly, sagely, and teacherly. "Robert, you're a poor little Black boy. As a poor little Black boy, you must be twice as good as a White boy to get the same things: opportunities, jobs, a position on the team, and recognition in your life. It's not fair, but that's just the way it is. It's not fair, but that's just how it is."

What Mom said didn't discourage me, frustrate me, cause me to lose a beat, or have negative thoughts. Instead, in her attempt to prepare me for the real world, she let me know what realities and challenges of life I would face in the day and age I lived. I thought her comment was governed by me starting to compete in sports, getting older, and doing more things on my own. Mom and Dad constantly taught and prepared my siblings and me for life. As Mom spoke, I looked into her face and heard the harmonics of her concern and sincerity residing in her voice. I immediately knew what Mom conveyed was essential for my success and paid close attention to what she said.

Because I have an analytical mind, although Mom didn't know it, in what she said, she also gave me the key to success in my life. Mom gave me a number, the number 2, that is, twice. That was the number I needed to obtain my goals, to be twice as good as the White boy to get ahead. If I practiced, worked hard, studied hard, and disciplined myself. To be significantly better than any other person, especially my socially favored White counterpart with whom I was competing. I would get the spot, be it my position in a sport, placement in school, a job, or anything else. The quantitative number 2, which Mom unwittingly specified, gave me my goal and success target. That number was good news to me. I simplistically reasoned that I would get the rewards of life and my labors if I were twice as good as the next person. I received instantaneous relief, knowing how to obtain what I wanted and strove after. So Mom gave me the number and methodology to accomplish my goals.

I assume Mom spoke that specific number because it was a common saying that a Black man had to be twice as good as a White man to get the same job. I had heard that expression several times before when I was among my uncles, aunts, and other adults. However, before Mom spoke to me, it was a general expression I had heard and was aware of, but I did not know its ramifications and application. But on that particular evening, after Mom's illumination, it came alive! It became real! It was now the grounds on which I was to operate and play!

Mom grew up in racially segregated Texas during the Jim Crow era and experienced racism, segregation, and denigration against Black people, especially Black men, up close and personal. I don't know if this was a common saying in Texas when Mom grew up. But on more than one occasion, Mom remarked that the only free people in Texas were White men and Black women. My mother's grandparents were born in the Reconstruction era after the Civil War. Mom's mother, my grandmother, Mama Betty, for most of her life, worked as a domestic for various White families under the direction of the lady of the house. I certainly knew Mom didn't mean Black women were genuinely free, that is, having the freedom of White people. Rather, Mom spoke, having insider knowledge from my grandmother of White families' functional interaction and relationships. Thus, I interpreted Mom's meaning as Black women were freer, having more freedom than Black men. However, White women didn't have freedom comparable to White men. I also perceived that White women were more restrained in their husband-wife interactions and family relationships than Black women. Whether that was true or not, I don't know. But it is the understanding I walked away with.

It's sobering and strengthening for me to know the racial dislike, hatred, mistreatment, and denigration of my grandmother. And as well, Mom and her siblings, my aunts, and uncles, experienced while living and growing up in Texas never crippled their image of themselves. They never allowed what occurred to them and what others experienced to affect their self-esteem and self-worth. Nor did they allow hate or racial prejudice against White people to enter their hearts and minds. In all my life, I never heard any denigration of White men, White women, or any other ethnic people from my family members on either my mother's or father's side. On both sides of my family, people were people. Good, bad, or ordinary people!

When Mom commented that I needed to be twice as good as the White boy to succeed, she had recently experienced racial bias in California, which likely surfaced the topic. It occurred when she decided to go to work after my younger brother Daryl was old enough to go to school full time. Mom scored exceptionally well on several US Federal Government tests, but time after time, she was turned down following her face-to-face job interview, which she felt went very well. Her interviews were for civil service jobs in the San Francisco Bay area. Eventually, Mom and Dad saw and discussed the pattern of her losing job opportunity after job opportunity, following her face-to-face dialogues. They decided to involve our congressman once they recognized the job loss sequence. Mom, through a letter, solicited our US congressman's help.

Interestingly, after his prompt investigation, she "miraculously" got another interview and was offered a position, which she accepted at the Naval Supply Depot in Alameda, California.

Thus, Mom's comments to me on our front porch were like all of her and Dad's lessons. They weren't scripted and planned but occurred at opportune times to either solidify my values and character or prepare me for the *real world,* as was this one.

Except for two schools I attended when we moved to Fresno, a middle school to finish my eighth-grade year and a high school for my first or freshman year, all other schools I went to were overwhelmingly White. For example, during my sophomore year of high school, out of over 2,700 students, only twelve were Black. There were, however, significantly more Hispanics than Blacks, and by my senior year, the Black population had grown to about a hundred students. My high school's ethnic majority mimicked American society with some, but not many, elements of social privilege, White favoritism, racial prejudice, and bias. However, when confronted with those issues, my siblings and I handled them appropriately as our parents instructed. We got our parents involved or received further instruction as needed several times. However, because we managed each case properly, like Mom's job, every issue was quickly resolved and neutralized without adverse effects on anyone.

The overwhelming message and instruction from my parents were the following:

> Always treat people, no matter who they are, what they do to you, or how rich or poor they are, as people, with dignity and respect. You are no better than anyone else, and no one else is better than you! Know it and stand up to the fact that *no one is any better than you!* If prejudice, racism, or favoritism confronts you, raising its ugly head, or you are looked down upon or disgraced because of your color or economic status, then deal with it directly, person to person. Do not wallow in

self-pity, disgrace, shame, or embarrassment. Or stoop to their level and become prejudiced and racist yourself or throw back vindictive or "put-down" words to defend yourself. Do not take anyone's abuse and lack of respect either. But respond in defense of yourself as a person and as a person of value! If you need to elevate an issue to your teacher, principal, or us, immediately elevate it. Don't keep it to yourself or be afraid to report it. We will get involved and take it from there if necessary.

That message from my parents was essential and exceedingly valuable to me. It was coupled with permission from my father to say anything to people I wanted as long as I approached and spoke to them thoughtfully and respectfully in the proper manner, tone of voice, attitude, and selection of words. Pop's conditional permission significantly freed and matured me. It included treating even those who didn't like me or were racist and haters with respect—but holding them accountable for anything they said or did to me, including timely confronting them if they transgressed my person. This approach broke many barriers and delivered to me, in return, respect for myself. Surprisingly, it also returned respect and favor from those I confronted, corrected, and rebuked and others aware of the situation.

What additionally helped me was that my parents were involved and participated in all aspects of my life. They actively prioritized knowing all the authorities in my siblings' and my lives—school administrators, teachers, coaches, etc. As they said, they would quickly get involved in any problem or mistreatment that came our way. I developed great confidence in Mom and Dad's messages as I grew older. They became my messages, instilling a sense of character, integrity, and purpose that significantly increased my confidence and interaction with people. Ironically, their teachings contributed far more to my success than working twice as hard as the next person.

My Takeaway

- **There are certainly some things out of my control, and I will not always be treated fairly.**
- **There is nothing that can hold me back if I don't negatively react or give in to any "trash" thrown my way.**
- **I am to stay on the path I've been trained and taught to take. I am not to let others who hate or derogatorily criticize me get me off my track and onto theirs.**

Vignette 12

My Siblings' Rebellion against Me

One summer, when I was a preteen and still in elementary school, my three siblings, Beverly, Karen, Daryl, and I, were home from school on summer vacation. None of us attended summer school or camp that summer and remained home together all day. We could play in the backyard, but not in the front yard, nor could we leave the house or have any friends over until after Mom got home from work about 5:30 p.m. and permitted us. I became bored daily and looked at my siblings as my play toys. When I passed one of them in the hall or a room, I would nudge or hunch them with my shoulder or body. Because of my dad's restriction laws regarding hitting and playing rough with my sisters, I never pushed them with my hands and certainly not with my hands closed in a fist. Instead, I would brush them aside or gently into a wall, or I would purposely and rudely walk into them and over them if they fell or lost their balance without helping them up. Sometimes, I would fake what I did, saying, "I'm so sorry. It was an accident." If they were reading or sitting down watching TV, I would sit very close to them, bumping them with my upper body or pushing them over with my whole body in continuing annoyance until they got up and walked away. If I walked by them while seated, I would gently swipe one of their legs with one of my feet like a baseball shortstop or second baseman, using their leg and foot as second base and mimicking making a double play. I looked at my double-play maneuver as practicing my baseball skills. Whenever my parents were not at home, and I got bored or wanted to tease one of my siblings, I took my shot as soon as I saw the opportunity to catch one off guard.

I got an awful lot of opportunities. Every day that summer, whenever they weren't looking, I would do something irritating and disruptive to them but fun and stimulating to me. I spread out playing with each of my "sibling toys" evenly, showing no favorites as I impartially shared "my playtime" with them daily. I paid no attention to their yelling and screaming at me to stop and leave them alone. After all, in my bully attitude, I saw them as being there for my purpose. They were my personal "play toys" to use when I got bored or needed something to do. Their emotional intensity, anger, and frustration with me grew as the summer days progressed toward fall and school restart. Even before that summer, I had always teased my sisters throughout our recent school years. With my brother, now older, I had added him. They were now all my "play toys," my temporary diversion from boredom.

Even though I noticed when I teased and harassed my sisters, their attitudes bitterly changed toward me. I could not have cared less. Then a truth of life set in near the end of summer. That truth was I reaped what I sowed, or more accurately, I reaped what I had been sowing!

One afternoon, after I had had lunch and was sitting by myself peacefully in our den watching TV, I heard some whispering and looked in its direction. I saw my siblings caucusing in the living room. *Hum!* I thought. *What are they discussing together? Whatever it is, it's of no matter and importance to me. It's nothing I should be concerned about or anything I need to know.* I turned my head back to watch TV and didn't think about it. A few minutes later, all three entered the den with sweet, humble attitudes. Then suddenly, without warning, they attacked me. I jumped to my feet, and Daryl dived down to my feet and firmly locked his arms and body around my legs, holding them tightly so that I could not walk or move. Beverly grabbed my arms and pulled them behind me, locking them behind my back and preventing me from moving them. As I reacted to their vice grips, I immediately thought of breaking out of Beverly's and

Daryl's holds. But their clasps were extremely tight and secure, clenching me with all their strength. As I felt their power and immense effort to keep me stationary, I quickly decided that it would require a great deal of muscle and force on my part to break their gripes, and in so doing, I would probably hurt them. Therefore, I decided not to resist them strenuously.

Then suddenly, I found out what they had plotted. Karen had tied a face-sized circular knot into a large terry cloth bath towel. As Daryl and Beverly held me, Karen stood before me and started beating me viciously with the towel and knot. I kept turning my head to avoid the knot from hitting me squarely in the face as she beat me repeatedly, swinging that knot from left to right and then back right to the left with all her anger and might in each blow. Then Karen started bellowing words loudly and angrily through a gale of pent-up frustration as she continuously struck me with the knot.

In incredible rage, anger, bitterness, and frustration, Karen said, "We are sick and tired of you! We are sick and tired of you! We don't love you; we just endure you! Leave us alone, you old, Black thing!" Because of Dad's prohibitions, she couldn't curse me or call me anything derogatory, so she called me you old Black thing. Not a person but an old Black thing. When Karen blurted out, "We don't love you; we just endure you!" something immediately died in me. Her words and their potency shattered my heart.

Upon hearing her words, I had no more fight in me. I kept moving my head to keep that knot from landing squarely in my face. But Karen's words had shattered my heart to the core of my being. I no longer had the will to resist from that point on. My siblings crushed me. They got me! Their words took life's air out of me, and something in me died. I loved my siblings. I considered them my "play toys" but loved them dearly. I regularly took my "baby" brother to the park and taught him how to catch and play baseball; when we played pickup games, I chose him on my team, and he quickly excelled above his peers due to playing with the older boys. As Julius Caesar asked of Brutus, I thought, *Daryl, even you? It's one thing for the girls to hate me, but you too?* I was severely wounded emotionally.

I kept my composure and kept moving, bobbing and weaving my head to avoid that knot as Karen continued to mercilessly beat me with her weaponized towel and bombardment of caustic words. When she completed her onslaught, Beverly and Daryl released me. I didn't say anything. Instead, I went into my bedroom, got some money from my piggy bank, went outside into the backyard, got my dog Queenie, and ran away from home. As I was walking down the street, my composure broke. I couldn't contain Karen's words any longer. I cried deep down in my gut and emotions, continually thinking, *They don't love me; they endure me. They just endure me*, and feeling a deep pain of rejection!

I was away from home for about nine hours. From an elevated position in our neighborhood, I saw my dad in his green Ford looking for me continuously for hours after he got home from work. My dog Queenie knew the car, and I constrained her from running after him. After dark, between 9:00 and 10:00 p.m., I tried to sneak into the house through my bedroom window and then through our back pantry door when I couldn't open my bedroom window. I needed my jacket and the rest of my piggy bank money. I had not considered how cold it got when the sun went down, plus Queenie and I were hungry. My mother caught me breaking in.

When Mom saw me, I could immediately see the worry and concern leave her. I was amazed she didn't yell at me as she settled into emotional relief. Instead, she told me to "get in the house" and then asked where I had gone and why. I was humble and submissive but not very responsive. She didn't force the issue but instead told me to feed Queenie. She then fixed my dinner plate, told me to eat, and said we would talk when Dad returned. As I ate, Mom waited patiently for Dad without pressuring me or prying further into why I ran away. My siblings never told our parents that they beat me severely or what they said to me or why I ran away. As Joseph's siblings did with their father Jacob after selling him into slavery, my siblings did the same (Gen. 37). They played innocent of their deeds and expressed ignorance of why I ran away and my whereabouts. I gloried because I never snitched on my sisters and brother under my parents' questioning. I never told them why I ran away, that my siblings had beaten me mercilessly and told me loudly and distinctly they didn't love me; they just endured me. My silence was my way of telling myself and my siblings that I genuinely did love them.

However, in my experience, I painfully found out that the old African Methodist Episcopal (AME) church adage "Sticks and stones may break my bones, but words will never break me" [14] *is not true.* Words seriously hurt me. They ripped my heart out! In my experience of severe pain, I found out the hard way that words can and did break me. Just like the book of Proverbs says, "Death and life are in the power of the tongue" (Prov. 18:21).

More than thirty-five years after the event occurred, my sister, Karen, was still living in the consciousness of what she did to me with my other two siblings. Finally, after all those years, she came to me in person and sincerely apologized, asking me to forgive her for what she said and the beating she gave me. About seven years after Karen apologized to me, I walked in on a conversation at my uncle Calvin's home, my dad's youngest brother. My brother Daryl was in the midst of a discussion with some of our cousins visiting from New Jersey. Daryl was telling them how I harassed him and my sisters the summer they beat me. His voice held great joy and glee, with accompanying facial expressions, manner, tone, and word selection, as if he were a victorious warrior. He told them he and my sisters had had enough of me that summer. They planned and plotted their strategy and suddenly rose like a special forces unit attacking and beating me severely, stopping my ill-mannered behavior toward them forever.

As I entered the room near the end of his dialogue and description, Daryl's words brought back a vivid memory of the event. And without any effort, I recalled the pain from what he and my sisters applied to me. It affected me emotionally. When he finished telling the story, he laughed loudly and joyously, saying, "We finally got Robert back for all he did to us." In their response to all Daryl said, my cousins laughed hilariously. Based on their laughter, it was evident that they agreed with the retribution my siblings dished out to me. I then spoke up and told my cousins, all women, that Karen was the only one of the three to come back years later, apologize for what she did, and then ask me to forgive her. When I said that, my brother again let his joy of victory over me come out. He said, "No! I'm not apologizing! You deserved all you got and then some! No! I'm not apologizing!" As he said that, I thought, *This dude has a long way to go. Daryl feels they were justified in doing what they did to me.*

Some months after writing this vignette, as I pondered some other aspects of my life, it dawned on me that I never considered, nor did any thought ever cross my mind, that I did anything wrong to my siblings. Let alone anything that I should accept their onslaught on me as poetic justice and apologize for what I did to them, asking their forgiveness. It had always been clear that I did nothing wrong to them in purpose and conscientiousness, nor did I hurt them. From the day they brutally assaulted me to that current moment. My thoughts had always been that my siblings gravely transgressed their relationships with me by violently beating me and then boldly proclaiming, right to my face, that they didn't love me. They only endured me. Everything I did to them was in play and love. Their response was wrath and retribution. Then they lied to our parents by not being forthright about what they did to me.

After those thoughts occurred to me, a mental and emotional image of myself as self-centered and arrogant soon followed. I recalled that I thought of my siblings as my personal "play toys" to pull off the shelf, play with when I was bored, and then put back on the shelf when I didn't need them. I believe the Lord revealed that I had downgraded my siblings to objects useful to me, only for my play and entertainment! I did owe them an apology for how I viewed and treated them. I did need to ask them to forgive me for mistreating them. Upon that revelation, shortly thereafter, I apologized to my sister Beverly and asked her to forgive me. I attempted to do the same with my brother. He passively heard me but had no response, and I didn't push it. Unfortunately, Karen had already passed away and was with the Lord when the revelation of my offense came to me.

My Takeaway

- **It's painful when it's time to pay the piper for your misdeeds and offenses.**
- **People will only take so much. When their limit has been exceeded, their response may not be something you can contain or bear up under.**
- **There is nobody who is your "play toy," who you can pick up and put down at your pleasure!**

Vignette 13

Lesson on Being a Gentleman

One day at school in late spring, when I was thirteen and nearing completion of the eighth grade, suddenly and unexpectedly, a girl I had seen at school but didn't know well approached me and asked me to escort her to an upcoming debutante ball that summer. She explained that the debutante ball was a formal affair, including our parents, and that she and I would have to undergo six weeks of etiquette and manners training and learn to waltz and do other formal social dances.

As she explained and described the ball to me and my role as her escort and date, I had no interest in it and quickly decided not to accept her offer. My parents, however, had taught me to be friendly, kind, considerate, and mannerly to all people, especially older women, ladies, and girls. Thus, I decided not to reject her offer and tell her no right then, but instead, wait a few days until after the upcoming weekend. Then she would think that I had seriously considered her request. I would then sincerely thank her for her offer and tell her, "No, unfortunately, I couldn't go because of my Babe Ruth League baseball practice and games." Therefore, when she finished her explanation, I thanked her for considering me and for her invitation, then told her I would get back to her with an answer in a couple of days. Although I had decided I would not accept her invitation as we parted, I strangely felt special that I had caught her attention, and she thought enough of me to ask me to be her escort. I then wondered if any of my other friends got invitations. I later found out that neither my friends nor close associates had. I then asked myself, "What was special about me? What did she see in me to ask me to take her to something that she noticeably considered very special and significant in her life?" However, even after thinking as I did, I didn't have the maturity to recognize the value she placed on me. Or appreciate the special consideration she gave me before exercising her option to ask me. My thoughts concerning her selection of me were superficial and shallow, with no depth or substance.

That Saturday afternoon, my friend Tommy, who went to a different school, was at our house. We were in our family room, and I mockingly and disrespectfully talked about the girl who asked me and the event itself. I told Tommy, "This girl asked me to be her escort and date to a debutante ball." I followed by telling him I was in no way going to go. My mother overheard us and spoke up from another room as I continued. Her interest caused her to stop what she was doing and enter the family room. I thought, *Oh man! What have I done?* I had no intention of mentioning any of this to Mom. I was unaware Mom was in the living room adjacent to us and heard everything I said. If I had known that, I would not have said anything. Indeed, if I had, I would not have been as disrespectful regarding my comments and attitude toward the girl and the event as I was. (Woe is me, and shame on me! It's amazing what I would say and do when my parents were not around and rephrase it when they were.) As Mom entered the family room, I saw a curious look on her face and her keen interest in what I was telling Tommy. Before Mom spoke again, I quickly thought, *Oh man, Robert, how could you have been so foolish to say what you said to Tommy where Mom could hear you? This debutante ball is girly stuff. I don't want anything to do with it or participate, and I surely don't want to spend six weeks of my time learning manners and "old folks" dances. You should not have talked aloud about this at home where Mom or your tattletale sisters could hear you.*

Mom abruptly stopped my thinking and scolding myself, for not being more careful. She said, "Robert, tell me more about this debutante ball." I replied, "Mom, don't be concerned about it. I'm not going to go!" She said, "No, tell me more about this ball."

So I explained to her that a girl I didn't know very well asked me to escort her to a debutante ball. I told Mom as much as I learned from the girl about the event. I described the required rehearsals, parent involvement, and participation, including the formal attire required for the debutante, her escort, and the parents, and the cost of participating and attending the ball. As I explained what I knew, Mom quickly said, to my surprise and horror, "No, you are going! Tell the girl yes, you will go and be her escort!"

I then desperately tried to get out of it. I reminded Mom that I had Babe Ruth League baseball practice and could not attend the rehearsals. Mom quickly responded to my excuse, "No! After baseball practice, I will pick you up in your uniform and take you to the rehearsals." At that point, I had no other get-of-jail cards to play. Early the next week, I informed the girl that my parents and I had accepted her offer and would escort her to the ball. She was delighted and appeared happily surprised at my reply, her countenance displaying a sense of relief as she heard my acceptance. I felt good that I had not disappointed her, and I immediately stopped complaining to myself that Mom forced me to do something I didn't want to do.

As Mom said she would, she picked me up after baseball practice and dropped me off on time for each debutante ball rehearsal. On the first day of training and practice, Mom walked me to the door and introduced us to the lady who met us at the door. She was our headteacher, trainer, and instructor. She was elegant, regal, formal, and very impressive. Her face was beautifully brown-skinned, her hair was in a neat, gorgeous bun, and her hands, fingers, and nails were feminine and well-manicured. Her dress, clothes, stockings, and shoes were immaculate and appropriate for the occasion. Her manner was very professional. Her voice was soft, feminine, and powerful, demanding my attention and respect. She was a "lady" in every sense of the word and its meaning. She reminded me of my mother's older sister, my aunt Carrie. When Mom introduced me to the lady, I was to her Mr. Auten, never Robert from that moment on. My remaining reluctance regarding being at rehearsal and participating in the ball was gone. I wanted to listen and quickly learn as much as possible from the lady. Just like I did with my baseball coach, I desired to obey and please her. I also wanted to do everything she instructed me to do the first time correctly. My mind even left baseball, as I realized this was essential, very important to me and my life. I much needed what I was being exposed to and learning. It was enjoyable and fun growing in the new things put before me. That is, understanding my society's culture, grace, dignity, and acceptable manners. I thought, *Mom was right in making me come here.* Over my course of training, I maintained deep and sustained gratitude and thankfulness to Mom and the girl who invited me to be her escort.

Over the six weeks, we learned how to talk to one another in a considerate, kind manner and tone. We were also instructed to greet one another with bows and curtsies. How, as men, we were to be genteel and politely assist in sitting our dates at the dinner table. And to thoughtfully and respectfully rise if they, another girl or lady, got up from the table or came back from the lady's room. Instructions were given on formal table place settings, the utensils to use, and their order of use. We were provided directives on basic table manners, conversation, and etiquette. We learned and practiced formal dances like the waltz, tango, samba, rumba, and cha-cha.

We were also given directions on properly greeting and respecting grown-ups and adults, as well as formal authority figures and our dates' parents. For example, as boys, we learned how to receive our dates' fathers and mothers properly. To properly look fathers in their eyes and firmly shake their right hands, addressing them as sir, mister, and doctor as appropriate. Similarly, we learned to respectfully greet our dates' mothers by pleasantly looking them in the face with a smile but never extending our hand to shake theirs unless they offered or extended their hand first. Then only to gently squeeze it. Never shake it like a handshake with a man. We learned these and other social and etiquette skills and social mores, which later added significantly to my confidence and self-assurance as I moved about our society's various social strata and economic and social variances.

Many things I learned at the rehearsals I already knew or had some partial knowledge and practice in because of what my parents, aunts, and uncles had taught me. For those things in particular, what the lady's teaching, instruction, training, and rehearsals did for me was to formalize and solidify them in my mind. They were no longer things I learned from my parents and elders but became confirmed principles. The training and education I received consolidated and fused into my mind what I now knew to be proper and acceptable social behavior and etiquette. I benefited greatly from my training, gaining a high degree of confidence in meeting, greeting, and being in the presence of anyone in society, regardless of their social or economic standing, ethnicity, position of responsibility, or authority. Without exaggeration, this experience made a huge difference in me. It prepared me to walk and maneuver in any social circle properly and confidently. Specifically, my overall confidence soared with the recognition that I had the knowledge and skills to walk acceptably among all people. Mom was right! I did indeed need the training I received.

We were well-trained, ready, and excited when the debutante ball evening arrived. The organization and execution of the ball were stunning. That is the luxury hotel venue, the formal dress, exquisite dinner and place settings, ballroom dancing, and the presentation of the debutantes to society. All were excellent, very professional, and quite memorable. I had a lot of fun, and my parents were very proud of me. I wore a black tuxedo and gave my date a beautiful corsage when I picked her up, with the chauffeur's aid of my dapper dad and beautiful mom. My partner wore a beautiful formal evening gown, and I took delight in her pinning a handsome boutonniere on me. My parents and her parents looked great in their formal wear. All of us had a great time.

I especially enjoyed the introduction of each debutante couple. The following is an example of the formal announcement by the master of ceremony of each debutant's entrance to the fully occupied formal dining area and ballroom. His proclamation was "Ladies and gentlemen, I now present Katheryn Rebecca Stevens, the daughter of Dr. John and Diana Stevens. Her escort is Robert Keith Auten Jr., the son of Robert and Dorothy Auten." It was a great introduction. My date looked beautiful. I was very proud to be her escort and grateful that she thought enough of me to give me the honor and privilege of escorting her.

The "Sophisticates"

After that year, I was again asked by two other girls when I was fourteen and fifteen years old to be their escorts to that summer's debutante ball. Mom and Dad wholeheartedly supported me and participated with me at those balls. My honed manners and gentlemanly qualities drew much attention from girls, other parents, and even a newly formed classy and suave boys club called the "Sophisticates." Early in my ninth-grade high school freshman year, the Sophisticates asked me to join their club. The boys in the club came from what were considered "good," two-parent families and homes. They were economically and socially middle to professional upper-middle class. The club consisted of about twelve members. All the boys in the club were older than me by one to three years. The boys in the club were like me in their values and character or, more accurately, since they invited me to join them, I was like them.

The Sophisticates were generally self-confident, especially in their academic, athletic, and social skills. However, no one I knew in the club considered themselves better or worse than anyone else. We were all Black of Afro-American ethnicity and, as such, had a range of skin colors from the lightest light to dark brown. Just like my parents trained and taught my siblings and me about who we were and who we were not, my club members had similar training from their parents or other mature adults. All, including myself, appeared to reject and repel society's racial stereotypes and denigration of Black people, such as being intellectually inferior to White people.

We were all well-rounded in associating with low-income, middle-class, and upper-middle-class people. Our friends and acquaintances came from these socioeconomic groups. Our city, Fresno, didn't have many wealthy people, and I knew no one considered rich. Our range of friends and acquaintances also covered our city's diverse population in the schools we attended. Specifically, our friends and acquaintances included Black, White, Mexican, Asian (primarily Japanese), Armenian, and even some hoods or hoodlums.

After my parents' interrogation and evaluation of the Sophisticates' values and purpose, they permitted me to join. As their youngest member, I felt honored and confident that I belonged. We were "kool," suave, debonair, and collected. My etiquette training, manners, good looks, personality, and how I carried myself got their attention. All of which favorably led to their consensus vote accepting me into the club's membership. When we went to a party or event together, we were the crème of the crop, an amazingly confident, well-rounded group of young gentlemen. We wore our semicustom powder blue blazers with our custom emblem on the left breast pocket. We were definitely "chick magnets" and very socially desirable at parties. I liked the attention and respect we received when we went to a party or an event as a group with our blazers on.

The primary lesson I got from my debutante ball experience was that it is highly beneficial to obey your parents! Following Mom's directive to accept that first girl's invitation to the debutante ball, with its six weeks of etiquette and manners training, paid massive behavioral, social acceptance, personal choice, and confidence dividends. It changed my thinking and behavior to highly valuing my siblings rather than thinking of and using them as my personal "play toys" to pull off the shelf, play with when I was bored, and then put back on the shelf when I didn't need them as I described in vignette 12. Additionally, the benefits rolled in and kept coming in after my first, second, and third balls. Those dividends appeared in the magnificent form of Pamela, Shirley, Theresa, Lynn, Patricia, Diane, Carolyn, Naomi, Barbara, and others. So again, Mom was right! Although her purpose was significantly different from mine, I did indeed need to participate in the debutante balls and reap the benefit of etiquette and social training.

My Takeaway

- **Obedience to your parents is critical to avoiding the pitfalls of life, overcoming immaturity and short-sightedness, and reaping the full benefits of your elders' knowledge and wisdom.**
- **Having manners and social etiquette makes a huge positive difference in one's life.**
- **Having social skills and knowing how to meet and greet persons of authority, adults, parents of dates, and people of all ethnic backgrounds and social strata dramatically increases your confidence and societal influence.**
- **Having social skills and etiquette gets you accepted to places that you usually would not have access to.**

Vignette 14

Lesson on Being a Gentleman

Sequel 1: The Man Paladin

This vignette is highly important because my life was significantly enriched and altered for good after my mother forced me to accept the escort invitation to my first debutante ball. After getting and taking escort invitations for the two other subsequent debutante balls, the repeated etiquette training continued to enhance my confidence and maturity, positively altering my life course.

Greatly helping my self-assurance were the "Sophisticates" asking me to join their club. Once I was a member, my senior brothers instructed me to design a personalized business card and order a set of cards from a company they recommended. The cards, in actuality, were not business cards but personal introduction "Flirt Cards." They were relatively inexpensive, and I could afford them with my allowance. Therefore, I didn't need to ask my parents for money or let them see my ideas before ordering my cards. The card idea came from the popular Western television series *Have Gun—Will Travel* starring Richard Boone.[15] By referencing that weekly TV series, the Sophisticates hooked me. After they gave me the *Have Gun—Will Travel* illustration, my face lit up with a huge smile and nonverbal reply of "I got this. I know what you're talking about." The hook that caught me was Boone's character. He was a man's man, a gentleman, and a professional gunfighter, a "hired gun." Boone never revealed his character's real name but called himself "Paladin." I strongly related to Paladin because my father identified with him. Paladin was Dad's fondest TV personality. When the show aired, the *Have Gun—Will Travel* series was nationally top-rated and Pop's favorite TV program. As a family, we had watched it regularly with Dad.

My Sophisticates brothers' direction to couple my business (flirt) cards and other values and aspirations with Paladin's persona readily garnered my total interest and commitment. Dad loved Paladin's character, integrity, and treatment of people. My great love and respect for my father made it easy for me to accept the Paladin ideals my older Sophisticate Club brothers espoused and pointed out. I didn't question them, nor was I questionable of the directions they gave me. On the contrary, they elevated my consciousness and brightened the light my dad had already placed on Paladin as a man's man—a man and role model for me to take after. Like Dad, the Sophisticates saw something quite admirable in Paladin, which caused me to focus intensely on his person and all aspects of his life and manliness. However, as it is in life, you learn as you go. I didn't comprehend that my personalized flirt cards and a new mindset of assertively going after what I wanted also fostered a self-centered mindset—a "Me, Myself, and I" mentality.

In the TV series, Paladin was Boone's character's alias. He took it from Charlemagne's (Charles the Great's) elite body of knights. Thus, a paladin was a knight of knights—the best of Charlemagne's knights. In our terminology, he would be a Team 6, US Navy SEAL, or British Special Air Service (SAS) member. In scripture, he would be one of King David's "Mighty Thirty" (thirty-seven) described in 2 Samuel 23:8–39.

I'm spending time on Paladin because, although he was a fictitious TV personality, his persona, values, and character were honorable and authentic. Dad had already pointed him out to me, with the Sophisticates now referencing him as a role model. I no longer overlooked who Paladin personified. As such, I readily started modeling myself after him. Besides

Dad, Paladin has been the only role model I've consciously sought to emulate. In Paladin, I had a vivid image of the fruit of living an intellectual, highly skilled, disciplined life within the sphere of acceptable social values and proper etiquette. And like the formal etiquette training I received, taking Paladin as my role model solidified the numerous principles, warnings of life, instructions, and teachings I received from my parents. I got a panoramic view of life in Paladin and what I needed to do to succeed. It was unexpected, but my older Sophisticate brothers brought me face-to-face with my parents' teaching and warnings through Paladin's character, values, and attributes. They confirmed what my parents had said and taught me up to that point. For the first time in my young life, I knew and had a visual image of what, by my choice, I would commit and strive for and incorporate into my person. It was incredibly liberating mentally and emotionally when I understood what I wanted, no longer wondering or guessing what Mom and Dad wanted of me. I now had a clear picture of who I was and wanted to be, including my values, character, gifts, skills, and talents. More importantly, I recognized my parents had given me all I needed to get there.

Who Was Paladin That He So Greatly Influenced Me?

Per his alias, Paladin, first and foremost, was an elite warrior. He was a graduate of West Point and a Union officer in the Civil War. Post-Civil War, Paladin journeyed west and became an independent professional hired gun working on a request-only basis. He didn't take all clients who requested his help— only honest, ethical clients who had been unjustly wronged or bullied by those more powerful or richer. Paladin preferred to settle his clients' issues without violence if at all possible. However, if necessary, he was prepared for any confrontation. He excelled in fisticuffs and martial arts; as his profession demonstrated, he was also an accomplished gunfighter. Paladin charged huge fees per job for his professional consultant and problem-resolution services—about $27,000 per job in 2022 dollars ($1,000 in 1875 dollars).[16] Paladin, however, provided his services free to poor people who requested his help and were being unfairly oppressed or mistreated by those more powerful than them.

Paladin's permanent residence was the upscale Hotel Carlton in San Francisco. From outside appearances, his life was that of a successful businessman. He lived high on the social ladder with refined social skills and taste. He wore elegant custom-made suits, drank the finest wines, played piano, and attended opera and other cultural events. He wore a mantle of excellence, artistic refinement, education, and wealth for all to see, including well-read, and an expert at chess, poker, and swordsmanship. There were many things about Paladin I liked and wanted to emulate. Therefore, I accepted and learned to enjoy and appreciate the discipline required to get to the place of Richard Boone's character.

One attribute of Paladin that quickly caught my attention was Paladin's warrior mentality. From the time I was a small kid, ingrained in me was the desire to be a warrior. I firmly held a passion for the ability to defend myself and those I loved effectively. That desire increased as I learned of my father's and his three brothers' exceptional fist-fighting skills, which they acquired while young and honed as they matured into adults. They took their courage and love for our nation into the US military during WWII and the Korean War.

As a boy, I had a cap gun and holster set and practiced my "quick draw" and shoot skills over and over until I got bored and no longer desired it. I progressed to playing war games in our backyard with my younger brother and my dog, Queenie. Then I further advanced to more sophisticated wargames with my neighborhood friends. We dug foxholes in a vacant neighborhood lot after making custom rubber-band "firing" wood rifles and rock bombs. We then shot and launched these at each other from our respective foxholes. I then asked for and received boxing and fist-fighting lessons from my dad, which he gladly gave me. Thus, being a warrior was as natural to me as being a boy, and I readily identified with that attribute of Paladin.

It was also easy for me to accept Paladin's other attributes and skills, and I wanted the success and satisfaction of life that he openly displayed. Paladin was the visual image of who I wanted to be: a man of integrity and honesty with high performance, skills, and accomplishments, including those of a businessman with great financial success. Paladin was also a man of learning, a gentleman of manners and social graces. He was a protector and defender of the innocent and helpless. These were all virtues my parents taught me, and after my three debutante balls and etiquette training, I highly valued them all. As profoundly as I could perceive, what I viewed of Paladin was what being a man was all about. Paladin provided a solid model of the person and man I wanted to be.

After accepting the Paladin picture of myself, I was essentially immune to peer pressure. I took my academics seriously. Temptations of disobedience, rebellion, nonsubmission to my parents or societal authority, laziness, drinking, smoking, etc. did not affect me. Nor did any temptation to steal, lie, waste time in school, or be indifferent and undisciplined have a pull on me. Nor did negative suggestions and derogatory racial comments, such as I was less than a White man or not as smart or athletic as a White man. I knew who I was and sternly who I wanted to be. Being disciplined and single-minded to stay on my course was paramount to me. Although Dad didn't know it, he authored my Paladin image of myself. His acceptance of Paladin became my acceptance as soon as my Sophisticates

Club brothers drew my attention to him. Although I never talked to Dad about it, I'm sure he would have approved of my role model because Paladin personified the image and values he and Mom had continuously instilled in me. As such, Paladin's attributes and accomplishments after becoming a Sophisticate were what I very much wanted in my life. Paladin's business card was simple. It had the image of a chess game knight with the bold words

"Have Gun Will Travel"
Wire Paladin
San Francisco [15]

When Paladin gave out his calling card or when one was returned to him, it was time for business. That is when he changed into his all-black work clothes and boots, including his cowboy hat, gun belt, and holster.

My Takeaway

- **My Sophisticates Club membership and Paladin model gave me virtuous goals and skills to seek after.**
- **The Paladin model brought together and cemented the teachings I received from Mom and Dad.**
- **The vivid Paladin picture of the functional person and man I wanted to be immunized me against**
  - **peer pressure, hanging around the wrong crowd, rebellion and nonsubmission to authority, laziness, drinking, smoking, etc.**
  - **all temptations to steal, lie, cheat, waste time in school, be indifferent or undisciplined**
    - **I was disciplined and single-minded, with a mindset to stay on my prescribed course.**
  - **Unlike many African American teenage boys, nulled in me were the effects of White supremacy, low self-esteem, peer pressure, street life, gangsterism and hoodlumism, low ambition, and low scholarly achievement, in addition to degrading racial concepts and images of myself.**
    - **I knew who I was and who I wanted to become.**

Vignette 15

Lesson on Being a Gentleman

Sequel 2: A Girl Named Barbara

I was very impressed with Paladin's business card and the professionalism with which he went about his business. However, unlike Paladin, my business was not gunfighting. Instead, it was finding and attracting the magnificent "honeys" that I now had access to with my etiquette skills, confidence, membership in the Sophisticates club, and the Paladin image of myself firmly planted in my mind. So I went and ordered my introduction "Flirt Cards." But man! It would not have been pleasant if Mom knew how I perverted her good intentions and motivation for taking me to the debutante ball etiquette and manners training sessions.

Like business cards, the idea was to use my flirt cards to introduce the company and product I was selling: me! My strategy was to give the selected "honey" one of my cards to introduce myself and follow up shortly afterward. The rules of the game, however, were to be very selective. If I handed too many cards out, they would become meaningless. Eventually, when a girl got one of my cards and was excited about me taking an interest in her, someone would invariably say to her, "He gives those out to everybody. It's no big thing; don't think anything of it," thus killing her excitement for me.

On the other hand, if I gave cards out to girls who knew each other, especially if they were close friends, they could team up against me, place me in one of their "trick bags," publicly exposing and humiliating me, and "blow up my game." So my strategy was to give out my cards judiciously and selectively, distributing very few in my neighborhood social circle and the school I attended. My personalized cards came with a minimum order of five hundred. I put ten cards in my wallet and hid the remainder when they arrived. I was then ready for the illuminating moment when that special girl would catch my eye, and I couldn't leave her presence without making my introduction.

That situation occurred not long after I received my cards. I walked home through an unfamiliar portion of my school campus one afternoon after school. As a high school freshman, I knew relatively few students, and I glanced upon this amazing girl I had never seen before. As I walked a few steps after she caught my eye, it suddenly hit me that she was the one. The "honey" to give my first card to. I couldn't leave the incredible sight of her without introducing myself. She was a short distance away, talking to three other girls, and they appeared to be delightfully enjoying themselves. However, I didn't want to miss the opportunity set before me. As I quickly pondered the situation, the approach and manner to use became clear and distinct in an instant of recall from my etiquette training. I then turned and headed in her direction with bold confidence and composure. As I approached her, I had no fear of rebuke from her friends or rejection from her. Nor was I fearful or uncertain about what I was going to say. I pulled a card out of my wallet and walked directly toward the girls. As I entered their field of view, she and her friends turned and looked at me in astonishment. Their expressions were as if they were saying to themselves, "Who is this rude boy interrupting and crashing our conversation?" I stopped within a couple of feet of the girls, purposely looking at all four of them. Then speaking to all four, I politely excused myself for barging in and interrupting them.

Then I turned my face away from the other girls and gracefully focused on the young lady I was interested in. I sensed the three girls' facial expressions, body language, and piercing eye darts penetrating my back as I turned from them. Although out of sight, their emanating aura caused me to discern that their view of me had gruffly changed when I turned my back on them. My perception of their thoughts and what they were saying internally to themselves was "Who is this brazen, mannish boy with the audacity to barge in and take over our time and conversation? This dude is an incredibly bold, impudent, and arrogant boy who thinks he is somebody, a "lady-killer" and all that. He has the nerve and audacity to come between us and make a bold in-your-face pass at our friend, right in front of us. Who does he think he is?"

Although I felt they thought that, it didn't faze me. My full attention was on the girl who had caught my eye. First, I very mannerly let her know my name. Then with poise and manly grace, I told her she was lovely and had caught my attention, and I was very interested in her. Then I requested an opportunity to spend time together at her convenience. I wanted to know her and for her to know me. The person who grabbed my attention was a girl named Barbara. As I spoke to Barbara, I interpreted her initial thoughts to be similar to her three friends. But from her facial expression, her thoughts quickly transitioned into the moment and conveyed wonder and awe at my approach and gentlemanly confrontation. She had a pleasantly curious look on her face at my behavior toward her. However, not ruffled by me, she responded with dignity and composure. After completing my introduction, I pleasantly smiled, looking into Barbara's eyes, and gave her my card, nodding my thanks for receiving me. I then faced her three girlfriends and warmly thanked them for allowing me to interrupt their conversation and speak to their friend. Afterward, I turned and politely walked away in my Paladin confidence.

My flirt card was like any typical salesman's card. It had a logo, a catchy phrase, and a personal introduction. Unfortunately, as hard as I've tried, I haven't remembered my catchphrase or the logo I placed on my card. However, the logo I used might have been my Sophisticates Club logo. Whether it was, depicted below is an example of the flirt card I gave Barbara with a black stallion logo and my friend Tommy's catchphrase, which I remember.

THE BLACKER THE BERRY, THE SWEETER THE JUICE

I'M SWEET TO THE TASTE AND SOFT TO THE TOUCH

**I'M
Robert Auten**

After giving Barbara my card, I walked away pretty pleased with myself, knowing I had impressed her and her friends. Even with my back turned to them, I knew that for the next hour, or at least until they went their separate ways home, I would be the talk of their conversation.

I didn't put my phone number on my cards because that would have been bad for me. If I started getting a lot of calls from girls at home, Dad and Mom would have noticed it very quickly. They would have known that something was up and of a nature they needed to check out. Plus I never told my siblings about my cards. My tattletale sisters would have had a field day with me, and I would have never heard the end of it. First, they would have openly humiliated me before my parents. Then they would have embarrassed me in front of my cousins, aunts, and uncles when we got together.

The Saturday after giving Barbara my card, I was stunned when I came home and found Barbara talking to my older sister Beverly in our kitchen dining area. I had no idea she knew Beverly, let alone their friendship. I also found out, at that time, that Barbara was a junior upperclassman. When I saw her, I just saw a beautiful brown fox that I wanted to know, not thinking about or even considering her age to mine. To upper-class girls, I was a "lowly" freshman. Before I arrived home, Barbara had told Beverly what I had done and how I had impressed her. Although I didn't know Barbara, Barbara knew I was my sister's younger brother when I gave her my card. So when I walked into the house and got my surprise, Barbara pleasantly greeted me and reintroduced herself to me. She received me with grace and appreciation for my gestures toward her. Speaking of her delight and the honor to her, it was that I boldly singled her out in front of her friends. As her eyes glistened, she continued saying that what I did was pleasing, impressive, and cute.

Barbara didn't mock, patronize, belittle, or shame me to my sister. Instead, she spoke of the courtesy and manners I had extended to her and her friends. When I heard that, my rising anxiety about Barbara being in our home and conveying my actions to my sister subsided. It took all the teeth out of what Beverly could use against me if she told Dad and Mom what I did. Per Barbara's explanation, Dad and Mom would have expected no less of me, thereby leaving no ammunition for her to use against me.

Barbara also spoke to me politely and sincerely, letting me know that she cherished me taking an interest in her and giving her my card. However, she gently emphasized that I was too young for her. Barbara's proclamation that I was too young for her and my dad's regulation that I was not to date significantly older girls provided a graceful path for me to walk away from Barbara without my ego being affected. It peacefully and honorably ended my consideration of Barbara as a potential "catch."

Barbara Was Much More than An Image of Beauty

The fascinating thing about Barbara was up until that Saturday, even though she knew my sister, she had never come over to our home. However, she came over frequently after that day, becoming very close to my entire family. Per her visitations, I found that Barbara got up at 4:30 a.m. every weekday to work in her mother's restaurant, helping prepare for the morning breakfast crowd. She then got herself ready and went to school. On some days, after school, Barbara would go back and help her mom at the restaurant and work some mornings on Saturdays and Sundays. Oh my, that girl worked so much more than we did. Our lives were a breeze compared to Barbara's. As I understood more about her, I was incredibly impressed with her. I had never seen a girl as pretty, sweet, and kind, with a sense of humor and work ethic that beautifully complemented her personality as Barbara. She never complained or said anything negative about her predicament or her mom's demands. Her father was not actively involved in her life, which made Barbara even more impressive as I took notice of her discipline and all-around high performance. She kept her grades up, dress, appearance, demeanor, and what appeared to be everything else in her life. From looking at her, I would've never known she carried the weight of life she did. At some point, I stopped being impressed by Barbara and was awed by her!

I surmise Barbara started regularly coming to our home on weekends because she felt comfortable and at ease with our interaction and closeness once she met my family. It gave her a sense of family normality and an opportunity to unwind and relax—a break from her noncommunal family, all work, no play lifestyle. In support of that, it allowed her to talk to my parents. That was not unusual for me. My friends, as well as my sisters' friends, very much took to our parents. When my friends came over, invariably, at some point during their visit, I would look around for them, and they would have left me to talk to my dad, the same with Barbara. She would speak to my sisters but spend considerable time with Mom and Dad. Not always, but she usually talked to them separately. Mom and Dad never conveyed anything about their conversations with Barbara. Still, it appeared to be about things of life and Barbara's future desires and plans from the very little I overheard as I passed through the living, family, or kitchen dining room in which they were talking. Barbara discussed things a son or daughter would typically discuss with their parents as they matured and wanted to understand the world and their options. Mom and Dad likewise enjoyed talking to Barbara and held love and concern for her as if she were a close relative, seemingly drawing closer and closer to Barbara the more she visited.

After learning about Barbara and seriously considering who she was as a person. I saw the error of my ways and thinking. It occurred about a year after my induction into the Sophisticates Club and accepting Paladin as my role model. I realized I had a distorted Paladin image of myself. My subconscious told me that when I scoped Barbara out, it was solely her great looks and shapeliness, not her person or character, that caught my attention. It was the weakness of men I was born with, which Mom warned me of when I was eight. It was the involuntary, forceful, natural desire for the middle portion of a girl's anatomy. I was entering my midteens, and now that desire had surfaced. As I grew to know and appreciate Barbara, I felt compelled to look hard at myself and face the truth of my motivation to pursue her. Truth be known, my ultimate goal and silent unspoken ambition was to "get into Barbara's pants." My custom flirt card was the key designed to open her front door. My gentlemanly introduction was to get an invitation into her inner circle of trust. Once in her ring, my cultured and elegant persona, coupled with my subtle desire for her precious "fruit," at some time would produce the benefit I sought.

My recognition of the quality person Barbara was exposed and illuminated my motive of attraction to her. It cast a bright light on my primal sexual desire and the shallowness of my thinking. With only that one example of handing out my flirt card, I could see where I was heading if I continued in my Sophisticates Club brotherhood methodology and Paladin image. The reflection of light from Barbara exposed me, "Robert Keith Auten Jr.," as to who I could become if I didn't heed the warning. Namely, I could become a hound, "a dog," as Mom called them, always looking for a meal but not caring for the girl. I targeted Barbara without knowing anything about her or her excellent reputation. Her person didn't catch my interest; instead, it was her looks, figure, and subliminally, the middle part of her anatomy.

It's mysterious how complex life is. I was convinced my Paladin image of myself and membership in the Sophisticates Club placed me on top of the world. I indeed believed that I had what I needed to succeed in life. However, after getting to know Barbara, her life, and what she had been going through, I felt guilty and self-conscious concerning the path I was on. I was initially unaware. But my growing libido was causing me to misuse valuable lessons from Mom and Dad, along with my powerful Paladin persona, to go after and fulfill my wants and desires in assertive, self-centered, and narrow-minded ways. But thank God, I recognized I was heading the wrong way!

Once uncloaked, I recognized that all my sophisticated planning, preparation, and training were my primal nature and my body's strategy to get the fruit in the middle of a girl's anatomy. Mom had warned me that this intention would be my greatest weakness when I was eight and that I was not to let it control me. It was a horrible thing to see in myself. I didn't like what I was becoming. I was intelligent, observant, analytical, and ambitious. But I was going in the wrong direction. I felt it, and I internally knew it! I knew it because, besides making my bold pass for Barbara. During my freshman year in high school, the following incidents showed me that I needed to change my life:

- I had a Paladin-style, full-on street fistfight in the defense and honor of one of my sisters. During school, a boy disparagingly named-called my sister and publicly said other ugly things about her after my sister told him she wasn't interested in him. Like Paladin, I nonviolently chastised the boy and thought that was the end. I assume, however, because of his ego and then being egged on by his friends after telling them what I said, he challenged me to meet him off campus after school. I met him per his invitation, dressed in all black like Paladin. However, I wore a black leather beanie instead of a cowboy hat.
- On another occasion after school, but on campus, I initiated a Paladin-style confrontation with a boy, which was stopped by a coach who separated us just before it went physical. The boy, an ex-boyfriend of one of my sisters, needed to be held accountable for his words and actions, and I was determined to defend my sister's honor.
- I initiated a verbal Paladin confrontation between me, a high school freshman, five feet, seven inches tall, and a six-foot, four-inch high school senior varsity

basketball player with a seventy-pound advantage. Due to a request for help from an ex-girlfriend (which she should have taken to her father), I seriously warned him about how to treat girls and women in a facial confrontation. Irrespective that I was no physical match for the basketball player from outside appearances, I meant what I said, and he knew it! Fortunately, he let me and my assertive warrior manner slide, saying very little in response to my words. Soon after, he broke up with my ex-girlfriend.

- I had a confrontation with a six-foot, two-inch, very athletic high school junior with a sixty-pound advantage, who confronted me over flirting with his girlfriend. I did it in ignorance, not knowing she was his girlfriend. He knew I played baseball, and we respected each other. The confrontation ended peacefully, with an apology from me for my transgression. He was an outstanding baseball player and signed with the California Angels after his high school graduation.

- I confronted a boy who had taken a jacket from me. I found him at lunchtime and planned to beat him up right then and there on the school grounds if he didn't pay me back for it (he no longer had the jacket) or give me one of his shoes or socks as collateral. But thank God, an upperclassman in the crowd, which had gathered, asked me to give the guy some time. Since I was acquainted with the upperclassman, I yielded to his request. But man! What kind of insane Paladin, law, and order thinking was I doing? Thank God He sees everything and "protects fools and babies" like me. He sent that upperclassman to get me out of the fool's hole I had dug for myself.

Near the end of my freshman year, my history teacher, Mr. Gonas, saw me doing something foolish and talked to me after class. My older sister had him the year before I did, and he knew my parents and what they stood for. He seriously checked my thinking and attitude right then and there. He also called my parents and informed them of what he observed in me. He then strongly recommended that I transfer to another high school. He believed I was too comfortable in my school environment, and what he saw growing in me would not play out for my good. He also saw too much potential in me not to say something to my parents. Mom met with Mr. Gonas an evening or two later while Dad was still at work. After their meeting, Mom sat me down and spoke seriously in her calm, sage way. I got the message. She let me decide whether to take Mr. Gonas's strong suggestion that I transfer to another school. I thought about it and decided I needed to make a change.

The Sophisticates Club stuff, the Paladin attitude I had developed, and what I saw in myself through my mirror of Barbara let me know that I had to change. I had too much popularity at that school; I had compromised and perverted my sense of values and, indeed, needed to make a change. Thus, I told Mom I would like to change schools and what school I wanted to attend across town. Therefore, Mom reviewed the school transfer guidelines and submitted the paperwork to the school district. I switched to Theodore Roosevelt High from Thomas Edison High in Fresno for my sophomore through senior years. I chose Roosevelt because it had a great baseball program and coach, Jake Abbott.[17] Under Coach Abbott, Roosevelt's baseball program was the best in Fresno and Central California's San Joaquin Valley. Once I started at Roosevelt, I let the Paladin, "Man in Black" image of myself gradually die. However, as I described in vignette 4, the desire for sex didn't die but grew.

I also allowed my involvement with the Sophisticates Club to fade as the older members and club officers started going to college and getting involved with other parts of life. I also purposely didn't hand out any more flirt cards after Barbara. I felt like they were much too powerful. I came to that conclusion after considering my card's effect on Barbara. After giving Barbara my card, I planned to find Barbara on another day at school and pick up where I had left off. That didn't happen. My card greatly stimulated Barbara. It may have awakened her suppressed feelings and thoughts of herself, hopes, and dreams. It possibly also encouraged and reminded her of her value and self-worth.

Barbara didn't wait for me to contact her. Instead, she tracked me down and found me. Thus, after considering that and listening to Barbara's feedback on how my card and approach affected her. In my thoughts, I reasoned that some girl not as stable emotionally or as secure as Barbara could easily mistake my gestures, coupled with her need or desire to be loved or romanced, and fall in love with me. I had heard of situations like that. That was not at all what I wanted. I wanted no part in any committed boyfriend-girlfriend relationship. I was much too young for that. And I had too many other fabulous things planned for my life. I just wanted to "hit" and move on.

I have not seen or talked to Barbara since her elegant wedding at the iconic Frank Lloyd Wright Jr.-designed Wayfarers Chapel in Rancho Palos Verdes, California, and following reception over forty-five years ago. But I would not be surprised if she has kept my card as a "charming" keepsake from the mannish and arrogant high school freshman who hit on her. Barbara remains special. She is the only woman I've ever approached and introduced myself to in the extraordinarily assertive and confident manner I did. After high school, I destroyed all my remaining flirt cards before leaving home and heading to the University of Santa Clara (now Santa Clara University).

When I was a senior in college, one day, my younger brother Daryl said to me, "Bro! You used to be so *kool!* What happened to you?" I heard him, but I never responded to him because I thought the answer was too involved. However, the short answer to his question is the following:

- In the mirror of Barbara, I saw a reflection of myself. Barbara gave me a clear image of myself and where I was heading. It made me think, take inventory of myself, and grow up. Being a "player" and allowing my weakness (i.e., my desire for the middle part of a girl's anatomy) to lead, rule, and control me was not where I wanted to go!
- The Paladin "Man in Black" attitude I had toward correcting injustices was outdated for our society and was thus leading me to be a thug. In two of my freshman confrontations, I was grossly outsized and physically overmatched but didn't back off. Continuing that path would bring me to possibly seriously hurting someone and going to jail or someone seriously hurting me or ending my life. From "the commonsense" wisdom God gave me, it was time for me to abandon the "Man in Black" attitude and methods.
- As a godsend, toward the end of my ninth-grade year, Mr. Gonas, my history teacher, confronted me regarding the "problem" path he saw me on. He took the time to illuminate where "the road" I was on would take me if I continued on its way. His concern for me carried over to him immediately notifying my parents and pointing them and me to a path of escape. Dad and Mom gave me a choice and supported and financed my way out and onto the escape path to another school, as Mr. Gonas highly recommended.
- God, who watched and orchestrated everything that occurred to me for His purpose and my benefit, opened my eyes and understanding to see that a change in my life was necessary.

I also believe the Lord manipulated my debonair card handout to Barbara for her well-being. The door my card opened allowed her to develop an incredibly healthy and beneficial relationship with my parents. When Barbara graduated from high school, she applied, was accepted, and became a flight attendant for one of the major airlines. As a family, especially my parents, we were very proud of her and happy for her breakout to independence. The basis for my family's joy was "Now Barbara can finally have a life of her own." She can do what she wants and have time to enjoy life and other people outside all the work and time she has been putting into her mother's restaurant since she was a little girl. Barbara was now traveling throughout the United States, the Caribbean, and the world, seeing and experiencing people, places, and things. She was excellent at what she did; Barbara's years of joint school and restaurant responsibilities, work ethic, efficiency, and excellence lavishly provided her with the skills needed to enter the professional workforce and her chosen career as a flight attendant. Barbara was very bright, quick on her feet, and composed. From her restaurant experience, she knew very well how to handle, converse, and communicate effectively with all types of people. Adding to all that were her great looks, a great smile, a cheerful personality, and a sense of humor and laughter that invited others to join in.

I learned from Mom and Dad that Barbara progressed quickly in her promotions and assignments through her delightful personality and skills. Barbara stayed in touch with my parents and visited them when she was in town to see her mother and siblings. She also arranged and provided my parents with an employee family airline pass until she received a heated objection from her mother and felt compelled to withdraw it. The lasting image I have in my mind of Barbara is seeing her form, facial beauty, happiness, and radiance as I viewed her in her flight attendant uniform. The smile on her face and the joy all over her was astonishing. Barbara loved her job! You could see and hear it on her face as she talked about it. Except for my daughter's achievements, I don't think I've been as happy with anyone's accomplishments as Barbara's. What an amazing girl and treasure I happened upon when I first saw her, and an even more incredible young lady when she freed herself to grow, bloom, and blossom!

My Takeaway

- **I had to release my Paladin method of physical confrontation in support of helping others. Paladin's method is outdated in our modern society.**
- **I was clearly on my way to selfishly abusing my social skills, etiquette, and training had Barbara's high personal value and character not checked me.**
- **Had not God intervened through Mr. Gonas and my parents, my life, as well as the lives of others, could have been shipwrecked.**

Vignette 16

Lesson on Being a Gentleman

Sequel 3: A Question to Myself

After writing the previous two vignettes, I looked back at the history and events of my high school freshman year. I wondered why I was so impressionable and quick to take on and absorb Paladin's persona, demeanor, and lifestyle as literally as I did. My other Sophisticates Club members were not nearly as impressionable as I was, although I recognized they were also significantly older than me. As I later discovered, a one-to three-year difference in age during your teen years is significant in maturity and understanding. I saw the difference in myself as my thinking and behavior changed between the start of my freshman year and the end of my sophomore year. However, recalling the Paladin image I held of myself in the ninth grade caused me to notice that I am very impressionable by nature, even to this day. And it's probably why I've learned to be cautious regarding what I purposely see, speak, and hear. I don't watch or discuss scary, horror, dark drama, mass murder, or bloody movies. Nor do I listen to nonedifying songs and music. Because of its popularity at the time and my former wife wanting to see it, I let my guard down once and saw the Sigourney Weaver movie *Alien*. It was a bad mistake on my part. Later that night, I had a horrible nightmare and woke up in a sweat, screaming in fear at an alien confronting me.

Another incident of my impressionability occurred some years ago when my church, Faithful Central Bible Church (FCBC), owned the Forum in Inglewood. The Forum was the former home of the Los Angeles Lakers and Kings professional basketball and ice hockey teams. One Sunday morning in service, I sat with my daughter, Johanna. My daughter's best friend, Brandi, watched us from the other side of the Forum, where she was sitting. During worship, I was praising and worshipping the Lord like everyone else. Later that week, Brandi told Johanna in their phone conversation that she saw me worshipping during service and that I had no rhythm. She made a big thing of it in her discussion with my daughter. After their conversation, Johanna jokingly teased me about what Brandi said. Then based on what she herself had seen in my dance moves, she laughed and confirmed what Brandi had said. I took great umbrage and offense at what Brandi said and even more so after Johanna, to my face, dared to agree with Brandi's assessment of my skills. It was hugely offensive to me! I'm a "brother," Black, of African descent, born with natural rhythm and dance skills from the motherland. I was an outstanding athlete. No way do I not have rhythm! That is just plain ridiculous. Also, what was Brandi doing watching me? As a congregation, we were in the worship of the Lord, our God! I was worshipping the Lord. She should have also been praising the Lord and not looking at me. I looked at her comment as "hitting me below the belt" because her comment was a critique of my sincere worship, which I presented to the Lord. I'm confident that the Lord received my praise.

A few weeks later, Brandi visited Johanna at my house. After a while, I finished what I was doing upstairs, then came downstairs to greet Brandi and converse with her and Johanna. Soon after, I remembered what Brandi had said to Johanna about my church service rhythm. So humorously, I mentioned it to her. Why did I do that? I was not expecting or ready for her response. I expected to get from her an "Oh Mr. Auten, I was just kidding. It was great to see you worshipping the Lord." Instead, as she recalled her comment, she took off in hyperbolic words of jest and mockery about me having "no rhythm." She repeatedly said, "Mr. Auten, you have no rhythm." Then adding insult to insult, she upped her tone and volume, saying, "Mr.

Auten, you have no rhythm! I think! I think! I think, Mr. Auten, your new name is Rhythmless Nation. That's it! Your new name is Rhythmless Nation." As she said it, she and my daughter fell out laughing. For the time I remained with them, they seemed not to get enough of mocking me and continuously repeating their humor and laughter with joke after joke about my "no rhythm moves" and their designated "Rhythmless Nation" new name for me. At some point, I had enough of their mockery, making fun, and laughing at my expense. I said good night and went upstairs to my bedroom.

As I said, I'm very impressionable, as life would have it. Sometime in the wee hours of the morning, as I was sleeping, a very vivid dream started unfolding in my mind. In the dream, I was in a very excited mood with high anticipation on my way to this amazing and exclusive dance club. As I arrived in glee and anticipation, I went straight to the front of the long waiting line at the entrance. When the security guard saw me, he nodded, removed the velvet rope, and let me through. The music was popping and amazing as I walked into the packed club. I immediately started gyrating and smoothly moving to the music, heading straight to the crowded dance floor. As I moved toward the dance floor, I saw a young lady and asked her to dance as I continued walking. As we took our place on the floor, I started doing my thing. All my rhythm movements and great dance steps came alive and immediately caught everyone's attention. After a few minutes, people on the floor were awed and intimidated by me and stopped dancing. They started staring at me and moving to the outer edge of the floor, letting me have it all. They were awed and dazzled at my moves and steps. My partner realized she couldn't hang with me, and as the floor cleared, she joined them. I just had too much soul and rhythm, and it was all coupled into amazing dance steps with fluidity. I was doing my solo thing like John Travolta in *Saturday Night Fever.*

Standing on the floor edge to my left was this tall, very dark-skinned Black guy. From the aura coming from him and the respect the whole room appeared to give him. He was the "dance master/virtuoso" of the club. His eyes glued on me with an expression of wow and awe. As if he was saying, "I ain't never seen anything like this!" As I briefly scanned him and his facial expressions, I surmised that he was studying my moves to incorporate into his repertoire and wondering, *How is he moving and grooving like that?* I reasoned he was attempting to get a mental picture to copy me precisely.

As I continued to scan around the circle of people watching me, my head came to an abrupt stop. In front of me, slightly to my right, was this incredibly "fine" White girl. Oh my! That girl was "fine." Her legs, her hips, her amazing figure, her face, her eyes, and her hair. She was gorgeous and staring intensely at me. Then I started to get the impression that she was the female counterpart of the tall, dark Black guy. She likewise had an aura of crowd respect surrounding her, and I accepted that she was the female "dance virtuoso" of the club. Her rigid attentiveness to my dance moves struck me and grabbed my full attention. I was glued to her gorgeous face as she observed everything I did in the closest detail. She was also awed by my rhythmic style and dance moves. Enraptured by her looks and figure, I started thinking, *Man! She likes me. She is unearthed treasure, laid out here just for me!* Within the final seconds of the song to which I was dancing, I thought, *When this song ends, I'm heading to her. I've delighted her. She is an opportunity meant solely for me, and I wholeheartedly accept her.* I further thought, *When my extraordinary dance exhibition ends, while people are verbally wowing and loudly clapping my acclaim, I'll gracefully and confidently walk over to her and make my introduction.* The music stopped as I finished thinking those thoughts, and I rhythmically took my first step toward the girl. As I stepped, I quickly turned my head to the tall Black guy and saw the admiration for my performance on his face. He was still fully focused on me, having maintained, but with amplification, his expression of "wow and awe!" He was still mesmerized by my moves and mouthing, "I ain't never seen nothin' like that." I then turned my head from him back to the girl and took my next step. Then the tall Black guy made a shocking pronouncement. In an authoritative, loud, booming voice, he heralded, *"No! He ain't one of us!"* As I was looking at the girl, I heard him. She simultaneously heard his words, violently taking her eyes off me, and in an instant snapped her head, looking directly at him with a very stern, unpleasant, and serious expression. Then she responded as loudly as he did, with a defiant attitude, saying thunderously so that everyone in the club would hear, *"He sure ain't one of us!"* In her attitude, facial expression, body language, and loud booming vocal retort, she made it abundantly clear to the tall Black guy that neither he nor anyone else in the club should so much as imply that I was "White" and one of them. Namely, I was "White" because of my no-rhythm, non-"Black" dance moves.

When she said that, and I saw the incredibly stern "no-nonsense" look on her face, I felt a sharp dagger of rejection go through my heart. Neither "Black" nor "White" claimed me. The visual instantly went from a highly pleasurable experience to a horrifying nightmare, and I woke up screaming and sweating. My scream was so loud it greatly startled and woke my daughter. Hearing my yell, Johanna ran into my bedroom full of concern, asking me, "Daddy, what's wrong? What's wrong, Daddy?" I immediately rebuked her for what she and Brandi had planted in my mind, repeatedly mocking and calling me "Rhythmless Nation" over and over again.

It is clear that I'm very impressionable and have to watch closely what goes into my ear and eye gates.

My Takeaway

- **Knowing by experience that I'm very impressionable, I have to watch closely what I give my attention to and allow into my eyes and ears.**
- **As a precaution, the connotation of the "hear no evil, speak no evil, see no evil" Chinese proverb of the three wise monkeys is something I must keep in mind.**

Vignette 17

The Mighty Tongue: A Woman's Weakness and Greatest Weapon

The New Testament epistle writer James, the son of Mary and Joseph by birth and the half brother of our Lord Jesus Christ, said,

> When we put bits into the mouths of horses to make them obey us, we can turn the whole animal. Or take ships as an example. Although they are so large and are driven by strong winds, they are steered by a very small rudder wherever the pilot wants to go. Likewise the tongue is a small part of the body, but it makes great boasts. Consider what a great forest is set on fire by a small spark. The tongue also is a fire, a world of evil among the parts of the body. It corrupts the whole person, sets the whole course of his life on fire, and is itself set on fire by hell. All kinds of animals, birds, reptiles and creatures of the sea are being tamed and have been tamed by man, but no man can tame the tongue. It is a restless evil, full of deadly poison. With the tongue we praise our Lord and Father, and with it we curse men, who have been made in God's likeness. Out of the same mouth come praise and cursing. My brothers, this should not be. (James 3:3–10 NIV)

King Solomon said,

> Death and life are in the power of the tongue, and those who love it will eat its fruit. (Prov. 18:21)

When I was a teenager in high school, Mom talked to me about a woman's tongue. She warned me what a woman or my eventual wife could do to me with her words in the heat of battle. Mom elaborated, letting me know that the woman's tongue would likely be her weapon of choice in anger and rage toward me during a heated argument or opinionated disagreement. She did this as part of her parental rhythm of ongoing lessons to prepare me for life. She warned me of the potential intensity of a woman's anger so that I would not be surprised and caught off guard when it happened. In Mom's mind, I would receive a girl's or woman's sharp tongue at some point. Her warning was strictly preventative so that when it occurred, I would not allow myself to be provoked to anger and rage in a retort or response of fighting back by initiating a violent physical or verbally abusive reaction against her.

From mother to son, Mom's purpose was to educate and protect me. I was not to allow any woman's words to get to me and break down my self-confidence, manliness, or emotional stability, no matter how hateful and derogatory they were. It was evident in her and Dad's teaching that as the man, I was always to be the head, the lead, and maintain my composure and restraint regardless of the pressure put on me or the situation I found myself in. No matter what, I was to keep and hold my temper and, as they called it, "keep a level head" to soberly assess my situation to make the right decision. Independently, they clarified that this was my duty and responsibility as a man, not anyone else's.

I continued in my teenage years, gaining experience and learning many things about girls and women independently. As well as confirming several things Mom told and taught me about them. Including her vignette 3 message that "the weakness of the woman is money." After combining the whole body of knowledge regarding women I obtained from Mom, my aunts, and others with the knowledge I gained from observance and my experiences, I wondered if the tongue, rather than money, was the woman's greatest weakness. I started seeing that what came out of the mouth, as James said, was indeed challenging to control. As I matriculated through high school, I noticed that holding their tongue was a significant challenge or weakness in some girls and women. Therefore, I had to keep it in mind when choosing a girlfriend and, infinitely more important later, when selecting a wife. Mom's warning was to be aware of a woman's tongue. It could be kind and sweet but also highly flammable and lethal. Maybe because I wasn't around money, to see its full power and effect on women is why the tongue surfaced to me as the more prominent weakness of women.

I unpleasantly observed the power of "death" in the words of several girls and women in my formative teenage and young adult years. I heard fierce, fiery words directed at some boys and men I knew and some I didn't know. Knowing this placed a natural caution in me and alerted me to step up my game regarding my perception skills concerning who I should date, befriend, and with whom I should exercise great caution! From what I observed, I saw that beauty could genuinely be only skin deep.

As I grew older and saw more and more human interactions, I observed certain situations when a passionate woman felt the need or necessity to defend herself or her position. Then she decides to "take over the floor," so to speak, from her boyfriend or husband, to protect what she thinks and feels about strongly.

The dynamics of that conversation can quickly change, so he can no longer get a word in edgewise. He then asks her to pause and says, "Please allow me to say something," or says, "Please, stop and listen to me," or says, "Please, be quiet and listen to me." If her refusal to yield leads him to utter frustration, he removes his mannerly gloves and says, "Keep quiet and listen to me!"

I've observed that if the dynamics digress to the point where the man does have to boldly insert himself into the woman's forceful monologue to get a word in. It could be pretty hazardous to the goal of peacefully settling or compromising on their differences. Depending on the woman's personality, what he says, how he says it, and the tenor of voice he uses when he says it. Or the aspect or point of importance to the woman when interrupted. Or the level of emotion and passion she's residing in when he utters his interrupting words. He could quickly get his head blown off with a loud category 5 hurricane retort, "You wait until I'm finished!" or "I'm not finished yet!" or "Don't tell me to keep quiet! You keep quiet!" Followed by a deafening angry reply of words seasoned with piercing adjectives with his name on them but describing someone he doesn't even know. Or she, with inflexible sternness, continues ignoring his request, and he still cannot get a word in edgewise.

Even if the female does yield, going silent when asked, from what I've observed, she wasn't silent in her mind, patiently listening to her man as he explained his point of view or considerations. Instead, she was planning and conjuring up her next point to make. Or her rebuttal to his "wrong thinking" and what he said. Unfortunately, I've witnessed these female-male interactions on more than one occasion. I've beheld them in my extended family, as well as between other adult couples outside my family.

I've additionally seen, heard, and personally experienced the rapier-sharp slashes and pinpoint stabs of a woman's tongue when she has had enough, whatever enough for her was. Without exaggeration, I've never heard of anything nonlethal, as sharp, vicious, and poisonous as a woman's tongue when sent purposely to cut its target and victim down to size. Then before her tongue comes to rest, it completes its verbal and relentless assaults by ripping some portion of her partner's self-esteem or manliness guts out. It appears that women know the power and ability of their tongues and how to destroy a man or "put him in his place" if they so desire.

I am very grateful that many women bring their tongues under control and carefully watch what they say to their boyfriends and husbands in the heat of battle or when stressed from the lack of some need or want. I'm also glad many women know the potential healing power of their words and how to say, "Baby, I'm so sorry, so very sorry! Please forgive me for ..." When they know or realize they've sent a dagger to their man, they can't take back. If most women did not, I don't know where we men would be. From my observations, I've noticed, but can't say with certainty because I'm not a woman, women's tongues on each other are not nearly as effective and "deadly" as they are on men.

Speaking from experience, I've heard and felt the deadly oral rapier slashes from females, then their final verbal sword thrust into my "gut." It came multiple times from my two sisters when I was a preteenager. It happened when I exceeded my sisters' tolerance limits by teasing and harassing them. Their rapier tongues were drawn from their scabbards faster than lightning when I breached their limit without further warning. On more than one occasion, I left their presence in a hurry, not wanting them to see me cry and break down. But unfortunately, their rapier tongues had found their marks and got to me. I can't tell you the pain I felt. It was far worse than when they used their fist and hauled off and hit me as hard as they could on my back as I walked away or started running away when I saw how angry I had made them. I quickly recovered from those blows and laughed as the pain and discomfort subsided. However, not at all so, with my sisters targeted vicious, mean-spirited verbal assaults on me. Those words pierced me deeply, bypassing my body and five senses and penetrating deep into my soul and whole being. In truth, my sisters' pinpoint, hurtful words raised doubts about whether I was loved and, indeed, whether they truly loved me.

Additionally, their words, with their intended purpose aimed at my mind and emotions, hit my self-esteem and self-worth and injected questions into me about whether I was valuable to them. Additionally, it affected my glee, happiness, and outward demeanor for days after. Even now, with being as accomplished and mature as I am and further knowing that my sisters did love me. I still tear up and feel sorry for myself if something triggers a memory of something they said to me during one of those attacks. Especially if it is a memory of something my younger sister, Karen, told me. Karen seemed to have a Greek mythology Amazon warrior's mind-to-tongue rapier skills of precision and sharpness. When I exceeded her limit, oh my, that girl, without further consideration, would mercilessly cut me to the bone with her tongue and metaphorically leave me for the vultures.

OK, OK! I get it! I get it! Many women will say to me regarding my sisters, "You got what you deserved! You pushed your sisters to a dead end with nowhere to go. You left them no option but to fight. They were only defending themselves. Unfortunately, they used their tongues as their weapon of choice. But you pushed them to it. Why did you tease and harass your sisters mercilessly as you did and then continue goading them after they told you and told you, over and over again, to stop? Why didn't you leave them alone?

"Additionally, once it happened to you, why did you repeatedly tease and harass them to the breaking point again and again? You deserved what you got! You deserved every bit of what you got! Hopefully, you learned your lesson from your sisters and have never pushed another woman to draw her sword and cut you into pieces defending herself."

All I can say is I truly loved and cared for my sisters. However, I did tease, harass, and toy with them whenever an opportune time arose or they said or did something I could exploit. I don't know why I did it. It came naturally as part of my boyishness to see them as target practice for my jokes, a convenience to relieve my boredom, and play toys to pull "off the shelf" and play with as I desired. After filling my emotional emptiness at their expense, I quietly placed them back "on the shelf," leaving them alone and walking away until I again needed them. I meant no harm and did them no physical hurt. I loved them but considered them as being there for my convenience.

However, as described in vignette 12, I experienced firsthand, in their retribution, how they viewed my jocularity. As President Franklin Delano Roosevelt said, that day was a "day of infamy" for me. I'll never forget the pain or the memory of it. It will forever live in me. I did, however, eventually learn to respect and value my sisters. The transition occurred early in my teen years after Mom compelled me to take etiquette training through a series of debutante balls and the resulting Paladin image I bloomed to view myself (vignettes 13 and 14). Thus, as a result of my excruciatingly painful experiences with my sisters, coupled with my gentleman training and maturity, I've learned my lesson very well and have never pushed a woman to pull her rapier tongue sword out of its sheath on me. Thank God!

My mother's warning of what a woman or my future wife could do to me with her words in a verbal confrontation was a clear message of warning to me. However, it should be emphasized that the above-referenced verses from James are written to and apply equally to men and women. Once, in a conversation, I told a lady about my experiences and life lessons regarding the power and damage caused and inflicted by a woman's tongue. After hearing all I said, she responded with noticeable meekness and humility, saying, "Men hurt with their mouths too." I acknowledged the absolute truth of her statement as her body language and facial expressions vividly told me that she had been hurt severely by some man's tongue. It was very sad to see.

When Is Enough, Enough?

After I graduated college and started working, a work friend in his midthirties told me of an issue in the marriage of one of his close friends. He considered himself a mentor to me and wanted to prepare me for the real world and marriage. I had no aspirations of marriage at that time. However, his story caught my attention and significantly impacted me regarding the power of a woman's tongue, especially considering what I knew and needed to consider before choosing a wife. It also brought back to mind what Mom taught me about marriage and the possible challenges that may come my way.

My friend said his close friend and his wife were in a heated discussion. She got right up in his face; he could not talk or give feedback due to her intense and unyielding verbal pommeling. Finally, after constant bombardment, he made a quarter or ninety-degree turn to the right to put some distance between them. As he turned, she continued her nonstop verbal onslaught, following him and then parking herself nose-to-nose in front of him again when he stopped. After some time, he made another quarter turn to the right, now 180 degrees from his starting position. Yet she repeated and followed him, continuously talking and parking herself nose-to-nose in front of him when he stopped. I assume, in her mind, she had to, at all costs, get her point across to him. Whatever it was.

After some time, he made another quarter turn to the right, now 270 degrees from his starting position. Again, the man's wife repeated her manner of following him, continuously talking and parking nose-to-nose directly in front of him. After some time, he again made a quarter turn to the right. Now he was back to his starting position, having revolved a full 360 degrees. Without halting, pausing for a breather, or stopping her verbal barrage, she again followed him, parking herself nose-to-nose directly in front of him. Finally, he had enough and assertedly backed away from her. He then, with vigor, walked to and out their front door. He slammed the door behind him with her inside the house. He then got into his car and drove out of their driveway, putting the pedal to the metal and onto a place of peace.

The end of the story was this: My friend's friend left his home for more than three hours, hopefully giving his wife adequate time to cool off and think a little more soberly, considerately, and lovingly. He hoped they could settle and resolve their issues cooperatively when he returned home.

When he arrived home, his wife heard him pull into the driveway and put his key in the door. Contrary to his desire, she met him when he opened the door, picking up where she had left off more than three hours earlier. For her, nothing had changed. She was back in his face, nose-to-nose, as he entered his home. On further thought, it's more appropriate to say when he entered his house. I'm not sure you can call it "home" under his living circumstances.

My Takeaway

- **The tongue is a small part of a woman's body, but it can set a great forest on fire. Or if controlled, put out an even greater forest fire.**
- **Choose a woman with control over her tongue to put out the fires of life and not start any!**

Vignette 18

Every Woman, at Some Time, Will Attempt to Take the Lead from Her Husband

I remember a lesson my mom pointedly gave me as a teenager. In her sage, casual way, she said to me one day,

Robert, deep down inside, every woman wants her husband to be the head of her home. However, every woman will also, at some point, for whatever reason, attempt to take the lead from her husband. She doesn't want him to give in and give it up in her heart, but she will surely take it if he does. In most cases, if he yields and gives in, turning the household leadership over to her, that home will not be balanced and will eventually show its weakness and possibly crumble. For certain, know that, at some point, your wife will challenge you for the lead. Be aware that this will happen. Be prepared. Don't be surprised or caught off guard; be ready for it! You are to be the head but not rule over and dominate your wife. Your wife has an equal voice and input in everything, including money. But if necessary, and it comes down to it, you have the last say! Don't let your wife intimidate you with her words or attitude. You are the "man of the house," and God has given you the lead. You are to be the example for your home and respect your wife. You don't know everything! In some things, she will be smarter and wiser than you are. In those cases, you should submit to her and take her advice as best for your family.

This lesson from Mom was short and, like all of Mom's messages given to me, was without any fanfare or follow-up. However, none was needed. Her message was clear, to the point, and very powerful. I had already observed some things in Mom's interaction with Dad that testified to what she said. Ironically, I witnessed Mom do to Dad what she just told me to guard against with my future wife. On more than one occasion, Mom attempted to take the leadership from Dad. On one of her attempts, she responded like a petulant little girl when Dad put his foot down on a family decision.

I also saw Mom on more than one occasion, and it grieved me immensely, to tactically put Dad down in a sly challenge to his thinking and reasoning ability. Following his older brothers as soon as possible, Pop dropped out of school before completing high school to join the navy during WWII. Mom completed high school and had about two years of college. Mom had actively encouraged Dad to return to school and continue his education and training up until my teenage years. Although Dad was good at basic math, I believe a lack of confidence prevented him from returning to school and picking up where he left off. Unfortunately, as I later found out, my grandmother had injected that lack of academic faith and self-doubt into him. During Pop's upbringing, she verbally scolded, embarrassed, and belittled Dad because he struggled in reading and writing subjects like history and literature compared to his older siblings.

Although Mom was very sensitive to what Dad's mother did to him, describing Dad as the "black sheep" of his family, she did the same thing to Pop more subtly. It was customary in our home during dinner or after while we relaxed, had dessert, or watched TV together as a family for Dad, and sometimes Mom, to put before us a subject for discussion on life, school, or a national or global news event. Dad nearly always initiated the debate and encouraged us to speak up and give our opinions on the subject or question he or Mom put before us. Our responses were always positively encouraged and received nonjudgmentally. Dad and Mom would, either before my siblings and I spoke or after, also provide their opinions. Very discouraging to me on more occasions than I want to recall was an act of Mom. After Dad expressed his thoughts and opinion, Mom sometimes made very sly comments to belittle Dad's thinking, ideas, or assessment of the issue.

Although sly on her part, I could see the word knives Mom used to cut at Pop's confidence regarding what he was thinking and saying. In a negatively emphasized tone and manner, Mom's typical ploy was "Bob, do you actually believe that?" Mom did it to highlight her thinking, solution, or answer as superior to Dad's. In her overtone, she implied Pop's reply or response was simplistic and not up to par. A put-down to humble Dad and emphasize her thinking, approach, and opinion over his. Every occasion I saw and heard Mom do this, I grieved seeing my dad put down like that. Again, it was very sly, but I could see its effect on my father. I didn't know if my siblings noticed it, but I did, and it hurt me deeply. Dad never countered. He would passively back off supporting his position and become silent, intently listening to Mom and us give our opinions.

I reasoned that because of Dad's lack of education, he didn't have the confidence to counter Mom. He sure loved and respected Mom too much to let his ego get the best of him and go after Mom in any derogatory or denigrating way. He just took it. I never said anything to Mom as to why she would do that. I just thought that her subtle undercutting of Dad was cruel and unloving. I determined within myself that I would never, ever let a woman do me like that. For that matter, I would never let a woman or man, no matter who they were or the position they held, belittle me, tear me or my self-worth down, or emasculate me. What I painfully witnessed from Mom reinforced my life's requirement to be highly educated, well-learned, well-read, and well-traveled, with the ability to articulate and defend my thoughts and positions powerfully.

I had noticed that most women in the circle of people I came in contact with were more articulate than the men and could control and dominate verbal skirmishes. I couldn't allow that to happen to me. I had also observed that women fight with their tongues and cunning much more readily than their brawn. They know they don't have the physical strength, power, and ability to overtake a man or go one-on-one with him. Thus, they don't come to men head-on in battle or full-out war as men do with each other. Instead, they come with their tongues tactically, subtly, but aggressively, targeting their victim's biggest intellectual or emotional insecurity and weakness. Their manner of fighting is potentially more destructive, hurtful, and deadly to a man's self-esteem than cursing him out or hitting him. That is how I viewed the effect of Mom's performance on Dad. I stood in great pain each time it occurred, silently pulling for my dad. Saying to him in my mind only, "Pop, please fight back, please fight back. Mom doesn't have all the answers." Dad never fought to defend his position and thinking; he just took it. Pop only faced off with Mom, putting his foot down, on a few situations where he strongly and confidently felt he knew where he wanted his family to go.

As I said, I never knew how Mom's belittling Dad affected my siblings. But about four years ago, I talked to my older sister Beverly about Mom's virtues. Beverly silently agreed with what I said. But then her facial expression gradually changed to a solemn look of sadness, with water puddling in her eyes and slowly streaming down her cheeks. Then as she started wiping her tears away, she said, "But I didn't like how Mom sometimes treated Daddy!"

After Mom's marital relationship lesson and warning, I took more interest in examining male-female relationships, starting with those of my extended family, such as my aunts and uncles' and much older cousins' marriages and intercommunication. Mom's warning activated a watchful alarm in me to be careful about who I choose as a girlfriend and what negative characteristics to look for before selecting her as a wife in my future. My focus until then was only on a girl's outward personality, how she spoke to me, and her attitude. My uppermost interest was how pretty, shapely, sexy, and overall "fine" she was. Not at all to her character, motives, and hidden personality. Thus, Mom's message and my witness of her talking to Daddy in a put-down, belittling manner woke me to another reality of life. That reality was my wife, by her words and other methods, could subtly or aggressively compete or war with me for the leadership of our home. The older I got and the more I knew, the more of life's reality set in, and with it, knowledge of how complicated life kept getting. Nothing was as it appeared, not even the girl who blows your mind with her exceptional beauty and awesomeness. It was becoming clear that there is always something else behind the door coming your way when people are involved. You never know every issue or obstacle you are dealing with or what's in the future!

The seriousness of Mom's conversation caused me to consider what I had heard about Dad's mother. My paternal grandmother's last contact with me was as a baby, six months old before my parents moved back to California from Dad's birthplace and family home in New Brunswick, New Jersey. But from what I heard directly from Mom and ascertained from my grandpop, Dad's father, my grandmother was a dominating woman who "ruled the roost" absolutely. Years after Grandma died, from discussions I had with my grandpa when he visited us in Fresno, one summer, Grandma was so dominating and unyielding that he eventually gave her the leadership of their home. He then extended his work hours away from home with daily bar visits, socially drinking much more than he should have. As an idiom, it's accurate to say from what I heard, my paternal grandmother was literally "the queen bee" of her family hive.

Mom's message also caused me to recall my growing-up experience with my sister Beverly, which I never wanted to experience or go through again. From that experience, I learned firsthand what it was like to experience someone's dominance over me. As I grew up, Beverly was smart and bossy. She was always steps ahead of me. I lacked confidence in my thinking ability to counter her, argue with her, or disregard her ordering me about or directing me around. I felt like she unwittingly oppressed me. Although I never said anything to her or anyone else about her dominance or how I felt. From my early youth, year after year, I thought, *Someday, I will get out of this! Someday, I will feel confident enough in myself and my decisions to throw off her bossiness and end her ordering me around.* I cannot tell you what it was like when my emancipation day came. It came sometime after my tenth birthday. That day, I woke up knowing this was the day I no longer needed my sister's leadership and direction. I woke up confident I could make my own decisions. I no longer feared Beverly or needed or wanted her to make decisions for me. Nor did I need to comply with her commands; I could stand and make my own decisions. I could tell her, "No, I won't do what you want me to do! No, I don't want to go there. No! I'm going here! No! No! No! Leave me alone!"

Even now. To this very day, without any exaggeration, other than the day I accepted Jesus as my Lord and Savior. That day, by far, is the most significant day of my remembrance. Of course, it was personal, and I didn't then, nor have I, until now, shared it with anyone. But I don't have words to describe the joy I felt with the full release from the bonds and mental bondage of my older sister's dominance over me. Finally, I was mentally and emotionally free from being tied to her quick and bright mind. No longer was I her captive little brother. She was unaware of her effect on me, but oh man! I certainly was. Looking back, I can relate to the old African American spiritual "Free at Last." Namely, I could personalize the song with a loud shout and sing triumphantly, "Free at last! Free at last! Thank God Almighty, I am free at last!"

Looking back as I write this vignette, in my youth, Beverly's dominance and control over me took effect when neither our parents nor other grown-ups were around. That is when her bossiness, "I know what I'm doing. You be quiet and do what I tell you" attitude took over.

After receiving Mom's lesson, I retained my interest in examining male-female relationships until I married. Thus, whenever the thought occurred to me, I purposely observed the interaction of married couples to see how they related to each other. For example, I saw some wives dominate their husbands by mastery of persuasive language. Some women appeared to be more aggressive or assertive than their husbands. In other scenarios, women, by personality, dominated their husbands, setting a tone in the household of their control. Others did the same using their higher education and intelligence compared to their husbands. I unpleasantly noticed this latter behavior in the wife-husband interaction in a family with whom our family had a close relationship.

In my discoveries, I heard but didn't personally witness that some women who had been abused by men early in life, or grew up impoverished without material things and had learned to fend for themselves, steadfastly determined they would not be dependent on a man or anyone else to be head over them or be their provision source. Additionally, it was brought to my attention that some women who had those experiences were also prone to marry men they could dominate and control. And in some cases, they would physically and verbally abuse their mate if he got too far out of alignment.

Again, as I think back to my teenage years, after receiving Mom's message and hearing Grandpa's experience with Grandma and what I observed, read, and heard on my own. It was deeply ingrained in my mind to be extremely cautious regarding who I marry. I certainly didn't want to marry someone like my paternal grandmother. I thought it would be a miserable life and existence if I married someone with her personality and character.

As I entered my twenties, I learned some confirming things about husband-wife relationships that I added to Mom's lesson. I gathered, directly and indirectly, male-female relationship information from other men, single and married. Considering that Mom's message was specifically directed to me, I only looked at her message and the associated knowledge I gained from my perspective. Not how a woman or my potential wife would view or assess me as the lead or head of our home. As I pieced together what I knew, it became clear that women use various tactics to take the lead or garner the headship from their husbands if they so desire. A small set of tactics I found are the following:

- manipulating their husbands by giving sex or withholding sex from them
  - rewarding their husbands with sex when they do what they want
  - withholding sex from their husbands when they miss their mark

- Some women use the tactic of deceivingly agreeing with their husbands about something but, in their mind and heart, do not agree but instead think, *I'll change him* or *No way am I or are we going to do that. I'll change these plans.*
- Some wives never overtly take the lead or assertedly express their will to take over as the primary influencer of their family. However, she gradually usurps the headship over time by using various methods.
  - She uses her husband's sensitivity to her feigned feminine weakness to get what she wants from him or him to do for her.
  - She manipulates her husband's love for her as a ploy to get him to do what she wants him to do or when she wants him to do it.

In summary, what I learned from my simple observance and listening was, like Mom told me, if I'm not careful, there can be a yin and yang in my marriage as to who is in control or the head of the family.

Mom's message to me was short, simple, and straightforward. She gave me a lot of insight into a practical aspect of marriage that I had to consider. I learned a lot from her telling and teaching me what to be aware of and prepared for as I matured, contemplated marriage, and later married. I was delighted Mom pointed out this realistic attribute of men-women relationships to me. It forced me to look deeper into girls I was attracted to before their beauty and sex appeal took me over. And it also caused me to ask myself, "What is she really like? What is she like when she gets angry or doesn't get her way? Or when you tell her no?" I knew I didn't want a domineering, controlling, "I'm calling the shots," manipulative, nonsubmissive woman as my girlfriend or wife. She may be suitable for someone else, but not for me!

When taken in the context of everything Dad and Mom taught me about being the head of my family, this lesson was one of the top tutorials. My parents prepared me to be responsible, knowledgeable, and highly educated. To enter a profession where I could make a better-than-average living for my family, travel broadly, be well-rounded, be stimulated in life, and be diligent and knowledgeable regarding my duties and responsibilities, not lazy or a slacker. To be an excellent father to our children and husband to my wife, "going the extra mile" with her in consideration, kindness, and patience when those occasions arose. My dad was strong on those qualities and instilled them in me. So in addition to planting and drilling into me, "my wife and family came first." As the head of my family, I also knew what was required and expected of me.

Additionally, Mom's message notified me that no matter how well I performed as a husband, there was a possibility that a challenge for the headship of our home could come from my wife.

Throughout my extended family, among my relatives, it was readily established and understood as we grew up that if you were not qualified to lead or less mature than someone else, step aside and let the best or most knowledgeable person take the lead, and back them up supportively. Thus, within my extended family, leadership was not an inherent right. Therefore, implied in Mom's lesson was her directive to be well prepared to lead my family when I decided to take a wife.

My Takeaway

- **Prepare yourself to be the lead and head of your family.**
- **My wife is an equal partner with me, with an equal say in all matters. However, if a situation or family direction came to a point. I was to have the final say in full consideration of her views and my love for her.**
- **For whatever reason, at some point in our marriage, my wife will attempt to manipulate me to get something she wants or assert herself to take all or some manner of the lead or headship of our family.**
  - ○ **When and if it occurs, be prepared to handle it properly with love and consideration.**
  - ○ **If possible, note why she is or has decided to take the lead and make any necessary or helpful corrections as needed.**

Vignette 19

Love Always Finds a Way

I was a varsity baseball player in high school. When I was a senior, our great baseball coach, Jake Abbott, left to pursue other career opportunities. Our school, Roosevelt High, in Fresno, won seven consecutive North Yosemite League (NYL) baseball championships during his tenure. During baseball season, Coach Abbott didn't allow us to cross-train or participate in another sport. However, his replacement, Coach Jack Wheldon, permitted some of us with track and field ability to participate on our school's track and field team on a noninterrupting basis. As our baseball season was ending, it became inevitable we would not win the championship that year. As such, Coach Wheldon granted permission to us to join the track and field team on the condition that we also played our remaining games. Our track coach, Coach Dose, was ecstatic that some of us joined his team. He had pursued me and some other baseball team members for the previous two years. I was incredibly fast, and he wanted me for the one-hundred-yard dash and the 4 X 110-yard relay team. I boastfully thought my time to challenge Jessie Owen's high school one-hundred-yard dash record of 9.4 seconds had finally come. When Coach Wheldon released us to join the track team, the Fresno City track and field championship meet was scheduled only a short time away. Therefore, I had only about ten days to practice coming out of the starting blocks and my baton handoffs with the relay team. In caution, however, I didn't go full-out or run my scheduled race distances at top speed during training due to the possibility of straining or pulling a leg muscle in practice.

My Time to Shine

Since track and field are individual competitions compared to team competitions in baseball, I thought, *This is my time to shine and get personal recognition for my performance. I'm going to show the whole city who I am.* I had starred in baseball and football and had league-wide recognition from the schools in the NYL and the *Fresno Bee* newspaper. However, this was different; I alone was going to be on display, and I cherished thinking about my upcoming crowning.

Unfortunately, my dad worked evenings and nights and could not attend the meet. I was shocked and disappointed when Mom told me she and my siblings wouldn't be there either. There was a higher-than-usual admission fee for the event, and Mom said we didn't have the money. Even though she said she wouldn't be there, I believed wholeheartedly she would find a way to get there. I never asked why we didn't have the money, but looking back at it. I'm sure it was due to my older sister Beverly's expenses. She lived in Los Angeles, was going to college, and needed support from our parents.

Time for the Gun to Sound and Me to Shine

During the track meet, while warming up, I kept looking up into the stands, expecting to find Mom, but I didn't. When called to the starting blocks for the one-hundred-yard dash, I again looked for my mom. But I didn't see her, my sister Karen, or my brother Daryl. I then accepted that she and my siblings were not there. I swallowed my disappointment and focused on the business "at hand." That business was to blow my competitors away by running a 9.4–9.6-second one-hundred-yard dash. When the starting official said, "Take your marks, set," and the gun blasted, I was gone! The first out of the blocks. Like a flash of light, I was gone! None of those guys who had been running the one-hundred-yard dash all track season were even close.

I blasted out of the blocks, and neither felt nor sensed anyone close or coming up behind me. Through fifty yards, I was out front. I thought, *Stay relaxed, don't tighten up, run through the tape, don't slow down at the tape.* Then suddenly, between the fifty- and sixty-yard mark, I felt like I was carrying a backpack. As I took more strides, that backpack got even heavier, as if it were now a piano. Then swish: one, then two, then three runners, out the corner of my eyes, flashed by me. I started sensing that my body was under intense labor.

My legs were fading fast. I couldn't get enough air. I had blown my "wad." As I saw out the corners of my eyes and heard the swish of others passing me, I knew I would not win the race. My thinking switched too. *Don't come in last; give it all you've got.* That is just what I did. I gave all I had left within me. As I approached the finish line, I felt like I was neck and neck with two other runners. I leaned forward in the hope of not coming in last. My legs then wholly gave out on me. As I crossed the finish line, I fell flat as a pancake, face down in my lane. Expended in energy and strength, I was gasping desperately for air and breathing the dust of the ground; I had given all that I had.

I was keenly conscious of my total humiliation as I lay flat on my face, panting and puffing hard and rapidly! The lack of oxygen, physical pain, and discomfort I was experiencing was entirely overwhelmed by the recognition of my utter failure, humiliation, and embarrassment! My thoughts were *What are the people in the stands thinking? What is Coach Dose thinking?* For two years, Coach Dose begged Coach Abbott to let me run. He now gets me, and I utterly fail. I thought, *I've embarrassed him and let him down. I've also let down my track and baseball teammates, who were rooting and pulling for me and my success.* I came nowhere close to my expectations. I was an utter failure and a humiliation to myself, my team, and my school!

But God! That's all I can say. But God! I used all my remaining strength to lift myself from the ground with the help of some others. As I raised my head, I saw my mother standing directly in front of me in my lane, as if it had extended through the wire mesh fence separating the stadium from the parking lot. Mom was outside the stadium in the parking lot, viewing me through the wire mesh partition. With an unobstructed view, she saw everything! The thoughts shot through my mind. *She didn't have the money to get into the stadium, but she found a way to see me.* Just like my first day of school in kindergarten (vignette 1), when I clutched Mom's waist and cried and cried, begging her not to leave me. Mom assuring me that she would come back for me. Just like that day, Mom again came back for me. She didn't leave me alone! She found a way to get to me! To see me and for me to see her! I failed miserably, and Mom saw it all, but more importantly, I saw her. I *saw her!* Her presence and face reflected love, concern, and hope—everything I needed!

I Could Now Live with Myself and My Defeat

I sternly felt my humiliation and embarrassment. I let myself down and the many people who were pulling for me. I reasoned that my performance and inglorious ending embarrassed my coach and track and baseball teammates. As I rose from the ground, that was my awareness. But by the grace of God, when I saw my mother, all that thinking and the sullenness of my failure, disappointment, and embarrassment instantly vanished, and I knew I could live with myself and my defeat. After seeing Mom and her love and support for me, I felt deep down in my internal "knower" that I had enough of whatever I needed to face myself in the mirror and face others, as a man without shame, knowing that I utterly failed, but I gave it my all. I could indeed live with my defeat, utter embarrassment, and humiliation. I accepted that my sole victory was "I gave it my all, all I had!"

I can't fully explain what it did for me to see Mom staring lovingly and very caringly at me through that fence. But it did something for me far beyond my ability to explain it. It transformed me; it didn't change my circumstances but raised me above my situation. I suddenly felt highly secure and confident that I could live with my humiliation and embarrassment. Mom's love and concern for me lifted me far above my experience and circumstance. At that moment, I knew that my mother loved me, and I greatly needed her! Without hesitation, I opened my heart and received all of her love at that moment and instant in time. My mother loved me, and that was all I needed. I was foundationally supported at my emotional roots and could now continue my life! Mom didn't have the money to get into the stadium, but she found a way to see and be seen by her son. Due to my limitations, I know the words I've used to express what seeing my mother did to me only partially illuminates what occurred within my heart that day.

However, at the expense of being redundant, Mom being there completely obliterated my failure, humiliation, and embarrassment. That incident has not negatively affected me or resided in my mind as a bad memory from that moment to now! Paul was right when he said, "The greatest of these is love" (1 Cor. 13:13). My mom's love for me was demonstrated by her finding a way to see me and placing herself in my line of sight to see her as I looked up from my utter defeat. Her love slew and buried everything the devil, his demons, or anyone else could throw at me. All Satan's darts and arrows, with their warheads of negative thoughts and depressive emotions, were destroyed in flight and buried, not even arriving at my mind's door after I saw my mom.

I tend to analyze everything. As such, I noticed later as I thought about what had occurred. Mom found a way to see me without breaking our family budget or cheating. She didn't attempt to enter the stadium without a ticket. My parents were ethical. That was the standard my dad upheld for our family. Mom would sometimes refer to Dad as "Honest John" because of the steps she saw him go through to return excess money he received from a pay telephone booth or a store clerk.

However, it's interesting that my siblings Karen and Daryl weren't ethical that day. They left Mom and found a place in the fence to cheat by climbing over and into the stadium. I didn't know it then, but they were in the stands and watched the race from its start to my inglorious finish, hearing all of the crowd's comments regarding me. Then when the track meet was over, they ran down to me on the field and gave me some up-close, personal encouragement and comfort that I very much appreciated. They didn't then, nor have they to this day, ever teased or ridiculed me regarding my performance that day.

That was the last time I ran track. After examining my failure, it became apparent that running a full-out one-hundred-yard dash required more training and stamina than I had acquired playing baseball. Baseball necessitated me to run all out for thirty yards (ninety feet). That track experience glaringly illustrated my stamina breakdown at fifty yards, pointing out my limit. I did great up to fifty yards, then fell like a rock dropped off a cliff.

My Takeaway

- **Pride goes before a fall! All my arrogance and self aggrandizement were crushed at my utter track failure**
- **Love always finds a way! Nothing will or can stop it!**
- **My mother's love, care, and encouragement were much mightier than my failure, humiliation, and embarrassment. It nullified all of the devil's potentially destructive darts thrown at me!**
- **My parents were ethical. Dad set the moral standard for our home, and Mom found a way to see me without cheating or attempting to enter the stadium without a ticket.**

Vignette 20

My Change from a Teenager to Thinking Like a Man

Late in my teenage years, I was with my mother at a mall, and she had to go to the restroom. She came out soon after and was very frantic. She was calling and waving for me to hurry and come into the bathroom. I wanted to know what was happening but was reluctant to enter the women's restroom. Mom, however, demanded that I come right in, and then she rushed back into the bathroom. When I walked in, I saw a girl in her early twenties crying, in pain, with an expression of fear on her face, sitting on a toilet. As I entered, Mom waved for me to hurry over to her and the woman. She told me the woman was having a baby. But the baby was stillborn and attached to its umbilical cord, pulling on its mother, causing great pain as she attempted to rise from the toilet seat. The baby was hanging down, with its legs and lower torso in the toilet water. Mom had called me into the bathroom to assist as she helped the woman. In an act unimaginable to me and infinitely far out of my comfort zone, Mom commanded me to stick my hands under the woman, grab hold, and pull the baby out of the toilet as she helped the lady rise and stand up, reiterating that the baby was lifeless. As I did and touched the baby, it was dead weight, relatively cold, and indeed without life. The baby was dead!

To be sure, I hate, and I say again, I hate, recalling this experience. I hate even more writing about it. However, I'm pressed into action with confidence that the Lord has directed me to write this vignette with all its pertinent truth. Up until now, I've deliberately and unequivocally blocked the whole experience out of my mind. I haven't even considered it since I expelled it from my consciousness with all its accompanying emotional feelings and thoughts more than fifty years ago. However, as the Lord would have it, out of the blue, about a week ago, I was firmly pressed to write about it. Even after I was sure the Lord prompted me, it's taken a week for me to follow through and do it.

There is no way I can adequately explain what went through my whole being as I reached under the girl and touched her baby's solid, lifeless body. As soon as I felt it, I immediately clamped shut my eyes. I didn't want to see the baby; I consciously did not want its sight in my mind and memory. It was a traumatic and horrific experience for me. As I held the baby under its armpits, it felt fully developed. I sensed its rigid form with no heat emanating from its body. It felt strong and solid in my hands, and I, with purpose, held myself back from relating to or identifying with the baby. Then as a faint curiosity rose in my mind to see the baby, I hardened my heart and steadfastly refused to look at it. But oh my! As I held that girl's baby in my hands, I fought against my brain's attempt to paint a picture of the baby in my mind. This experience was such an emotional ordeal I've refused to think, recall, or talk about it to anyone. And I do mean anyone, even my dad, until this writing.

As I lifted the baby, it allowed the girl to stand up. Mom then protected the girl's modesty and privacy by wrapping her coat and the girl's coat around her and her baby. The girl leaned on Mom for assistance, then in unison, with me holding the baby as close to the girl as possible. We next started walking to our car, with me shuffling my feet in pace with the girl to prevent the umbilical cord from pulling on her. We worked our way out of the building to our car. We rushed the girl to the hospital with Mom driving and the girl and me in the backseat. I continued holding the baby and sat close to the girl to prevent the baby from pulling on the umbilical cord.

Once we got to the hospital, Mom ran in to get help, and the nursing staff rushed out with a gurney for the young lady and her baby. My job was over. However, I walked into the hospital to wash my hands and arms and waited as Mom parked the car. Mom wanted to stay and ensure the girl was OK before we left. She felt a strong responsibility for the girl. There was also the issue of notifying the girl's family. Mom wanted the girl to have somewhere to go and be taken care of after leaving the hospital. As time passed, I wondered if the girl was considered a legal adult and could check herself out of the hospital. However, that thought became a moot point because her family was contacted, and her mother and family showed up and joined us in the waiting area. Not too long after, but before Mom and I left, a doctor came out of surgery to talk to the girl's family. I stood back away from the huddle but could hear what was said.

The doctor said the baby was aborted and died via a sharp implement like a metal fireplace poker plunged into its skull. At that time in California, abortions were illegal, and my mind took off with the assumption that the girl found some back-alley practitioner to abort and kill her baby. Per the doctor's explicit description of the baby's cause of death, my stomach churned as he continued saying the baby was a boy. I cannot tell you how sick and angry I felt after hearing what he said; he gave the baby an identity. I then started resisting horrendous impressions of the baby's pain, torture, and death shooting through my mind. My focused thoughts were *I touched and held that baby. He was a real human being.* Although I didn't see the baby and tried not to identify with him, the doctor's proclamation that he was a boy crushed my resistance to blocking the baby from my mind. I remembered his solid, well-formed, cold body in my hands. Hearing the doctor tell her family that the girl killed her own baby was shocking, horrifying, and too much for me. However, as much as I wanted to turn and walk away, wanting no more of what I was hearing or the girl, I didn't. Mom needed comfort but was lending her support to the girl's family. Mom was also highly interested in the girl's well-being. Therefore, I stayed to be a brace to my mother.

The doctor further explained to the girl's family that abortions were illegal in California, and as stipulated by law, he and the hospital were required to notify the police. He had a sorrowful and compassionate look, seemingly having great sympathy and concern for the family as he noticed their reaction to his news. He patiently spent time with the family, filling them in on the girl's condition and answering their questions and inquiries.

Although Mom was lending her support to the family, as I said, I didn't want to hear anymore, nor was I interested in anything else the doctor said to the family. My mind was not on them anymore. All I could think about was that girl killed her baby, her very own baby! How dare she do that. That was a baby, a real innocent baby. I felt her baby. I touched her baby. They killed it! She and whoever she hired killed her very own baby! I just wanted to go. I wanted to go home and cry and grieve for that baby. I had seen and heard enough. I knew and experienced rejection and feeling unloved by my siblings. I grieved for that baby. It's one thing when your siblings reject you and tell you they don't love you. But it's entirely different when your mother doesn't want you and kills you.

After hearing what I heard, I just wanted to get out of that hospital as quickly as possible. Get to my bedroom and grieve and cry for that baby. I related to him. After all, I had been beaten, rejected, and unloved by my siblings because I was a nuisance to them (vignette 12). However, this mother's deed was eons beyond what I experienced with my siblings. I couldn't fathom it. From my mother's demonstrated love for my siblings and me, I neither cognitively nor emotionally had any identification with the baby's mother. Without question, to that point, that experience was the most traumatic of my life.

Interestingly, however, it was also a turning point in my life. I didn't see it coming, but that day and event changed me. It separated me from a boy into a man. The mantle of manhood fell upon me that day. Although I desperately wanted to go home and be by myself and cry and grieve for that baby. I firmly realized that now was not the time for me. My mother needed me. My mother needed me to help her. If what we had just gone through was traumatic for me. What must it have been for her? Oh my! What came up inside me was a sense of manliness and responsibility. I needed to be there for my mother. My dad was at work and not there. I needed to be there for my mother. This moment was not a time for me to be emotional and close up by myself. It was not a time for me to cry and grieve by myself. It was a time for me to be there with and for my mother. If what I saw and experienced was traumatic for me. How much more for Mom? Mom walked in and saw that girl there. Mom has children, including two daughters. What must this be like for her? She helped that girl as best as she could, and then when Mom needed help, she called me into the bathroom to help her and help that girl. Now it was my time to help Mom. I determined that I would stay close to Mom until Dad came home. As we drove home together, I did and said everything I knew to be a strength and encouragement to Mom. For me, that baby was a turning point in my life. It was time for me to stop looking at life through the eyes of "me, myself, and I." That baby was a wake-up call. No! Not so! More accurately, it was a loud, high-pitched alarm clock that woke me up in recognition that Mom and Dad had done their job with me. I was now a man and needed to start thinking like a man.

As part of the God, father, and mother triune partnership identified by Jewish sages,[18] my parents brought me to where

God wanted me to be. Just as Moses brought the children of Israel to God at Mount Sinai, metaphorically, my parents had brought me to God at "Mount Hospital." God, through Jesus Christ, would take over for the remainder of my upbringing and life. Dad and Mom had done their job! As part of my relationship with them, it was time for me to start thinking like a man! It was my time to look after Mom and hold back my tears and grief for that baby until Mom was OK! Mom now needed me!

Interestingly, within about a year and a half after this occurrence, my sense of accountability to God significantly increased around age twenty, as I explained in vignette 5.

My Takeaway

- **Life is nothing to play with. All actions have consequences and impact and affect others. Even the innocent unborn are caught in our actions.**
- **Although I don't think about that day and what occurred. In my heart, I'll never forget that baby, and I know that I'll see him again in the arms of Jesus someday.**
- **In two traumatic hours, my life changed. I quickly went from a "Me, myself and I" teenager to a young man starting to think like a man.**
- **My parents did an exceptional job raising me. They brought me, in God's timing, metaphorically to Mount Sinai. They didn't know it, but on the day this vignette speaks of, they handed me over to the Lord Himself.**

Vignette 21

The Bond of Love between a
Mother and Her Son

From birth, I lived deep within the relational experience of acceptance, comfort, loving warmth, safety, and protection from my mother until her departure to God. My relationship with my mother was close, personal, and unique from as early as I can remember. I'm sure my sisters and brother Daryl would say the same about their relationship with Mom. However, in speaking specifically about the bond between a mother and her son, I've observed that many mothers have a unique tie with their sons. I've observed it up close and personal in my church's eight-month boys' Rites of Passage (ROP) program. Year-to-year, about 75 percent of the thirty to fifty participating boys are raised in single-parent homes by their mothers or grandmothers, with little or no active father participation. Seeing the love bond between the boy and his mother week-to-week is fantastic. But especially during the program's annual Mother's Day Ceremony. On that day, each boy reads, for all to hear, his personally written heartfelt poem, message, or love and appreciation letter to his mother or grandmother. Upon hearing their sons speak of their love for them and their appreciation for all they do for them, the mothers break with tears and the warmest embraces of their sons at their conclusion. It's incredibly uplifting to see and hear.

Additionally, I've seen the mother-son bonding relationships in a Little League baseball park near my house. It generally grabs and holds my attention for the whole period of my observance when I see a mother with her son talking and walking side-by-side or arm-in-arm to or from their car. Or when I see her pitching balls for him to hit or her throwing ground balls to pick up as he practices. As I observe the mother and her son in those cherished moments, the question never occurs to me: where is the father? I assume that thought doesn't come to mind because I'm pleasantly fixated on what I see. The esteemed love relationship between a mother and her son is indeed unique. I'm sure a great deal of the pleasure I sense and derive from watching them is me vicariously experiencing my relationship with my mom again through them.

The Bond between Jesus and His Mother, Mary

Before discussing the bond between Jesus and His mother, Mary, I should define it in consideration of what is of "utmost" importance to the Lord our God. With that in mind, we are to believe in Him and the truth, the veritas that Jesus is the Christ, the Messiah our Savior. And we understand that God is love, and His expected reciprocation from us is that we love Him in return with all our being. Jesus is God, and He is the Word of God (John 1:1). Specifically telling us we are to love God (Him) with all our heart, soul, mind, and strength, that is, with all our effort and might. Additionally, He repeatedly tells us to honor and reverence our parents (Ex. 20:12; Lev. 19:3; Deut. 5:16; and Matt. 15:4 and 19:19). Jesus's bond with Mary was a love link from God (Him) to Mary and from Mary back to Him (God). So with Him being the Son of God, the Son of man, the Son of Mary, Jesus honored and reverenced His mother just as He told us to do. This fusion of love was admirably illustrated at Jesus's crucifixion.

However, before further illuminating the bond between Jesus and His mother, I'll present two contrasting realities of love. One is unrequited love for God from His creation and the other is dishonor and ill reverence for one's parent. Many are familiar with both examples.

I'll start with the following. Can you imagine God, who is pure love (1 John 4:8, 16), having loved Lucifer (the "Shining One," now the devil and Satan) perfectly? But Lucifer allowed his admiration and pride in himself to germinate and grow unchecked. Then his pride burst forth with a love of himself that greatly exceeded his love of God, if he indeed still loved God, his Creator, at that point in his deterioration. In either case, Satan viewed himself as God's equal with an accompanying desire to usurp God's created order. His desire to "be like the Most High" was an apparent attempt to elevate or insert himself into the Godhead. Lucifer was created with unimaginable beauty, majesty, skills, and ability as an archangel, far above other angels. Even Michael didn't challenge him, his power, or his ability when Satan contended with him for the body of Moses. Michael said, "The Lord rebuke you" (Jude 1:9). God loved Lucifer with perfect love. For God is love, but Lucifer rejected God and God's will for him to love Him, "the Most High," with all his being, including with all his effort and might. In his immense pride and love of and for himself, Lucifer rebelled against God, wanting and desirous to sit on God's throne (Isa. 14:12–14). In his rebellion against God, Lucifer convinced one-third of the host of heaven to join him.

As I now move on from Lucifer. I pick up at King David's son Absalom. However, setting aside Absalom's justifiable emotional issues and bitterness with his father for not protecting and defending his daughter and Absalom's sister Tamar from rape by their half-brother Amnon. Instead, I view Absalom as the epitome of a son dishonoring and irreverent to his father. He, similar to Lucifer, desired to take his father's throne, using methods akin to Lucifer's in his rebellion. I make that assumption by comparing the scripture description of Absalom's person and his rebellion against his father to Lucifer and his rebellion against God. From the scripture presentation of both, it sure appears that Absalom is a type of Lucifer.

First, he was extraordinarily handsome in looks far above all others, from the soles of his feet to the top of his head (2 Sam. 14:25). Second, he was bright, highly intelligent, and gifted, triumphantly recruiting those his father had offended, such as Ahithophel, King David's chief counselor and Bathsheba's grandfather. Yes, the same Bathsheba whom David, in his lust, took in adultery and then killed her husband Uriah, who by marriage was also Ahithophel's grandson-in-law. In Absalom's cleverness, he used personal issues against the king, such as Ahithophel's utter bitterness and unforgiveness for David for what he did to his family, to successfully conspire and steal the people's loyalty from his father. Then with his deceptive theft of the people's affections accomplished, he openly rebelled in violence against his father, intending to take his throne by force and replace him as king. All similar to Lucifer convincing one-third of the angels to join him and Lucifer declaring, "I will ascend above the heights of the clouds. I will be like the Most High."

In getting another perspective of God's love through David, God calling David "a man after His own heart" (1 Sam. 13:14). It is enlightening to hear that when David heard about Absalom's rebellion and plan to take his place and throne, he didn't hate or disown Absalom or even speak evil of him. On the contrary, David still tremendously and very openly loved his son. He was grievously saddened when he heard that Absalom was dead, killed in the battle to take David's very own crown. David had an incredible love for Absalom, although Absalom was not worthy of it. Thus, using the David-Absalom analogy and biblically knowing God's nature of love. God had an undefinable love for Lucifer, just as He has for us. Therefore, I perceive that God grieved indescribably when He saw what Lucifer had become. Lucifer was never a threat to God, only to himself. By God's justice, judgment, and wisdom, He rejected Lucifer as a resident of heaven and his position of authority, forcibly casting him out of heaven (Luke 10:18). The undefinable attribute, if one can realistically call God's love "an attribute" (for God is love), is that even though Lucifer definitely didn't deserve God's love at his fall and certainly doesn't deserve God's love now. God still loves him because God is Love. God, however, has judged and cast a sentence on Lucifer, Satan, the accuser. Satan no longer has God's grace, mercy, and forgiveness but has acquired His judgment and wrath. He has become evil to its fullest extent, as the Lord identifies him in John 8:44, and he has been condemned and damned to hell for all eternity!

Still, after all the times I've read it, I'm always amazed at how soberly and respectfully the Lord talked to Satan in the Garden of Eden when He punished the serpent for tempting the innocent, childlike Eve. As Solomon would say, I know it is my thinking as a man under the sun. But if God had left it to me, when confronting Satan over what he had deceptively done, my words and actions in anger toward Satan would have been so hot and furious that the Garden of Eden would have been the most arid, burned-out desert imaginable when I finished with him. Then in my anger, I would have wholly obliterated Satan's existence. But of course, I have a finite mind, understanding, and limited love ability.

Our message of God is that He doesn't love us because we deserve it or because we love Him, but rather because He is love. We are quite different; we love Him because He first loved us (1 John 4:19). Or saying it another way, God loved us before we loved Him, and just like with Satan, there is nothing we can do to stop God from loving us. We can only forfeit His grace, mercy, and forgiveness by not accepting His salvation. Incurring His resulting wrath for our sin of willfully choosing not to love Him and consequently rejecting Him and His rule over us. Like Satan has.

With God, Love for Him Is Where the Rubber of Our Lives Meets the Road

Before continuing to describe the bond of love between Jesus and His mother, Mary, I want to nail down, via example, God's love for us and the love He sincerely wants in return from us. Knowing this is key to understanding the consideration and value Jesus placed on His mother and how He honored her at His crucifixion and death. The exemplification is depicted in the restoration of Simon Peter after Peter denied Him.

From The Pure Word (TPW) translation:

> Then when they had dined, Jesus said, Oh Simon Peter, son of Jonas, are you Loving (agape, pure unselfish love) Me greater than these? He said to Him, Emphatically Yes, Oh Lord, You Spiritually Know that I affectionately love (phileo, brotherly love) You. He said to him, you must Feed My Lambs.
>
> He said to him the second time, Oh Simon Jonas, are you Loving (agape) Me? He said to Him, Emphatically Yes, Oh Lord, You Spiritually Know that I affectionately love (phileo) You. He said to him, you must Shepherd My Sheep.
>
> He said to him, again, the third time, Oh Simon Peter, do you affectionately love (phileo) Me? Peter was made grieved, because He spoke to him the third time, Are you affectionately loving (phileo) Me? So then he spoke to Him, Oh Lord, You Spiritually Know all things,

> You know that I affectionately love (phileo)
> You. Jesus said to him, Feed My Sheep. (John
> 21:15–17 TPW)

It's clear from the Lord's conversation with Peter that the Lord very much wanted Peter to love Him much more than he loved anyone else and with pure, unselfish, agape love. Namely, He wanted Peter to love Him with all his heart, soul, mind, and strength. Peter didn't. He grieved but admitted that he only loved the Lord with a brotherly phileo love. Interestingly, the Lord ended that part of the conversation, accepting what Peter could give Him then. But as the Lord continues talking to Peter, in John 21:18–19, He spoke regarding how Peter would die for Him, and I accept that Peter's love did grow to agape love for the Lord. Because the Lord Himself said,

> Greater love has no one than this than to lay
> down one's life for his friends. (John 15:13)

Peter laid his life down in a painful upside-down crucifixion for Jesus, his Lord and Savior.

(It should be noted, however, that first-century writings have not confirmed passed-down reports of Peter's crucifixion in Rome being upside-down versus the typical head-up manner, although John appears to insinuate it in John 21:18–19.)

The Lord Says What He Means and Means What He Says

When the Lord tells us to love Him with all our heart, soul, mind, and strength (Mark 12:30), He means exactly that and nothing less! Interestingly, throughout Jesus's entire earthy ministry, continuing through His crucifixion and resurrection. The Lord's four half brothers, James, Joses (Joseph), Simon, and Judas (Jude) (Matt. 13:55), didn't believe in Him or love Him with all their being. In their unbelief and lack of agape love for their half-brother, they did not commit to Jesus, His will, or purpose. They refused to accept their Brother as God's Anointed, the Messiah, and the Prophet spoken of by Moses. Scripture speaks explicitly of Jesus's brothers' unbelief in Him.

> For even His brothers did not believe in Him (John 7:5).

In acknowledgment of their unbelief, Jesus did not recognize them as His brothers. They were not "born again." They had not submitted to God's will, as described in Mark 3:31–35.

> Then His brothers and His mother came, and standing outside they sent to Him, calling Him. And a multitude was sitting around Him; and they said to Him, "Look, Your mother and Your brothers are outside seeking You." But He answered them, saying, "Who is My mother, or My brothers?" And He looked around in a circle at those who sat about Him, and said, "Here are My mother and My brothers! For whoever does the will of God is My brother and My sister and mother. (Mark 3:31–35)

Jesus said what He meant and meant what He said regarding who His "true" brothers were. James, Joses, Simon, and Judas were not "born of water and the Spirit" at the time of Jesus's crucifixion (John 3:3–5). Thus, they were His brothers in the flesh only at the time of His crucifixion.

However, the Lord's mother, Mary, was "born again." She believed that her Son, Jesus, impregnated in her through the Holy Spirit, was the Messiah, the Son of God. The angel Gabriel had spoken one-on-one to her about her future virgin pregnancy and who her Baby would be. Shortly after conversing with Gabriel, God confirmed to Mary, via the Holy Spirit, through her relative Elizabeth, who was pregnant with John the Baptist, who her forthcoming child would be because she had believed God. Mary also received confirmation from others of who Jesus was at His birth and forty days later at His temple dedication (Matt. 2:1–2, Luke 2:25–32).

The Lord's half-brothers didn't believe in Him until after His resurrection. After His resurrection, Jesus appeared to and spoke to his brother James (1 Cor. 15:7). After James's conversion, scripture records James as a pillar in the church and the author of the Epistle of James. It also records the Epistle of Jude written by Jesus's brother Jude.

Now Back to the Bond between Jesus and His Mother, Mary

In returning to the special bond between a boy and his mother, I said all of the above to fully illuminate God's love and display the love, consideration, and honor Jesus gave His mother before His death. The earthly aspect of honor and care for His mother came to the forefront of Jesus's mind as His impending death approached. As Jesus's crucifixion drew near, I'm sure He thoroughly thought who He would entrust with the care and protection of His precious mother. Jesus was the eldest son and the Man of His family at His death. The provisioning and safekeeping of His mother was His responsibility. He, indeed, was not going to commit her to an outsider. Someone outside His family, the family of God. Or to a member of His "born-again" family of God, who could not be trusted to love and care for His mother wholeheartedly.

Thus, after all His considerations, in a manner that only God can. Jesus committed and entrusted Mary, His mother, to His *real* brother, "born of water and the Spirit." His disciple and chosen apostle, John, "John the beloved." It wasn't an afterthought that Jesus gave her to John. John was called a son of thunder, but conversely, in his Gospel, he refers to himself repeatedly as the disciple "whom Jesus loved" (John 13:23). As recorded in his Gospel, he was exceptionally close to Jesus and comfortable in His presence, leaning back on His bosom at the Last Supper. He was "John the beloved."

Christian tradition and early church theologian Tertullian tell us God miraculously delivered John unscathed from a Roman pot of boiling oil. Emperor Domitian then banished John to the Greek island of Patmos, where Jesus revealed the book of Revelation to him. Then after his exile, God further blessed John by extending his life into his nineties, he being the only apostle to die a natural death.

God's purpose for us is to love Him and love Him first and foremost. He lost Lucifer and a third of His angels because of pride and love of self. God looks at our hearts, not our outward appearance. He's looking to see who loves Him "with all their heart, soul, mind and strength." On the cross, just before He gave up His Spirit, Jesus looked upon His mother, the woman the Father chose for His conception and nurturing. She was standing below Him and looking up at Him. He saw John standing near her. If we go back to the Garden of Eden, He, who was now on the cross, is who God spoke of in the garden when He told the serpent (Satan), "And I will put enmity between you and the woman, and between your offspring and hers; He will crush your head, and you will strike His heel (Gen.

3:15 NIV)." Namely, this Son of Mary, Mary's Seed, was who God spoke of that day. Now Jesus, right then and there on the cross, as God said, was about to crush the head of the serpent, the head of Satan, the once mighty and glorious Lucifer. Lucifer withdrew his love from God and placed it on himself. Now his head was on the block and minutes away from being crushed at the death of Jesus. At Jesus's death, God would take back all authority Adam gave Satan.

But interestingly, Jesus, the Seed of the woman, the Seed of His mother, Mary. In doing the preeminent deed of all creation. What God, His Father, explicitly sent Him to do and had promised through Moses and the prophets suddenly paused His death. Per God, the crucifixion is the utmost event in all creation, for it is written, "For God so loved the world that he gave his only begotten son" (John 3:16). However, Jesus, in crucifixion, in excruciating pain from the spikes in His wrist and feet—along with His back having been ripped open, possibly down to the exposure of His blood vessels and muscles from the terribly brutal flogging by the Roman soldiers.[19] His face, perhaps unrecognizable from the beating He also took from the Roman soldiers along with the humiliation of voluminous spit spat on Him. In addition to the pain and bleeding from the crown of thorns laid and pressed into His head with the agonizing asphyxiation, He was suffering from being stretched out on the vertical cross, making it extremely difficult to breathe. All in addition to the entirety of the world's sins poured into Him, from Adam and Eve to mine, Robert K. Auten Jr., and humanity's last-born child. Then, absorbing the undefinable magnitude of God's wrath poured on Him, followed by God's abandonment of Him. Jesus, the Christ, the Lamb of God, even with all the excruciating pain and suffering He was undergoing and God's forsaking Him, paused His death to entrust His mother, the woman of His birth, whose breast He suckled as an infant, to the one who agape loved Him. To John, the one called "the beloved," who had leaned on His breast at the Last Supper.

Judas betrayed Jesus. Peter denied Him. All others whom Jesus called His friends (John 15:15) deserted Him, fearing for their lives. But John was at His trials, at His sentencing, and now at His execution. From the biblical report, there is no mention of Jesus's half-brothers being at His crucifixion. If so, they weren't even there to support their mother. But John the beloved was there as a living testimony that "Perfect love casts out fear" (1 John 4:18). He was to whom Jesus, God incarnate, entrusted His mother's care. What son doesn't *greatly* honor and appreciate his mother, ensuring she is well taken care of when he no longer can! So as Jesus died, He gave His mother to John. To him, who agape loved Him!

I sincerely thank God for my mother, our relationship, and my pleasant remembrance of her. The love between a mother and her son is indeed unique and highly precious!

My Takeaway

- **God is love (1 John 4:8).**
- **I shall, and I do, love the Lord my God, Jesus my Savior, with all my heart, soul, mind, and strength (effort and might).**
- **"These three remain: faith, hope, and love. But the greatest of these is love" (1 Cor. 13:13 NIV).**

Part 2

Lessons from My Father

My son, hear the instruction of your father ...
for they will be graceful ornaments on
your head, and chains about your neck.
—Proverbs 1:8–9

Part 2

Lessons from My Father

Vignette 1

The Measure of a Man

My mother taught and prepared me through her experiences and observance of life's reality. On the other hand, my father trained and disciplined me, instilled my values, and enforced the character he wanted in me. Much of what he taught me was how to treat and respect others and vice versa. That is, how others were to treat and respect me, including how I was to rebuke those who did not properly treat or respect me. To better understand the lessons I received from my father, I believe it's prudent first to introduce my dad and his background and personality. My father, Robert K. Auten, was born and raised in New Brunswick, New Jersey. I am a junior named after my dad. Pop came from a family of four boys and four girls and was the sixth child and third oldest boy. All the boys were very close and taught to defend themselves with their fists as needed from an early age. They were outstanding boxers. Their skills were enhanced by the neighborhood fire station, which as a community outreach organized boxing and training lessons for the boys at the station. My dad's youngest brother, my uncle Calvin, became a Golden Gloves champion through the fire department's program and fought in Madison Square Garden in New York City, New York.

Dad's neighborhood was racially mixed, consisting primarily of an ethnic blend of Jews, Italians, Polish, and Blacks. As part of their norm, it was common for Dad and his brothers to go to their neighborhood park and play ball. It was just as customary whether the Jewish, Italian, or Polish boys arrived first. When either of the other groups came, there would be a challenge for "first-come-first-served" park privileges, and then they would start fighting for those privileges if an issue arose. Even their dogs would be fighting each other.

As Dad explained, this neighborhood behavior between the boys was typical. What heightened my siblings' and my interest was that even their dog Nip, a black-and-white spotted Dalmatian (firehouse dog), was a super fighter, and he would go at it with the other kids' dogs. After fighting, they would choose teams and play ball together. After playing ball, they would commonly sit down, talk, joke, and have lunch together. From what we gleaned, this behavior and group interaction was customary among the boys in their area. Even though the boys fought, they were still friends and considered themselves one neighborhood. Thus, Pop said, if outsiders from another district came to the park, they would join together and fight against the outsiders driving them out. Their community was tightly bound and close-knit, with sincere and caring bonds among families. They looked out for and helped one another as needs arose.

My father told us a story that occurred when he was young and ventured off several blocks away from his home. A Jewish lady looked out of her window and saw him. She yelled at him, "Bobby, what are you doing here so far away from home? Does Bea (my dad's mother, Beatrice) know where you are? Come up here!" She called him up a flight of stairs into her home. She asked him again if his mother, Bea, knew where he was. She scolded, spanked, and sent him home when he said she didn't. Surprisingly, when he arrived home, he found out she had called his mother and told her he was as far down as her house. That said, Pop got a second scolding and spanking from his mom. He said that's how he and his siblings grew up as part of a two-parent, eight-children, close-knit family in an ethnically mixed immigrant neighborhood.

There was no racial prejudice or racism in Dad's neighborhood, and they did not view any race or ethnicity as any better or worse than any other. They all got along together, and even their fights were "boys will be boys," with no hard feelings or retribution afterward. Dad's two older brothers, James (Buddy) and Albert, joined the US Navy during the start of World War II in Europe after Hitler attacked Poland and before the US entered the war. Uncle Buddy was on one of the US naval ships in Pearl Harbor and was instantaneously blown off the deck of his boat into the harbor waters by a bomb's percussion or shock wave blast. The bomb made a direct hit on his ship during the Japanese attack on Pearl Harbor on December 7, 1941. Thank God that Uncle Buddy was not in a confined area, constrained, or hit anything when the blast instantaneously lifted and accelerated him off the ship's deck and into the water. Like my two eldest uncles, many boys in their neighborhood joined the United States military in their love for, and allegiance to, our nation when they also came of age just before or after the US entered World War II.

After the US entered the war, when Dad was seventeen years old, he lied about his age, left school, and joined the navy following his older brothers. The same was true with several of his neighborhood pals and associates. Once turning seventeen or close to the recruiting age of eighteen, they also fictitiously upped their age, joining the military, following their older brothers or their own WWII patriotic desires. Because of Dad's family upbringing and close multiethnic neighborhood affiliation, he knew in his heart and mind who he was and was not, nationally and racially. He was very secure knowing that America was his country and home, and he owed no one an explanation, defense, or apology for his person, ethnicity, or nationality.

Being who he was, Pop had no tolerance for racial hatred, racial prejudice, bias, racism, racial denigration, racially derogatory jokes, or for that matter, the mistreatment of anyone—man or woman, boy or girl—for any reason. As such, Dad was anathema to wife or child abuse, racial segregation, Jim Crow activity, laws, and behavior. In Dad's mind and heart, people were people, and there was no racial distinction between people. You treat people with the same consideration you want for yourself, judging them only by their values, character, and respect for others. He taught us that if a person did something or trespassed our person and needed rebuking, you rebuked them properly and moved on. Similarly, if they needed your help, and it was within your means to help them, you helped them and then moved on.

Mom commented, tearing up as she told me one day that Dad was the black sheep of his family. According to her, Dad was verbally abused and mistreated by his mother because he didn't excel in school to the level his mother expected. His mother's verbal abuse, along with things Mom knew she said to Dad, deeply hurt her and is what led Mom to believe that Pop was the black sheep of his family. As part of her belittling, my grandmother considered Dad the least likely among his siblings to succeed. This lack of love, affection, and consideration deeply affected Dad; however, he never spoke of it. But you could tell it affected him from the emotions that accompanied some things he did and didn't say. There was a gaping hole of love and respect that he wanted from his mom but never received. Dad rarely spoke or mentioned his mother, and when he did, it was very brief and emotionally neutral, with no soft, warming mother-son stories. The only detailed story about his mother I heard was from Dad's two older brothers when my daughter and I visited them in New Jersey some years after Dad passed away.

The story his brothers shared was Dad came home with them one day, and they reported that he had a fight with a boy, and the boy got the best of him. When his mom heard he had lost the confrontation, she became outraged. She spanked my father and ordered him to find the boy immediately and beat him up. He was not to come back home until he did. So Pop and his elder brothers left to find the boy. When they saw him, Dad unleashed a tirade on the boy, leaving no doubt that he bested the boy, much to his brothers' satisfaction. Their report greatly pleased my grandmother when they returned home, who then let my dad out of her "doghouse." My paternal grandmother was a "queen bee" and iron-handedly ruled and controlled their household.

Minutes after Dad passed away, Mom and I drove away from the hospital. Mom murmured with tears in her eyes, "Your grandmother may not have thought much of your father, but I can attest to him as a husband, a man of character and values. Even more so as a father to you and your siblings. He was an excellent provider, teacher, and trainer, ensuring you all graduated from excellent universities." She commented, "He might have been the black sheep of his family, but he was more successful than all his siblings."

My Takeaway

- **Treat all people with love and respect as people and equivalent to myself.**
- **If someone needs or requires correction, then properly and respectfully correct them.**
- **If someone needs help, then provide it as much as I am able.**
- **Don't mistreat or favor people with respect to their race, color, ethnic origin, or social position.**
- **I am not any better or superior to anyone else, nor is anyone any better or superior to me.**

Vignette 2

A Lesson of Love and Grace

When I was six or seven, my cousin Bobbie, a twenty-year-old college student, came to live with us because of tension and issues between her and her stepmother. Bobbie was close to my mom, her aunt, and her father's youngest sister. She was likewise very close to Dad as well. My siblings and I loved Bobbie dearly and had a great deal of love and respect for her. We loved that she now lived with us and regarded her as our older sister. After living with us for months, summertime arrived, and we were out of school. I had been practicing jumping up and grabbing an overhanging branch on a large tree in our backyard, then climbing up to the top branches. The branch I had been practicing on extended about ten feet from the tree's base. However, it was low enough for me to jump high and grab it. I had been practicing running as fast as possible and then jumping high, grasping the branch with both hands and allowing my forward momentum to swing me up onto the limb on my feet. I then gathered my balance and climbed the branches higher up into the tree.

One Saturday afternoon, Bobbie requested that my siblings and I go to our bedrooms and take a nap. For a reason and an accompanying attitude I have no recollection of, I rebelled against Bobbie in utter defiance. My parents were not home, and when she insisted, my obstinance took its stand. I refused to obey Bobbie, turned, and ran out of our house through the back door into the backyard. In a flash, I was gone. I intended to get away from her in the manner I had been practicing all week. Namely, to run fast, grab the tree branch, rotate onto the limb with my feet, and then quickly climb high up into the tree away from Bobbie and her grasp.

I knew I couldn't afford to miss the branch and needed some distance between her and me to give me time to execute my maneuver. I knew I wouldn't get a second chance, but I thought confidently, *There is no way this old lady can catch me.* Those were the thoughts in my mind as I ran out of our back door. However, as I jumped off the rear door porch, I surprisingly felt Bobbie close behind me. As I landed, I saw my baseball bat lying on the grass in front of me, so I grabbed it and turned in one motion to face Bobbie. She was too close for me to get away from her. Much to my shock and horror, she was faster than I imagined. However, I maintained composure and started waving my bat at Bobbie to keep her away from me. She quickly jumped up and down and stepped left and right to avoid the bat as I swung it back and forth. As my bat went by her, she would step forward and reach out with her hands, attempting to grab me. Then she retreated or leaped left to right or right to left to avoid the bat as I swung it back, keeping her away from touching me. I purposely let her see the bat to keep from hitting her.

My thoughts turned to alarm as I saw how determined Bobbie was to get me. I realized with growing concern that as old as Bobbie was, she was much quicker than I thought. Bobbie continued to jump high or leap this way and that way to stay away from the bat and me hitting her. I interpreted Bobbie's stern, determined look as her saying, "Robert, you're not going to get away with this. I'm going to get you!" After interpreting her facial language, for the first time during the incident, I feared she would catch me and my behind would be mush. Until then, I was "cool, calm, and collected," feeling in complete control and much more agile, fast, and athletic than the "old woman" Bobbie was. I then thought with genuine concern, *She's going to get me if I don't get some separation distance from her now! Robert, you've got to do something. Get away from her now!*

As those thoughts entered my mind, so did my escape plan. While continuously waving the bat at high rotational velocity. I elevated it to Bobbie's face level so she would greatly fear the possibility of it hitting her face. I wanted her further away from me and more conscious of the harm the bat could do to her. I needed Bobbie's attention on the bat, not on me. As soon as I detected her fixation on the bat, I released it straight at her waist. It was a perfect plan. When I saw her progress toward me, instantly halt, and she initiated her jump safely out of the way of the projectile, I knew I had the separation time I needed. I turned and was gone like a ball shot out of a cannon.

When I got to the tree, I jumped high, grabbing the tree branch just as I had practiced. My momentum swing was perfect as my body rotated from its feet on the ground, vertical position, through a horizontal position, with my arms and legs fully extended out as I swung, clutching the branch with my hands. As I continued my rotation, I started anticipating its completion by getting my feet ready to land on the tree stem. My mind was hyperactive, in expectancy of stopping my body's rotation and repositioning it as soon as I landed vertically on my feet. I knew I needed to quickly gain my balance on the limb and instantly accelerate my climb up the tree. I had to get high enough safely before Bobbie got to the tree and leaped up to grab my ankles, pulling me back down. As I swung up and through the horizontal position, my confidence, which I had temporarily lost, suddenly returned to me. I knew I had gotten away!

Then suddenly, with great fright and horror, I felt Bobbie's two hands simultaneously grab my left and right waists. Her grab occurred as my body laid out past its horizontal position before I started rotating on my last forty-five-degree path onto the branch. Bobbie's hands caught me just before my waist turned up and out of her reach. With her hands secured like vice grips around my waist, she pulled me to the ground, breaking my handgrip on the tree branch. I couldn't believe it when I felt her hands lock onto my hips! I could not believe it! I was so shocked that I didn't even feel or notice the violent thump on the ground my body absorbed when I landed. My mind was exploding with, *No! No! No! How could this old woman catch me? I'm much too fast! How did this old lady catch me?* All my fear and the horror of feeling Bobbie's hands on my waist suddenly were replaced by my shock, stun, and bewilderment that this "old lady" actually caught me. All my concentration centered on that thought. *How could this old lady have caught me?* I couldn't get it out of my mind; it kept repeating, *This old lady caught me! How could she?*

After Bobbie pulled me down from the tree and picked me up from the ground, she took me back into the house and spanked my behind, giving it all I deserved. However, when she spanked me, I cried, but I didn't feel any pain. Instead, I felt bewilderment, with the sustained shock that "Bobbie caught me." I could not reconcile the reality of what Bobbie had done with who I was. It was mesmerizing to me. As Bobbie spanked me, I not only didn't feel the pain of the belt, but neither did I hear her words of chastisement while she laid her punitive correction and justice on me. All I heard in my mind was *I was much faster than you; how could you have caught me? You are much too old to have caught me. How could that have happened?*

I apparently had a highly magnified ego and a very high opinion of my brain, thinking, and athletic ability, even at that early age. Maybe that is what Mom pointed out with her sage comments in part 1, vignette 2. However, to be sure, my superiority over Bobbie was all that my mind fixated on, not my rebellion, disobedience, the sting of the belt, or her words, but rather my bewilderment and shock that she caught me. That realism and fact siphoned all the air and fight out of me. It left me with the sense that I had been utterly *defeated!* Bobbie was the victor. I had no more fight residing in me. It was all gone!

The seriousness of my defiance and rebellion didn't come to my mind until several minutes after my spanking. After I finally accepted the truth that Bobbie had caught me, that she was faster and smarter than me. When it arrived, it came thunderously. The seriousness of my offense didn't enter my mind as a light that suddenly turned on. But as a nuclear blast! It hit suddenly and horrifically as the consequences of my disobedience and actions exploded in my mind. When those thoughts hit me, it became frighteningly real what would happen to me when Dad got home and found out what I did. It had never entered my mind during my rebellion. Now it was front and center. I knew when Bobbie or one of my siblings told Dad what I did. His rage and infuriation with me and for what I did would be quick, without mercy, and dreadfully painful to my ears and hindquarters.

My awakened consciousness regarding the seriousness of my act of threatening Bobbie with my baseball bat. Together with my overt defiance, rebellion, disobedience, and disrespect of her. All brought about a fear that frantically gripped me and released a set of vivid imaginations. I knew I was staring down at "death" as I started thinking about Dad's anger coming my way, and after its release, Dad not even being able to tolerate the sight of me!

As my mind shifted to my father, my imagination took over. I knew that the time I was now on was "borrowed time," as I had heard in some gangster movies on television. I also now clearly understood what being on "borrowed time" meant. It told me I was now on "death row," and my time would soon end after Daddy got home. I learned about death row, its purpose, and its ultimate end because, at that time, California had an infamous prisoner named Caryl Chessman on death row, heading for imminent execution and death by way of the "gas chamber." [1] It was on the television news and in the newspapers. In addition, I had heard my parents talk about him and what would happen. Thus, when I came to my senses and my imagination took over my view of life, I knew I was in serious trouble as soon as my father got home. All I could do now was wait on "death row" just like Chessman did until his date and time came. Because I knew my sisters, I also knew if Bobbie didn't beat them to it, they, in a blast of excitement, were going to blurt out what I did to Dad and Mom as soon as they opened the front door and walked into the house. I was in serious trouble, and I knew it.

As I expected, when my parents got home, one of my sisters eagerly blurted out and told them what had happened as they entered the house and closed the door. My trial started on the spot without my parents taking another step. The whole family, including my younger brother Daryl, was at my "trial." I stood a few feet away, about waist-high from my dad, the judge, jury, and executioner, "a dead man walking." I didn't want to look into Dad's face, so I focused on his chest area as he gathered himself from the surprise of what he had just heard. As he did, he asked Bobbie to explain the incident and what I had done. She filled him in on what happened and all the details. Man! As she did, I could feel the heat of the executioner's anger rise in intensity, and with a glance up, I could see my dad's face getting redder and redder. Pop had light skin, and as he was changing from David Banner into the Incredible Hulk, his skin tone didn't go green but crimson blood red! As Bobbie continued, he got madder and madder and redder and redder with every descriptive word of my defiance and disobedience. Finally, Bobbie described how I raised and swung my bat at high speed back and forth and then threw it at her. I glinted and glanced at my father as Bobbie briefed him on my behavior and rebellion. As my heart pounded profusely, I fully accepted what I did, having repeated thoughts. *I am dead! My time and end have come! My life is over!* After Bobbie told Dad and Mom what happened and all that I did. Pop turned from Bobbie to face me, and the blood-red-faced Hulk took his first step toward me.

My time had run out; Dad's face told me he was hearing no more witnesses! His judgment was being rendered. His turning from Bobbie and taking his first step toward me was the proclamation of his verdict. As he turned from Bobbie, I looked up directly at him and into his blood-red face with wrath and anger in his eyes. The executioner was coming, with no hesitation, straight for me. My end was here! I couldn't run, I couldn't scream, I couldn't ask for help. Worst of all, I couldn't ask for mercy. I did everything the witness and victim of my disobedience said I did. I had nowhere to go or anyone to run to. In submitting to the consequences of my actions, my emotions were suppressed, including the release of fear and crying. I prepared in my heart and mind for my deserved end.

I said nothing. I made no sound. I didn't look to my mom for help. I had no defense or excuse. My silence confessed to the accusations brought against me. They were true and accurate. I accepted that it was time to face the consequences of my deeds and actions. I voluntarily did everything I had been accused of by my choice and will. I was guilty as charged! I was ready to go. I was in total submission to the judge and executioner's judgment. I rightfully deserved what I was going to get, and my executioner was in motion just two or three steps away.

Then suddenly and unexpectedly, Bobbie, to my utter and absolute amazement and shock, launched herself between Dad and me. Even though I had openly defied Bobbie, swinging and throwing my bat at her, she still loved me. In her love for me and respect for my father, Bobbie, with determined resolve, without touching my dad or me, bolted herself into the space between us with a cat's speed and quickness.

Like she had done seconds ago in her testimony, her words grabbed and held all of my dad's attention. She, fervently and emotionally, without tears, earnestly interceded for me. Her body language, spoken word selection, voice tone, powerful and emotionally passionate love, and concern for me stopped Dad in his tracks! The emotion, love, and care for me poured out of her. I didn't know what it was then, but I could see and hear in her emotional appeal and voice tones that she had already completely forgiven me for what I did.

Bobbie always called Dad "Bob," like Mom and other adults did to distinguish him from me. Me being Dad's junior. She strongly petitioned Dad, saying, "Bob, I spanked Robert! I spanked him well! He got what he deserved! I don't believe you need to spank him again! I handled it! Robert's a good boy! He is a good boy! I believe he won't do it again!" With a stunning look, my father halted his aggressive advance toward me. Without saying anything to Bobbie, he studied her for what seemed like seconds on top of seconds. Finally, after his silent study and thought period, he accepted her appeal and backed off while silently staring intensively at me. As Dad pierced me with his eyes, he saw the stark fear on my face and my complete submission to the judgment and wrath I saw coming my way seconds earlier. I knew I was guilty, deserving every bit of the sentence, penalty, and pain owed me.

Before we dispersed, Dad said something to me, but I don't remember his words. Instead, I remember his prolonged, intense staring at me. Within his sharp observation, he seemingly sensed and convinced himself that I had gotten the message. His intense look at me also let me know that he had accepted Bobbie's intercession for me. His face and eyes additionally told me that I had better not do anything like I did ever again! Not ever again! There would be no second chance! I didn't know what it was then, but I had experienced and received unmerited mercy. I didn't get what I deserved and walked away knowing it. My experience humbled me beyond anything else to which I can compare.

I surely didn't intellectually know what mercy was at that age, but I knew I had experienced it. I experienced something I couldn't expound on or explain. But I felt it and knew I lived because of it. So when Dad dismissed me, and I went to my bedroom, I cried like a baby. It was deep, deep down, boohooing with gushers of tears. I wept as a release of my fear. I wept in thankfulness to Bobbie for saving me from annihilation. I cried and cried and cried because I knew I didn't deserve what Bobbie did for me. However, I also wept in relief that I was given another chance.

My life was not over. Bobbie's determinate and passionately intense intercessional plea saved me. I cried because the disaster that was imminently coming to me had been averted. I didn't receive or experience the dreadful outpouring of my father's wrath and anger. That one experience of my defiance occurred six or seven years after my birth, during my days of innocence and complete dependence on my parents. It has left an indelible imprint on me. My respectful fear of my father, with its accompanying emotions, thoughts, and imagery, is permanently etched in my psyche. Now that I know the Lord, that everlasting experience has helped me accept the message from the writer of Hebrews that says,

> It is a fearful thing to fall into the hands of the living God. (Heb. 10:31)

I recognize that facing my father's wrath for my sin of disobedience, defiance, and rebellion cannot be compared to being confronted with the rage and anger of God for the same offenses. Thus, I know that under no circumstances or desire for anything in this world do I want to fall into the anger and wrath of God almighty! I want none of it!

It's interesting that after telling my daughter this story a few years ago. She immediately said, "Dad, those were not Bobbie's hands that pulled you down from that tree. Those were God's hands that pulled you down. He would not let you get away with what you did."

Wow! What she said cleared up the decades-old puzzle of how that "old lady" Bobbie could have caught me. Now I knew! "God transported her like He did Phillip the Evangelist (Acts 8:39), from her position to the tree." I knew I was faster than that old lady.

My Takeaway

- Over the years, my cousin Bobbie's loving and sincere statement that "Robert is a good boy" has stayed with me and very deeply affected me beneficially. It inspired a desire to be what she thought of me.
- Bobbie showed me that when I'm my worst and see little or no value in myself, there is someone who still loves and highly values me.
- I am loved even when I don't feel loved or feel that I should be loved.
- God's love, mercy, forgiveness, and grace are real and will always find me no matter how badly I mess up or sin.
- From Hebrews 10:31 and my close encounter and experience with my dad's anger, rage, and wrath. I know I don't want to face the anger, rage, and wrath of God!

Vignette 3

A Lesson of Love and Grace

Sequel: What Did Bobbie See in Me That I Didn't See in Myself?

In my bedroom, after my dad, my judge, jury, and executioner, pardoned me with his accompanying eye warning that I better not ever do what I did again. And after, the fear of what could have happened to me subsided. My most in-depth thinking, soulful crying, and emotions transitioned from my fear of Daddy's wrath and judgment to what Bobbie did for me. As the transition occurred, I recalled seeing Bobbie step between Dad and me and her passionate facial expressions, voice tones, and fervent intercession to Dad on my behalf. I couldn't understand why Bobbie mediated for me and why with so much determination and zeal. Who am I that she would do that for me? I was mystified beyond reason as I wondered how Bobbie could think enough of me to do that.

Without question, I knew I was wrong for defying her. I knew my actions were terrible. I defiantly ran from her, then threw my bat at her. When I threw the bat at her, I knew I ensured she saw it to avoid it. But she didn't know that! As far as she knew, I was trying to hurt her. Yet! She passionately interceded for me. Bobbie told my father repeatedly that I was a "good boy." How could she tell him that? I was no "good boy," and I knew I was not a "good boy"! In no way was I a "good boy"! Why did she say that? What did she see in me that I didn't see in myself?

When she spoke to Dad, she had such heartfelt love and concern for me in her voice. I believe those buckets of tears I was now shedding were coming because I realized I had utterly failed someone who truly loved me. And worse still, I didn't place the value on Bobbie she put on me. I know it's repetition, *but what did Bobbie see in me?* Her words haunted and sobered me for a long time. I could not figure out what she saw in me that caused her to do what she did for me. What did she see in me that I didn't?

I knew I had not been a "good boy." When the bat event occurred, I had a history of consistently doing things that I should not have been doing. We lived in an apartment on the second floor when I was four. Suddenly, Mom heard girls screaming. She knew my older sister Beverly and I were outside in front of our apartment. Upon hearing the girls' screams, Mom ran to the window to check on our safety and shockingly found out what was happening. As she peered out the window, she saw a small group of girls screaming and running frantically on the sidewalk outside our apartment. I was behind, chasing the girls, with my pants unzipped, trying to tee-tee on them.

I additionally had painted my sisters' tea table red. I painted their cat red. I could no longer play with their cat or use their table. I broke their dolls, trying to see how they worked and were put together, and soon after that, I was forbidden to touch their dolls.

I filled our car's gas tank with water, playing service station attendant, while my older sister and I washed the car before leaving for a Saturday evening family outing. When the time came for us to go, the car wouldn't start. After Dad tried and failed to start the car, he checked under the hood, didn't find anything, but still couldn't get the car started. Finally, he asked my sister and me if we had done something other than wash the car. My sister told him we played "gas station," and I filled our car's tank with water. Pop had noticed the gas gauge showing the tank filled and thought Mom had gassed up the car. On Sunday, Dad attempted to drain the car's tank of its excess water. However, early Monday morning, the car engine blew up in flames. The fire could have killed or seriously injured Dad and Mom as they attempted to get our vehicle started for Dad to go to work. When the fire flared up, Dad was under the engine's hood, and Mom was in the driver's seat, attempting to start the car at Dad's command. I'll never forget that morning.

Thank the Lord my parents weren't hurt, and the fire department quickly arrived and extinguished the fire. Afterward, the fireman captain talked to Dad and Mom regarding the cause of the fire, and they informed him of what I did. Then all three turned and started walking directly toward me. All I focused on was the fireman. He was in the middle of my parents. He was tall with high black boots, a long black fireman jacket, and a black captain's fireman hat. He was incredibly intimidating to me as he came closer one step at a time. All I saw was him and his long legs and black boots coming for me as they walked. I knew the party was over for me. My heart was pounding, and I wondered if I was going to jail for the rest of my life. The captain walked right up to me with those high black boots, and I looked up into his face. The captain possessed a strong presence of authority, and I was very much intimidated by him as he talked to me about what I did and how it nearly cost my parents their lives. As he spoke to me, I realized he cared for me and was conveying a sobering set of facts that he was very familiar with, and I had better pay close attention. My unthinking and foolish, playful act nearly cost my parents their lives and destroyed our car. He wasn't there to take me to jail but rather to reinforce the seriousness of what I did and plant in me the process of thinking before doing anything else that could harm me or someone else. After talking to me, he resumed speaking to my parents as they returned to his vehicle. Dad and Mom seemed very appreciative that he had spoken to me. I thought I would get a spanking after the fireman left, but I didn't.

I was always in trouble. As my troublesome behavior continued, I remember Mom and Dad taking me to a child specialist. I didn't know why I needed to see this "child specialist." I wasn't sick. However, they thought something was severely wrong with me. Later, as an adult, Mom and I discussed my childhood behavior and continuous mischief and trouble. Mom then told me that the doctor they took me to was, in fact, a child psychiatrist. His diagnosis of me was that I was a "normal boy." His concern after his evaluation of me was for Mom and Dad. They had allowed me and my conduct to place them in a mental, emotional, and frantically stressful state. He assessed that they were the ones who needed psychiatric help for not recognizing a boy's behavior. He assured them I would grow out of what they were witnessing.

Irrespective of whether my behavior was boyishly normal, I was always in trouble. But to be honest, in my formative years, Bobbie's loving and sincere statement that "Robert was a good boy" affected me much more than the memory of what I did and my fear of Dad's anger and rage toward me. Bobbie's attitude and words made me want to be a good boy. I didn't want to let her down. The thought *What did Bobbie see in me that I didn't see in myself?* returned to me repeatedly. I don't know what Bobbie saw in me, but her passion and love for me truly did change me.

Thank God for my cousin Bobbie! I experienced real love and forgiveness from her. I've never forgotten what she did for me that day. Now that I've accepted the Lord and I'm saved. I thank God for showing Bobbie something in me that caused her to step in front of my father and intercede on my behalf. Even though I was as young as I was, I have never forgotten the feelings, thoughts, and pardon I experienced and received that day because of her.

Bobbie died in May 2017. At her funeral, when I was offered, I took the opportunity to affirm my cousin Bobbie to all present, letting them know what she meant to me. I told everyone, "Bobbie saw something in me that I never saw in myself." She placed a value on me that I was not aware I had. With all my being, I thank God for my cousin Bobbie. I thank Him for the love, grace, and mercy she had for me. All of which compelled her to step between my father and me and fervently intercede on my behalf!

My Takeaway

- **God will never give up on me or forsake me.**
- **As I experienced with my cousin Bobbie, God, through His love, sees something of value in me and has redeemed me to Himself.**

Vignette 4

Lying and Stealing

Dad hated lying and stealing. When I say hated, I genuinely do mean hated! Whenever the issue arose because my siblings or I lied about something, his face would visually change. You could see "Bruce Banner" transforming into the Hulk, which was not pretty. The same would happen if we stole something or he suspected us of stealing something. Oh my. The anger on Dad's face exploded as he said, "I hate a liar, and I hate a thief! If you lie, you'll steal, and if you steal, you'll lie! I hate a thief, and I hate a liar!"

I don't know how many times I've heard that from Pop. I've listened to it enough times that it is ingrained in me. It is entrenched deeply in my mind.

Once, when I was about eight years old, he and I went to a Safeway supermarket for some groceries. As we walked down an aisle, Dad was ahead of me, pushing the grocery cart with his back to me. To our right was a large open bin of individually wrapped candy, like saltwater taffy. Oh man, my eyes popped wide open, and my pupils dilated when I saw it. I thought, *Dad can't see me*. As I walked past the display, like a snake strike, my right hand instantly grabbed a handful of the morsels. I looked at Dad; he was still facing straight ahead and didn't see me. I started feeling good that I got away with my prize and started thinking about hiding it from my siblings and enjoying it alone. As we reached the checkout counter and got in line, I was in front of Dad, thinking about my candy. As we inched up to the second position to the clerk, Dad said to me, "If you don't put that candy back, I'm going to tell the clerk that you stole it." I said in total shock and surprise, "What candy?" Dad didn't bat an eye. Instead, he said in the same tone and manner, "If you don't put that candy back, I will tell the clerk." Dad caught me red-handed, as the saying goes. How did he see me? All I saw was the back of his head. I said nothing more but went and put the candy back and rejoined Dad in line as the clerk rang up our groceries. After placing the groceries in the car trunk, we both got in.

Once we got into the car, I got an ear full before Pop started the engine. A calm, stern, poignant, very useful earful! Even though Pop hated stealing and equally hated my poor attempt to lie. Dad didn't let his immense hatred and anger for what I did distract him from soundly correcting me in a way and manner that got directly to the point of my transgression and simultaneously, very stingingly pierced my consciousness. It's amazing how my parents knew how to talk to me. In a sobering, disciplined manner, Dad spoke to me in a way that struck me emotionally and intellectually. As we returned to the car, I thought, *Dad is silent because we are in public. However, once we get into the car, I will get fire and brimstone from Daddy's eyes, nose, and mouth. When we get home, I will get the hardest and most painful whipping ever.* But I didn't. Pop dealt with me in a calm, collected voice of love and deep concern as if I were a straying juvenile delinquent.

A delinquent who knew better but refused to listen and learn! He delineated how, if I continued in my wayward ways, what would happen to me and where I would end up. He made it crystal clear how I had, in his presence, disrespected him, my mother, and my family unthoughtfully and disgracefully. He then continued enumerating in detail the consequences of my ways and actions and where they would lead me if I kept doing what I had just done. It was a very impactful and effective correction, chastisement, and message. As I remember, that was the last time I ever stole anything. It was also the last time I was tempted to take anything that didn't belong to me. That night, I started seeing stealing and lying in the same light as Pop. "I hate lying, and I hate stealing!"

It's thoughtful to reflect on this lesson and consider what I didn't know until years after I was grown: Dad had lied, dropping out of school and upping his age from seventeen to eighteen to join the navy during WWII to follow his two older brothers. I would have undoubtedly pointed it out to him if I had known about his lie when I was younger. If I had done that, I'm sure he would have quickly and very authoritatively responded with something like "I've made mistakes. You do as I say, not as I did or do!" That would have been his answer because I got the line "You do as I say, not as I did or do!" with a stern emphasis more than once. True to form, Dad and Mom never covered up their mistakes they felt we should know about. They, however, expected more from my siblings and me.

My Takeaway

- **Do not steal, and do not lie! The two sins are a couplet! If you steal, you will lie; if you lie, you will steal!**

Vignette 5

In All of Life's Circumstances, Treat People with Love and Respect

My father was highly sensitive as to how you treat other people. His sensitivity and desire to help others could have been due to the ill-treatment he received from his mom during his formative and teenage years. The following illustrates how much Dad valued people and his sensitivity to others, especially the disadvantaged and defenseless. It was a lesson I learned early in life, but it has stuck with me. However, the tutorial brought with it a notice. An awareness that I may need to come to the aid of another at some point in my life.

When I was about ten years old, a situation arose as we visited a family who invited us over for dinner. Mom and Dad had met the husband and wife the previous year and grew to like them. The couple with the last name of Boyd had a single child, a son named Jason, who was one year older than I was. Our entire family and the Boyd family grew closer and spent more time in each other's company. They had previously invited us to their house on a Saturday afternoon, and we had a great time. That occasion was for a fish fry, which was excellent in presentation, taste, and family fellowship. This occasion was also for a fish fry, and because we had such a good time before, we were excitedly looking forward to this get-together. They lived in a city about thirty miles from us. As we neared their house, we saw Jason playing in a creek with some friends. My siblings and I waved and shouted to get his attention, but he didn't notice us. When we got to Mr. and Mrs. Boyd's home, they were excitedly waiting for us and warmly greeted us. They had expected Jason to be home before we got there. We told them we saw him and that he was OK, playing with his friends in the creek near their home. They knew the stream, and Jason arrived home shortly after in wet clothes.

When he got home, it was clear from his parents' body language and verbal greeting that they were highly upset with Jason for disobeying them. His father and mother excused themselves and went with Jason into his bedroom. Soon after, we heard Jason screaming and crying as he got spanked. However, the chastisement we heard didn't sound like a spanking on his rear or behind with a belt. But like a whipping. From the sounds from the room, it sounded like his parents waited until he got his clothes off and started whipping him with an iron's electrical cord. His screams and crying were unbearable, and my siblings, mother, and I all started crying in sympathy for Jason.

My dad's anger exploded, and my mom said, "Bob, stop this! Dad bolted through Jason's closed bedroom door with my mom following and stopped Mr. Boyd. Dad told Mr. Boyd he would not allow him to strike Jason again! As I looked, I thought, *Mr. Boyd has allowed his anger to get the best of him, and Dad stopping him would bring him back to his senses.* But that was not what happened at all. Mr. and Mrs. Boyd retorted in anger that Jason was their son, and they knew how to discipline him. Then they commanded Dad and Mom to get out of their business and get out of the bedroom. I knew this was very serious and thought I would not let Mr. or Mrs. Boyd hurt Mom or Dad. Immediately, I started getting closer to the bedroom door to protect my mom. Dad had already taught me how to fight and when to fight. I, like my siblings, was in shock and unbelief at what was happening, especially among adults. However, my mind focused solely on protecting my mom, then my dad. I was only ten years old and probably would have been thrown aside like an old shoe by Mr. or Mrs. Boyd in an attempt to protect my parents, but that was my mindset. True to his word, Dad did not allow Mr.

Boyd to strike Jason again. Even being a head shorter than Mr. Boyd, Dad inserted himself between Jason and his father and readied himself to violently go fist-to-fist with Mr. Boyd if he attempted to strike Jason again. Mom stepped in and pulled Dad back, reminding him we were his number one concern and that he should immediately get us out of their house! When Mom said what she said to Dad, I took some offense, thinking, *I'm grown. I'm not like my sisters and brother. I'm going to protect you, Mom!*

I'm not sure what Dad did, but it put fear in Mr. Boyd, causing him to focus on Dad continually. From Mr. Boyd's body language, you could tell Pop got to him, and he knew Dad meant what he said and was a real threat to him. Dad further enhanced his boxing skills in the navy with formal boxing training and fight experience. I assume it all contributed to Dad having no fear at all and it being highly evident in his tone and manner that he meant what he said to Mr. Boyd. Mr. Boyd read Dad's eyes and facial expression and knew Dad was committed to what he told him and not spewing boastful words. He stopped his aggression toward Jason, and Mr. and Mrs. Boyd started yelling and demanding that we get out of their house, which Mom was hurrying Dad and us to do. As we were leaving, Dad kept his eyes fixed on Mr. Boyd, and Mr. Boyd continuously peered in anger at Dad. A constant stream of words was exchanged between them until we got into our car. As we drove away, I remember Mom, my sisters, and my brother were still shaken and crying. I'm sure their crying was from fear and the horror of what we had just witnessed and gone through. However, our primary concern as we drove off was what would happen to Jason. As I remember, my parents reported the Boyds to social services. However, when we asked our parents about Jason's welfare, they had no word about him, and that was the last time we saw and heard from Jason and Mr. and Mrs. Boyd.

We received spankings when we disobeyed, but it was apparent and made clear that we would receive spankings with a wide leather belt, about three inches in width, on our clothed behinds. To emphasize this and keep us on alert, Daddy left his wide leather strap on their bedroom outside door handle so we could see it as a reminder. Mom grew up in Texas, and she had personal experience with being commanded to go into the backyard and pull a switch off a tree with which to be spanked. She told us this was customary in Texas during her upbringing. As common, her friends and acquaintances got spanked with a peach or other thin branch. Or worse, with a clothes iron or other electrical appliance cords. Some kids she knew, like Jason, were stripped naked before being spanked, whipped, or beaten, depending on what adjective one wishes to describe the infliction. Both Mr. and Mrs. Boyd were from Texas. Thus, Mom was very familiar with their mindset and the method of corporal punishment they levied on Jason. She recognized that they brought it with them from Texas and, quite probably, was the method of discipline administered to each of them as children, and they accepted it as normal.

In 2014, the NFL Minnesota Vikings' All-Pro running back Adrian Peterson was indicted in Texas on child abuse charges for using a tree switch to spank his son.[2] Knowing what Mom had told us years earlier about Texas's widespread tree switch spanking practice, his disciplinary method was unsurprising. Be it as it may, this manner of spanking children was anathema to Mom, just as racial segregation, hatred, and Jim Crow laws and behavior were aversive and anathema to both her and Dad. Mom had sternly determined within herself that her kids, when necessary, would only be spanked with a wide belt on our behinds in moderation. Spanking was a "hotbed" issue with Mom. She was vocally very clear and definitive to Dad, my aunts, and my uncles about how we were to be spanked when needed. I heard her and Dad talking about it on more than one occasion and then later giving our babysitters/caretakers instructions on the rules for spanking. Including leaving the spankings to them if they couldn't do it "properly" or didn't want to do it.

I did something wrong when I was eleven or twelve and no longer cried from spankings. I don't remember what it was, but I knew it was wrong. I knew that what I did was wrong, as well as I knew my name was "Robert." Dad and I were in our living room, and as he verbally disciplined me about what I had done. His frustration and anger grew as he realized I knew my decisions and actions were wrong before doing whatever I did. Then in Dad's frustration, he suddenly reacted and gave me a backhand smack across my face. It totally surprised me, and in my reflex to avoid it, combined with its force, I was lifted off my feet and flew about six feet across the floor. Landing on my fanny, I instantly thought, *Wow! I'm a man now! Dad's treating me like he would treat a man! I've outgrown the belt!* It's incredible how fast my mind worked. As I thought those thoughts, I had a surge of emotional happiness that I had outgrown being a child. I thought, *I've outgrown Beverly (my older sister), who still gets spankings.* I felt no pain from the blow, just its surprise and my landing on the floor. I had a smidgeon of blood run from my nose that I wiped off with the back of my hand. Mom was in the kitchen cooking, a room away from us. As Dad verbally scolded and corrected me, she could hear us and was also stressed and concerned about what I did. When she suddenly heard the smack, and I hit the floor, she hurried into the living room to see what had happened. She instantly knew what had happened when she saw me on the ground with Dad standing over me. Mom then was a different person. She immediately became an intensely angry mother grizzly bear, defending her cub. In a flash, she was in Pop's face, eye-to-eye, letting him have it for putting his hands on me. I wasn't hurt, but when I saw her reaction, I took full advantage of Mom's "mother bear" response and started crying very loudly as if Dad had hit me in the head with a hammer, and I was in the most unbearable pain, dying. I cried louder and louder while at the same time, inside me, saying, "Get him, Mom! Get him! Don't mess with me! No! You don't want to mess with me! Sic him, Mom! Sic him! Give him all you got!"

Mom came over to check on me and my well-being when she finished her scorching verbal correction of Dad. I played the "I love you, Mom" innocent, defenseless little boy role with her. I ate it all up and flooded myself with her sympathy and concern. When she saw that I was OK, she returned to the kitchen. Having been satisfied that she let Daddy know that no matter how old I was, the belt on my behind was the only corporal punishment I was to receive. Dad and I didn't say anything more when Mom left the room. However, as Dad left the room, I felt incredibly secure in Mom's protection, saying to Dad in my mind, *Mess with me, yeah! Mess with me, and you know what you'll get!* It was terrific how secure I felt after seeing and hearing Mom's defense of me while knowing that what Dad did was really out of his love and concern for me. I knew I was loved and felt incredibly secure in Dad and Mom's love for me in different ways. I felt safe in Dad's love because he would not let me get away with doing something wrong, especially something I knew was wrong. Mom's love secured me because she still came to my protection and aid even when I was wrong and she knew I was wrong.

When everything was said and done, I realized Dad had never been both angry and frustrated with me like he was in his living room chastisement of me. His anger and frustration were all because he knew that I knew better. I knew better but still went on and made the wrong decision. I also realized that I had brought him and Mom into conflict over what I had done, which could have been horrific. However, after I stopped mocking Dad in my mind, I walked away with even greater respect for my dad. That respect came because as Mom poured out her verbal scorching and wrath on Pop, he just took it! He just looked at her, not saying anything back, letting her have her say. He did nothing to escalate the tension or add to the situation. When Mom returned to the kitchen, the whole incident was over! I don't recall any tension in the family regarding what I did or what Dad did. There were no aftereffects or events!

I never told anyone, but in truth, I needed that smack! It brought me into my next stage of manhood. Spanking was not effective with me anymore. My ego and probably my pride also had risen since I no longer yielded to the pain and sting of the belt. Quite possibly, Dad sensed my arrogance or "You can't hurt me!" look, looking back at him as he talked to me. Mom's spankings stopped hurting me years earlier. The last time Mom spanked me, her blows were as wisps of air. I allowed myself to cry, to not hurt her feelings or think she was ineffective. Thus, the smack I received from Dad was perfect for me. It was a volcanic wake-up call to me. I knew without a shadow of a doubt that I deserved it. That smack from Dad and Mom's reaction let me know I was responsible for making the right decisions and correcting myself. Belt and spanking discipline were now gone forever! I was directly responsible for stopping myself from doing wrong and improving myself when I did. Dad had already taught me the time would come if I didn't correct and discipline myself. The law would. I didn't want that. Nor did I ever want to bring my parents into conflict again!

My parents believed in spanking when they felt it justified, but not out of anger. Before spanking us, Dad would always explain what we did wrong and then have us respond to him and say why we did or didn't do what we were supposed to do or not do. Then we would have to assure Pop that we understood what we did was wrong and would not do it again. However, as I grew closer to outgrowing spankings, I felt the lesson and Dad's talking to me were far worse and more painful than the spanking itself. I once politely asked Dad if he would skip the discussion and go straight to my spanking. After hearing me, he retorted, "No, you're going to hear this! You're going to hear all of this!" He then went through the whole thing with me, and just like in the past, I had to tell him that I understood what I did wrong and wouldn't do again. As always, the actual spanking lasted seconds. The pain and sting from the spanking stayed a little longer. However, the prelecture seemed to last an excruciatingly long time and was very painful for me to listen to and endure. It was much more painful than the spanking I received.

My Takeaway

- **As with spanking and disciplining children, there is always a proper way and a wrong way to do things.**
  - **The proper way will always value the child and treat them in wisdom with love, kindness, respect, and human consideration.**
- **In wisdom, with proper consideration and approach, come to the aid of those being abused, used, or taken advantage of.**
- **There is a time when you must grow up, take responsibility for your decisions, lack of discipline, and correction of yourself!**

Vignette 6

Principle of the "Head," Part A

As the "head" and lead of our home, my dad would not tolerate racial prejudice, hatred, or mistreatment of people of any kind. If you had problems accepting people of another race or ethnicity, you were unwelcome at our home. Our house was not a house of racial hate or bigotry; it just was not! Dad's and Mom's friends, as well as my siblings and my friends, were ethnically mixed.

In being specific and going further, it was an absolute no-no for my siblings and me to use, say, or refer to each other in a racially derogatory manner, like so many in our race did and still unabashedly do. Nor could we call each other a "fool" or say in anger or retort to something done to us, "you fool." Those were grave spanking crimes. For different ethnicities, the same forbidden criteria and accountability also applied to us regarding Pop's prohibition of using any denigrating and derogatory ethnic or racial terms. In truth, Pop was very watchful and protective over how we treated each other and our treatment, respect, and interaction with others.

Similarly, Pop was highly observant and protective of how others, including authority, treated and respected my siblings and me. Per Dad's upbringing, sensitivity, and human values, he had no sufferance for hating or mistreating anyone outside hating someone's ill character, behavior, or attitude. However, in that regard, Pop emphasized that a person's harmful conduct should be timely and adequately dealt with if we were ever confronted by it.

As I matured, I pondered many of my parents' virtues. One that powerfully struck me as I meditated was my understanding of the principle of the "head" or the "lead" as I witnessed in my father. As I reflected on Pop's leadership, out of the blue, it suddenly became exceedingly clear why racial hatred and bigotry thrived and still exist in our country today. It surfaced from my thoughts that a person's moral integrity and love of their neighbor like themselves were not inbred; instead, like my siblings and me, constant teaching and instruction, training, and reinforcement had to instill those characteristics. The only thing that kept us from thinking and acting like many of our peers was Dad and Mom injecting and constantly reinforcing our values. This precept became more apparent as I reflected on the civil rights movement. TV coverage of the civil rights movement displayed an ugly aspect of America for the entire world to see. It visually and audibly showed the White supremacist thoughts and views so many Southern and other American Whites firmly held. It publicly exposed the deep racial hatred, denigration, and dehumanization of Black people in America since its inception. As a kid, it was horrific to hear and see on television White Southern governors, congressmen, ordinary people, and police speak and treat Black people of African heritage in the hateful, vile, disrespectful manner they openly and boastfully displayed. It was even more horrific to see those calling themselves police and law enforcement hatefully beat, dog-attack, firehose, shoot, and jail people. People law enforcement targeted for peacefully standing up for themselves as God's creation and human beings. Over the years, I've never gotten those images out of my mind. Now and then, they caused me to think about the source of all the hatred, denigration, and violent outflow that I saw.

However, the cause never came to me until that out-of-the-blue moment when I recalled my dad as the "head" of our family. Repeatedly laying down his stern moral base against hatred, racial prejudice, and the denigration of others, in conjunction with the proper treatment of people no matter who they were. As I thought about it, knowing the history of our country. From our start, it's evident that the love and respect for all men, that is, the love of your neighbor as yourself, was not in the hearts and minds of Christian heads and leaders, namely ministers and preachers, when they first hit the shores of America. Irrespective of how our history books and schools have portrayed them in their Puritan dress and high moral codes. They illustrated their lack of godly love and moral ethics for all people as they lived out their lives believing they were ethnically superior to Black Africans when they later hit the shores of America. Their ungodly, immoral deficiencies were passed on into the hearts and minds of our country's founders. The baton also passed into the hearts and minds of many Christian and governmental "heads" and leaders who followed them as our nation grew.

Founders, revolutionaries, and constitutionists, presidents George Washington and Thomas Jefferson believed slavery was morally wrong. But also, Blacks were inferior to Whites. Jefferson said Black people were "as incapable as children." [3] Even though they thought it was wrong, for financial advantages and possibly some social benefits, Washington and Jefferson enslaved people into the hundreds, ignoring the resistance of their accusing thoughts and convicting consciences for enslaving other human beings. They continued enslaving people until their deaths. George Washington was so troubled by it that he revised his last will and testament just months before his death, foolishly freeing his slaves upon his wife Martha's death. In his desire to get out from under the guilt and pain of his conscience before his death, I surmise that he didn't stop and think about the effect his will's pronouncement could have on Martha. In the proclamation of freeing his slaves upon Martha's death, Martha increasingly feared for her life. Thus, she released her inherited enslaved people about a year after George's death to remove the potential threat to her life and her fear of it. [4, 5]

Although Washington, through his conscience and guilt, was aware that he was missing the mark. He never corrected himself, and as the "head," Washington utterly failed morally regarding loving his brother as himself and leading his family and our nation out and away from slavery into biblical human oneness and mutual love, respect, treatment, and consideration of each other.

Similarly, for nearly all of our nation's history, executive, judicial, and legislative leadership failed miserably regarding slavery, freed slaves, and their descendants at the federal, commonwealth, and state levels. A direct example of this is nearly two hundred years after George Washington, Strom Thurmond, a close to fifty-year, tenured senator from South Carolina, maintained his notorious and robust segregation and Jim Crow views and support throughout his life. It was notoriously surprising that the then-Senate Minority Leader, Trent Lott, from Mississippi. In speaking at Thurman's one-hundredth birthday party celebration in December 2002, he vigorously agreed with Thurman and his separation-of-races views. Lott afterward was forced to give up his Senate Minority leadership position. Thurmond was a Dixiecrat, a Southern Democrat who had left the Democratic Party and joined the Republican Party over the issue of African American civil rights. In his 1948 bid for US president, Thurmond made his position on segregation very clear, to which Trent Lott, at Thurmond's birthday party, gave his affirmation too. What Thurman said in his 1948 bid for president was the following:

> I wanna tell you, ladies and gentlemen, that there's not enough troops in the army to force the southern people to break down segregation and admit the ****** race into our theaters and swimming pools, into our homes and into our churches.[6]

Strom Thurmond, although a strict segregationist in his upper head and mind, like Thomas Jefferson, who fathered several Black children,[7] Thurmond also was not one in his "lower head." While living in his parents' home in his early twenties, he fathered a girl with his parents' Black sixteen-year-old teenage housekeeper/maid.[8] It's also fascinating to note in Thurmond's 1948 quote above that he explicitly references the segregation of churches. Thurmond was a Southern Baptist. The Southern Baptist Church/Convention was founded in 1845 when it separated from the National Baptist Church over slavery.[9]

Interestingly, the saying "Eleven a.m. Sunday is the most segregated hour in America" is about the church. One month after enacting the Civil Rights Act on July 2, 1964, the *New York Times* published an article on August 2 titled "11 A.M. Sunday Is Our Most Segregated Hour" by Kyle Haselden.[10] Haselden wrote,

- The religious community in American society produced and sustained—sometimes on Biblical grounds—the anti-"African-American" bias which has permeated the American mind from the beginning of the nation until the present day. Out of the nation's religious community came Biblically and doctrinally supported theories of racial inferiority, and from this same source came immoral ethical codes which justified the exploitation of the "African-American" and demanded that the White man hold himself in sanctifying aloofness from the "African-American."
- Moreover, the patterns of segregation which divide the common life of the country racially had their beginning in the church before they found their perfection in the secular society. It was not the secular world which infused the church with contemptuous views of the "African-American" and imposed a segregated life on

the Christian community. These offenses appeared first in the religious community, even if we view the religious community in its narrowest definition. The white man distorted the Bible …

- The white Christian in the developing American culture confused Christianity with morality, morality with gentility and gentility with aloofness from the "African-American." As early as 1630, a bare 10 years after the arrival of the first "African-American" slaves, white Christians condemned the crossing of the racial line as an "abuse to the dishonor of God and shame of Christians."
- While systematized and legalized racial segregation in American secular life did not begin until 1877, a hundred years earlier there were churches in the United States in which free as well as slave "African-Americans" were isolated from whites in their common worship. In 1795, the John Street Methodist Episcopal Church in New York City, a mixed church including whites and both free and slave "African-Americans," restricted "African-Americans" to pews in the rear of the church marked "B.M." for "Black members" and discriminated against "African-Americans" in baptismal and communion services.

Interestingly, Haselden points out that racism in America started with and within the church. Not in the secular agnostic and unbelieving world but in the American Christian church. In the hearts and minds of White Christian believers who had experienced and fled from religious persecution in Europe. The question is "Who told White Christians that they were better than or superior to Black Africans?" Surely not scripture. No verse in scripture implies in any way that any race or ethnicity is any better or more gifted than another. The children of Israel, the Jews, were chosen and separated from all others (gentiles), including White Europeans, to ensure they worshiped and followed God only. However, gentiles who came as foreigners to live in Israel, loved God, and abided by His laws were treated equally and integrated with the Jews. Rahab, the Canaanite prostitute, and Ruth, the Moabite, both of whom are matriarchs of King David and our Lord Jesus Christ, testify of that. Eliam the Gilonite, Bathsheba's father, and Uriah the Hittite, Bathsheba's husband, were Canaanites and members of King David's mighty thirty-seven fighting men, also bear testimony to that fact. All men and women that walk the earth today came through Adam, Seth, and Noah. So the question remains "Who told White Christians that they were better than or superior to Black Africans?"

My conjecture is in the White Christians' desire to be "more like God," just as Lucifer (Satan) in his explosion of pride "to be like the Most High." By their will and choice, they followed the sinful path of Eve in accepting the devil's deception and distortion of God's Word. They chose to believe the "serpent," the devil's lie that they were the superior race, rather than God, who said we are all from one blood and He is no respecter of persons. Once they accepted the lie, they, like Eve, acted on it. Eve ate the forbidden fruit from the "tree of the knowledge of good and evil" and then passed it on to Adam to eat. Likewise, they ate the forbidden fruit of pride and passed it on to their contemporaries and following generations. All, taking on "airs" with the accompanying thoughts, character, and attitudes of superiority and White supremacy. However, thank God, not all White Christians consumed the fruit.

There has always been a "church within the church" throughout history and even now. There has always been a Joshua, a Caleb, and a Ruth who believe in God and His Word and committedly walk in His truth and love. During our nation's slavery years, two examples of "not all White Christians" and the "church within the church" are the Quakers and Presbyterians. The Quakers (the

Society of Friends), from England to America, strongly opposed slavery and the ill-treatment of Black people and any people for that matter. They believed in the scripture "that all people are created equal in the eyes of God." In support of Harriet Tubman, they were abolitionists, supporters, and "conductors" on the vast Underground Railroad network of Black and White people who helped fugitive slaves escape from the South to the North and Canada. One Quaker, Levi Coffin, is credited with having assisted more than 3,000 slaves to escape. George Washington complained that the Quakers helped one of his runaway slaves escape. After the Quakers, many White Presbyterians were abolitionists and part of the Underground Railroad network of people and conductors; however, by no means were all Presbyterians abolitionists. Many Presbyterian leaders and educators enslaved Black people and held strong racial views, arguing positively for enslavement. Presbyterian-founded Ivy League school Princeton University has a disturbing racial past, as disclosed by Princeton Professor of History Martha A. Sandweiss, founder and director of the 2017 Princeton & Slavery Project. [11A]

As mentioned above, thank God there is a "church within the church." John Rankin, a Presbyterian Minister, adamantly opposed slavery. He was a very active conductor and ran the Ohio Underground Railroad. Henry Ward Beecher, the brother of abolitionist Harriet Beecher Stowe, author of the book *Uncle Tom's Cabin,* when asked after the end of the Civil War, "Who abolished slavery?" he answered, "Reverend John Rankin and his sons did.[11B, 12] Unfortunately, however, enough White Christians believed, accepted, and acted on their ideas of White supremacy and Black inferiority such that that thinking took root as the prevailing conviction of our growing nation even into the twentieth century.

As Haselden says, "The White Christian in the developing American culture confused Christianity with morality, morality with gentility, and gentility with aloofness from the 'African-American.'" In plain language, their confused understanding of Christianity changed their view of themselves from what God said they and all humanity were to who the devil said they were. Just like the "serpent" (the devil) called God a liar, telling Eve,

> Has God indeed said, "You shall not eat of every tree of the garden?" And the woman (Eve) said to the serpent, "We may eat the fruit of the trees of the garden; but of the fruit of the tree which is in the midst of the garden, God has said, You shall not eat it, nor shall you touch it, lest you die." And the serpent said to the woman, "You will not surely die. For God knows that in the day you eat of it your eyes will be opened, and you will be like God, knowing good and evil." (Gen. 3:1–5)

Far too many White Christians, like Eve, hook, line, and sinker believed the devil also. They engulfed the lie that they were genetically and ethnically superior to Black Africans. In their demonic belief, as Haselden says, "White Christians condemned the crossing of the Black-White racial line as an 'abuse to the dishonor of God and shame of Christians.'" In so doing, they perverted the Person of God Himself by slandering and falsely speaking of Him. They also maligned and misrepresented the Gospel of our Lord Jesus Christ, as Peter did when he refused to eat with the Gentiles and was sternly rebuked by Paul for doing so (Gal. 2:11–21).

Those White Christians converted their "Christian" views into a false religion (a false set of beliefs), just like all other religions, including atheistic religions. In doing so, they practiced their ideas, code of ethics, and worship of God based on their views and notions. In particular, their religious perspectives were expressed in their superior evaluation and characterization of themselves in juxtaposition to their devaluation of Black Africans. Although identified or characterized as a religion, the absolute truth is Christianity is not a religion! It is not a fundamental set of beliefs and practices that a group of ancestral or contemporary people agrees upon in their worship, submission, sacrifice to, and adoration of God, gods, or supernatural divine beings. Christianity is a personal relationship with God, through His Holy Spirit, initiated and established solely by God Himself with people (John 6:44), His "image bearers." Who, individually, by their choice, accept Him and His conditions through His Person, His Son, Jesus Christ, the Creator of people and all things (John 1:1–3). As such, Christianity is a relationship! A personal relationship with God Himself through His Son, Jesus Christ. The relationship is highly interactive as one walks in God's grace through obedience to His Word, the Bible, with complete transparency of self and constant communication with God, the Father, through all forms of prayer, just as Jesus did. Christians don't have separate views or opinions from God, nor do they make up the rules, bylaws, dos, and don'ts! God is Sovereign! The Bible is His Word, which we are to "rightly divide," conform to, and obey!

The bedrock text from scripture that White Christians used to justify slavery was the "the Curse of Canaan," which they renamed the "the Curse of Ham" (Gen. 9:18–27). They distorted and falsified the biblical account by dropping the fact that Noah cursed Canaan. That is, they falsely applied Noah's curse to his son Ham rather than to his grandson, Canaan, who was the one condemned, as scripture plainly says.

Then he [Noah] said: "Cursed be Canaan; a servant of servants he shall be to his brethren." (Gen. 9:25)

Black Africans, like Egyptians and some other ethnicities, are descendants of Ham but from Ham's other sons, Cush, Mizraim, and Phut (or Put), not Canaan. Specifically, Black Africans are descendants of Cush. Once, White Christians marked Black Africans as "the accursed." They justified their "White supremacy" thinking and practices of subordinating, denigrating, cruelly mistreating, and enslaving Black Africans.

With covers pulled back and blinders removed, it's easy to see the deception, lie, and extreme wickedness that the White Christians Haselden speaks of operated in and executed to Satan's plan. They ignored or threw out the scriptural facts that God destroyed the Canaanite nations through His angels and Israel, giving their land to Israel (Ex. 23:20–33, Ps. 135:10–12) because of their idolatry, child sacrifices, incest, bestiality, and homosexuality, as explicitly explained in Leviticus 18. It bears repeating that Black Africans, Egyptians, and other African peoples, such as the Libyans, are not descendants of Canaan or part of Noah's curse but, as mentioned, are descendants of Ham's sons Cush, Mizraim, and Phut (Put) respectfully (Gen. 10:6–13). Ham has the same bloodline and ancestry as Noah's sons, Shem and Japheth. Per God's creation, Black Africans are no different from any other human on earth now (i.e., after the "flood of Noah"). We are all sons and daughters of Adam, Seth, and Noah. Therefore, being very specific about this, John 3:16 can be ethnically stated in truth and accuracy as

For God so loved the Black African that He gave His only begotten Son, that Black Africans and their descendants who believe

in Him should not perish but have everlasting
life. (Ethnic paraphrase of John 3:16)

Scripture convicts us as a nation for thinking and treating Black people as racially inferior to White persons. Hence, for slavery, racial hatred, denigration, segregation, and Jim Crow laws, attitudes, and suppressive treatment. The biblical conviction of this comes from the following:

If you really fulfill the royal law according
to the Scripture, "You shall love your neighbor
as yourself," you do well; but if you show
partiality [i.e., White favoritism and superiority
or derogatorily treat and suppress Black people],
you commit sin, and are convicted by the law
as transgressors. (James 2:8–9)

As the book of James stresses, loving your neighbor as yourself is the minimal magnitude of love, treatment, and consideration for another Christian to have. As a church body, as Haselden wrote and our history confirms, American White Christians have never loved Black people as themselves nor considered Black people with equal respect and dignity to themselves. Thus, as a church body, even today, a large portion of the White Christian church is in disobedience and nonconformity to God's Word. However, as Christians, their sin of rebellion and refusal to love Black people as they do themselves has been compounded by the Lord. Before His crucifixion, the Lord upped His "royal law," as James called it. He issued a new commandment with the ability to draw men and women to Himself if obeyed. He said to His disciples,

A new commandment I give to you, that you
love one another; as I have loved you, that you

also love one another. By this all will know that you are My disciples, if you have love for one another. (John 13:34-35)

In America, it's been White Christians from the start of our nation that Satan successfully used to release his hate and viciousness on a people for whom God loves and died for. What those White Christians refused to believe and accept was the Holy Spirit speaking directly to them, saying,

Beloved, let us love one another, for love is of God; and everyone who loves is born of God and knows God. He who does not love does not know God, for God is love. (1 John 4:7-8)

If someone says, "I love God," and hates his brother, he is a liar; for he who does not love his brother whom he has seen, how can he love God whom he has not seen? And this commandment we have from Him: that he who loves God must love his brother also. (1 John 4:20-21)

In those verses, the Holy Spirit has told White Christians to love those of African descent, Native Americans, and all others as brothers and sisters in as direct a manner as possible. However, the application of these verses has not been taught or practiced on a broad scale in White America or White American churches. This effect is still openly displayed as horrifically evidenced within the last ten years by the widely reported Trayvon Martin and Ahmaud Arbery killings and the numerous controversial police-on-Black killings. The thinking, values, and behavior of White superiority, White supremacy, and Black inferiority are still alive in our country. As the above scripture verses declare, that thinking is against God's Word and will. It also discards the knowledge and truth that we all came from Adam, Seth, and Noah; thus, we all came from one blood and are brothers and sisters of one blood. As scripture tells us,

> And He has made from one blood every nation of men to dwell on all the face of the earth, and has determined their preappointed times and the boundaries of their habitation. (Acts 17:26)

In another place, God says through the apostle Paul,

> As it is written: "There is none righteous, no, not one; there is none who understands; there is none who seeks after God. They have all gone out of the way; they have together become unprofitable; there is none who does good, no, not one." (Rom. 3:10–12)

These verses show that we all came from one blood and DNA source and are equally corrupted. Therefore, no one is inherently better, superior, or more gifted than another or worse than another. Instead, we all walk according to our upbringing, training, values, and choices. My ethnic DNA composition confirms these truths. I'm African American with a genetic makeup of 70 percent African (Nigerian, Cameroon/Congo/Bantu), 23 percent European (Ireland, Scotland, England/Wales), 4 percent Asian (Philippines), and 3 percent Native American based on Ancestry.com DNA testing.

When I read Numbers 12 and see Miriam as the instigator, it's engrossing to see her lead her brother Aaron into coming down very negatively on their younger brother Moses—criticizing and rebuking Moses for marrying an Ethiopian (in Hebrew: Cushite), a Black African woman. Much consideration and debate among Jewish rabbinical and Christian scholars have gone into who this woman is.[13] Is she the biblical Zipporah, Moses's Midian wife, with dark skin? Is she Zipporah with such incredible beauty that Numbers uses the word *Cushite* to set her beauty apart from other women? Or is she, from a literal interpretation of the scripture, a woman from the land of Cush (Ethiopia)? The Septuagint (LXX), the Greek version of the Hebrew Bible or Old Testament, whom Jesus and His apostles quoted from,[14] refers to Moses, in Numbers 12:1, as having, in fact, married an Ethiopian (Greek for Cushite or burned-skin people) woman. Thus, I believe first-century Jewish historian Josephus's account of Moses and his marriage to the Ethiopian woman as he describes in *The Antiquities of the Jews,* book 2, chapter 10. There, Josephus provides details of Moses's marriage to the Ethiopian woman, Tharbis, the daughter of the Ethiopian king.[15]

In Numbers 12, Miriam attempts to take leadership or authority away from Moses because of his Ethiopian wife. However, in His anger, suddenly the Lord lets Miriam and Aaron know that Moses speaks with Him face-to-face and very clearly! Not through visions and dreams as prophets see, nor through glass or a mirror dimly as our generation sees Him (1 Cor. 13:12), but face-to-face. The Lord also told them Moses had been faithful in "all of His house." What grabs my attention is the Lord essentially telling them that Moses saw as He, God, saw. Moses, like God, saw no ethnicity or color differences in people. That message is crystal clear to me in God's judgment on Miriam, which I find incredibly humorous and sends a loud, booming, unambiguous message to us all. Scripture reports that when God finished talking to Miriam and Aaron. He left Miriam a leper. The Word of God emphasized that she was "leprous, as White as snow." When I note the emphasis "as

White as snow," I hear God saying to Miriam, "You want to be White! I'll make you White! I'll give you all the White you want!" The account of the incident from Numbers is as follows:

> Then Miriam and Aaron spoke against Moses because of the Ethiopian woman whom he had married; for he had married an Ethiopian woman.
>
> And they said, "Has the LORD indeed spoken only through Moses? Has He not spoken through us also?" And the LORD heard it ... Suddenly the LORD said to Moses, Aaron, and Miriam, "Come out, you three, to the tabernacle of meeting!" So the three came out. Then the LORD came down in the pillar of cloud and stood in the door of the tabernacle, and called Aaron and Miriam. And they both went forward.
>
> Then He said, "Hear now My words: If there is a prophet among you, I, the LORD, make Myself known to him in a vision, and I speak to him in a dream. Not so with My servant Moses; he is faithful in all My house.
>
> I speak with him face to face, even plainly, and not in dark sayings; and he sees the form of the LORD. Why then were you not afraid to speak against My servant Moses?" So the anger of the LORD was aroused against them, and He departed. And when the cloud departed from above the tabernacle, suddenly

Miriam became leprous, as white as snow.
Then Aaron turned toward Miriam, and there
she was, a leper. (Num. 12:1–10)

Per Moses's cry for God to heal his sister, the Lord did heal Miriam through His grace and restored her after she remained exiled outside the camp of Israel for seven days.

God is not a respecter of persons, whether Asian, Black, Red, or White, Jew or gentile, man or woman. It's straightforward and clear from Numbers 12:1–10 that God, in His face-to-face conversations with Moses, true to His nature, had no issue with Moses marrying the Ethiopian or Black woman—however, White Christians, not all, but many of them. Just like Miriam and Aaron have been dragged into deception and disobedience by the devil. Kyle Haselden opens the curtain for us to see the conception of this evil desire in the hearts of many early American White Christians as he tells us,

> as early as 1630, a bare 10 years after the arrival of the first "African-American" slaves, White Christians condemned the crossing of the racial line as an "abuse to the dishonor of God and shame of Christians.

As I asked earlier, "Who told these White Christians that they were better than Black people? Some historians say superior racial thinking started in medieval Europe. White superiority over people of African descent wasn't present in the time of Christ or the early centuries after. From conjecture, it could have been a carry-over and pass-on from their personally experienced inferior/superior social status treatment of the environment in Europe they left behind. That is, Europe's conceptual and social structure that some people are better or more superior than others. To me, however, looking at it from a biblical perspective, their human or fleshly desire to be "better or superior" to others closely parallels Lucifer's (Satan's) desire to "be like the Most-High" (Isa. 14:14), to be the top and on top! However, no matter the original origin of their passion, "to be the most high," James tells us, it came from their hearts and their evil desire to view themselves as different and superior to others. Using the knowledge we gleaned from the Garden of Eden, it's clear to assume that their evil desires were ignited by the whispering embers of Satan when they saw Black Africans looking differently. Unfortunately, the White heads and leaders of their families, churches, and the government at all levels had itching and receptive ears to hear what Satan whispered to them, just like Eve did. James's explanation is

> But each one is tempted when, by his own evil desire, he is dragged away and enticed. Then after desire has conceived, it gives birth to sin; and sin, when it is full-grown, gives birth to death. (James 1:14–15 NIV)

In closing, highly regarded and widely read contemporary, theologian, professor, and author Wayne Grudem says that all humanity's uniqueness is derived from God making us in His image. He emphasizes that we are God's image bearers despite being smitten and marred by sin. Grudem writes,

> Every single human being, no matter how much the image of God is marred by sin, illness, weakness, age, or any other disability, still has the status of being in God's image and therefore must be treated with the dignity and respect that is due to God's image bearer.

> In addition, it is important to emphasize that people from every racial and ethnic background

are all "in the image of God" and thus worthy of our respect and care. This has profound implications for our conduct toward others. It means that people of every race and ethnicity deserve equal dignity and rights. It means that elderly people, those seriously ill, the mentally disabled, and children yet unborn, deserve full protection and honor as human beings. If we ever deny our unique status in creation as God's only image bearers, we will soon begin to depreciate the value of human life, will tend to see humans as merely a higher form of animal, and will begin to treat others as such. We will also lose much of our sense of meaning in life.[16]

My Takeaway

- **As my father's leadership of our home demonstrated, the head sets the tone for the group's values and their implementation and enforcement.**
- **Slavery, racial hatred, racism, segregation, Jim Crow, and the mistreatment of Black people in America all resulted from nonbiblical, immoral, and unethical consideration and treatment of Black people.**
  - **Not all, but in America's history, enough White Christian leaders have bought into the devil's White supremacy/Black inferiority lie to have caused our racial divide.**

- As all sin does, the White Christian's sin of not loving their Black African brothers as themselves grew into more sin. It produced Satan's by-products of
  - slave trafficking and African tribal wars with killing and human capturing in support of trafficking
  - the death and personal and cultural beatdown of millions of Black Africans through the transatlantic slave trade, physical and mental mistreatment, rape and abuse, slavery, denigration, segregation, and Jim Crow practices
- In Numbers 12, God demonstrated when He turned Miriam leprous, as "White as snow," when she rebuffed her brother Moses for marrying an Ethiopian woman. He is no respecter of persons by race (ethnicity).
- In essence, Christianity is *not* a religion but a personal relationship with God, the Father, through Jesus Christ, our Lord and Savior.

Vignette 7

Principle of the "Head," Part B

With a devastating impact on America's Black families mentally, emotionally, educationally, socially, and financially, the thinking of White superiority and supremacy has been passed down from generation to generation of White Christians. With that remark, it's important to emphasize again that not all White Christians. However, enough to have created the racial division, hatred, and White supremacy that has permeated and embedded itself into our United States democracy and history. It was the bedrock of Strom Thurman's thinking and has continuously lived in many White believers' hearts and minds. A stunning and painful example of this surfaced when I was a member of Crenshaw Christian Center (CCC) in Los Angeles, under the pastoral teaching ministry of Fredrick K. C. Price. During that time, the White supremacist views of Ken Hagin Jr., the son of the well-known, highly respected, and universally regarded preacher and teacher Kenneth E. Hagin, became publicly known via a taped sermon Ken Jr. preached. Pastor Price had a long, close, and loving spiritual father-son/mentor relationship with Ken Hagin Sr., who most of us congregants lovingly referred to as Brother Hagin. Brother Hagin founded Rhema Bible College and was a highly anointed and gifted teacher of faith, healing, and prosperity. It is no exaggeration to say how greatly loved and appreciated Brother Hagin was by the thousands of members of CCC and the millions across the nation, worldwide, and me. We profited greatly from God's anointing on his life and the resulting ministry, tapes, and books that came through his gifting. Whenever he came to CCC, we congregants and visitors attended as many of his services as possible. It was amazing to hear the Word of God spoken through him and the gifts of the Spirit flow through him.

Therefore, it was a tremendous shock and awe experience when the revelation of what Ken Jr. said in his sermon became widely known. To not rely on my memory and emotional reaction, I'll use the description of what Ken Jr. said and the resulting response of Pastor Price, as reported by Teresa Watanabe of the *Los Angeles Times.* In an article entitled "Rude Awakening on Racism Gave Minister New Mission," Teresa wrote the following on July 25, 1999: [17]

> But the younger Hagin—a nationally known minister, a man of God, a presumed believer in the one body of Christ—had been caught on tape telling his congregation that he did not believe in race-mixing and had taught his daughter from her kindergarten years that she was not to date Blacks.
>
> Price was dumbstruck. Devastated.
>
> He thought: "I've been standing next to you all these years and didn't know you had a gun to my head."
>
> After Hagin Jr. failed to recant his remarks, apologizing only for hurt feelings, Price launched a boycott—throwing out Hagin materials from his church bookstore, cutting off financial support and even removing the father's name from one of his buildings. Those actions prompted half of the African American ministers on the executive board of one of Price's organizations to resign in protest.
>
> (Price never publicly identified the pastor on the tape, which he aired in 1997, but Hagin

acknowledged it was him. Hagin declined to comment, but a spokesman said the remarks were misconstrued, and "we love everybody.")

In a Sunday church service, Pastor Price explained to us congregates why he initiated a boycott and the *"throwing out Hagin materials from his church's bookstore, cutting off financial support and even removing the father's name from one of his buildings."* Pastor Price had a one-on-one conversation with Brother Hagin. Much to his piercing and painful dismay and sadness, Brother Hagin didn't amend, offer, or agree to correct his son. Nor did he recant and distance himself from his son's comments. When I heard that, I analytically assumed that Brother Hagin, being the father, indicated with his response that the thoughts and views Ken Jr. expressed in the sermon were also his deep-seated views. Rightly or wrongly, I additionally reasoned that, in all likelihood, they were the thoughts and perspectives he had personally placed in his son, Ken Hagin Jr., from his youth. I further reasoned that from Brother Hagin's Southern Baptist roots, in all probability, those were also the beliefs his father and grandfather had also put in him from his youth, and now it was as if those beliefs were family in-bred. After his one-on-one with Brother Hagin, Pastor Price announced to the congregation that his close association with Brother Hagin had been terminated. As my memory serves, he felt compelled, per the principle Paul describes in 1 Corinthians 5:9–13, to not associate with those who profess to be Christians but do not live as Christ lived. The understanding I walked away with was Brother Hagin and Ken Hagin Jr., both by their own choices, chose not to renew their minds and conform to God's Word but rather, by their wills, decided to lean on their own understanding, viewing their White race or ethnicity as superior to those of Black ethnicity and discounting or ignoring the following commands and admonishments of the God they served.

And the second, like it, is this: "You shall love your neighbor as yourself." There is no other commandment greater than these. (Mark 12:31)

A new commandment I give to you, that you love one another; as I have loved you, that you also love one another. (John 13:34)

If someone says, "I love God," and hates his brother, he is a liar; for he who does not love his brother whom he has seen, how can he love God whom he has not seen? And this commandment we have from Him: that he who loves God must love his brother also." (1 John 4:20-21)

My brethren, do not hold the faith of our Lord Jesus Christ, the Lord of glory, with partiality. For if there should come into your assembly a White man (with gold rings, in fine apparel), and there should also come in a (poor) Black man (in filthy clothes), and you pay attention to the White one (wearing the fine clothes) and say to him, "You sit here in a good place," and say to the (poor) Black man, "You stand there," or "Sit here at my footstool," have you not shown partiality among yourselves, and become judges with evil thoughts?" (Paraphrase of James 2:1-4)

The questions that come to the surface are these: How could one of such an anointing and full of the revelation of God's

Word, as Brother Hagin was, be so entrapped with a lie from Satan to think they are any better or more superior to anyone else? How could he not correctly divide the Word of God when God has made it so clear?

> For there is no distinction between Jew and Greek, for the same Lord over all is rich to all who call upon Him. For whoever calls upon the name of the Lord shall be saved. (Rom. 10:12–13)

The word "Greek" used in Romans 10:12 refers to anyone who is not a Jew, that is, to gentiles, all of us, Black, White, rich, or poor non-Jews. This incident resulted in a tipping point that caused Pastor Price to initiate a contiguous seventy-six-week Sunday series entitled Race, Religion, and Racism, accompanied and followed by a multivolume set of recordings and books with the same title.[18] In agreement with the *Los Angeles Times,* I found the Sunday series to be the most meticulous and scholarly presentation on race and racism in America I had ever heard. The fact that sin like this can dwell in a believer is a mystery. However, I assume that knowing the power of deception and the weakness and insecurity of humans, some White Christians still would not call their attitude and inferior thinking of Black people a sin. However, Jesus tells us plainly what His desires are and what Satan's are. Thus, looking at the fruit produced from someone's thinking and pursuits provides a clear path to the source and origin of the passion and thoughts that produced the fruit. Just as illustrated by Jesus when He told the Jews,

> You are of your father the devil, and the desires of your father you want to do. He was a murderer from the beginning, and does not stand in the truth, because there is no truth in

him. When he speaks a lie, he speaks from his own resources, for he is a liar and the father of it. (John 8:44)

For out of the heart proceed evil thoughts, murders, adulteries, fornications, thefts, false witness, blasphemies. (Matt. 15:19)

Solomon further says,

Keep your heart with all diligence, for out of it spring the issues of life. (Prov. 4:23)

The issues of life that stemmed from those White Christians' hearts, who believed they were superior to Black Africans. Disastrously produced centuries of mass and individual murders, brutal beatings, human thief and debasement, rape, the cruelest form of slavery the world has ever known, lynchings, Jim Crow laws and attitudes. Unfortunately, the ill-treatment of human beings, God's Black "image bearers," didn't stop there. It continued into degrading segregation practices, such as inferior education, separate Black and White building entrances, bathrooms, drinking fountains, sitting and eating locations, etc. Accompanied by the self-esteem, emotional and psychological breakdown of a whole population of people God created, loved, and died for.

Although the exact numbers are controversial, a World Future Fund report [19] estimates that as many as 60 million Africans were killed (murdered) as a result of the White Christian slave trade. The following is a summary of their report:

- The largest slave trade in the history of the world was created by White Christian Europeans … as many as 60 million Africans would be killed for the profit of White

Christian imperialism ... Huge numbers of people died as they were marched to the coasts of Africa ... as well as in an endless series of wars produced by the quest for new slaves. Millions more would die in concentration camps ... and ... due to the appalling conditions on the slave ships.

- The estimate of the number killed during the transatlantic slave trade varies anywhere between 6–150 million. The official UN estimate is 17 million.
- During the entire period of the slave trade, Africa's population did not increase ... We believe the stagnation of Africa's population is a by-product of the transatlantic slave trade.

The following table was generated from the World Future Fund report. It shows Europe's and Asia's populations nearly doubled while *Africa's population lost more than 6 percent during the transatlantic slave trade from 1600 through 1800.*

World Population by Continent in Millions

Century	1600	1700	1800	Population Increase/ Decrease (%)
Asia	339	436	635	+87.3
Europe	111	125	203	+82.9
Africa	**114**	**106**	**107**	**-6.1**

My father's mature leadership of our family regarding the value of people and understanding relationships and interaction with all people flowed from his immigrant neighborhood, upbringing, and training. It spurred his utter intolerance for racial hatred, racism, racial denigration, and mistreatment of people for any reason. Bigotry was not tolerated in our home from an outsider and indeed not from us in our thinking, words, actions, or inaction. That included hatred of White people individually or as a group, no matter what we heard or saw some of them do or how some treated us personally. The only thing I ever heard my dad say with a racial overtone was "The White man will sell his own mother for a dollar!" He said that on several occasions, in emotional frustration with the prevalent greed and "Money first! Money foremost! Money now and forever!" business practices, he encountered and observed of the overwhelming number of White-male-owned and operated American corporate businesses. As for my siblings and me, we were strictly taught to treat people as people and how we wanted to be treated. That teaching emphasized that we were no better than anyone else, nor was anyone any better than us. It additionally taught us how to properly chastise and defend ourselves, if needed, when someone "crossed the line" or attempted to belittle or denigrate our person.

Thus, after growing up, maturing in life's experiences, and having the out-of-the-blue moment I spoke of in vignette 6, as I considered our country's issues, it was very apparent that many individual "heads" and "leaders" of families (fathers and mothers), churches (pastors and ministers), and government (federal, state, and local) were not high-moral leaders. Namely, without argument, America's "leadership and heads" have not been of sufficient moral integrity or obedience to God and His Word, the Bible, to bring us to our Pledge of Allegiance of being "One Nation under God, indivisible, with liberty and justice for all." Historical and social observation of our nation's nonconformance to that pledge is openly displayed in its love and preferential treatment of White people over Black and Native American people. Many of our leaders have refused by their will and choice to live by the nation's pledge. Not all our nation's "heads," "leaders," White Christians, or White people. But enough of them to have brought our country to this place in time. Looking at it subjectively, Native Americans and Black

Africans have been a test for America. Unfortunately, to this point, the American Christian church, which should be the most prominent leader in this area, has utterly failed the test.

The historical evidence of White America's persistent will to not love African Americans as they love themselves is easily seen in the aftermath of the US Civil War. In preparation for the Civil War's end. Against the strong resistance from many Republican Party members, who became known as "Radical Republicans." President Abraham Lincoln did not want the Union or US Government to penalize the South or bring retribution and reprisals on them for their rebellion. On the contrary, in his submitted "Ten Percent Plan," released about sixteen months before the war's end, Lincoln provided a lenient return to the Union for the Southern rebels with full pardons for all but the top military and Confederate government leaders. Lincoln's plan treated his Southern "White brethren" with mercy, grace, respect, and forgiveness. He wanted to make it easy for them to rejoin the union with only the conditions of emancipating their slaves and only 10 percent of their presecession voting population taking a binding oath of future allegiance to the US. But try as he did, Lincoln couldn't get his specified plan through his party. The sizeable coalition of radical Republicans viewed his plan as forgiving the Southern traitors, who had torn the country apart without guaranteeing civil rights to formerly enslaved people. Radical Republicans wanted to punish the South for what they did to our country with judgment and retribution and additionally protect the formerly enslaved people. All of which went significantly beyond Lincoln's "Ten Percent Plan."

After Lincoln's assassination, his replacement, Vice President Andrew Johnson, a Southern Democratic senator from Tennessee, a slave owner himself, who stayed loyal to the Union, maintaining his seat in Congress after Tennessee seceded from the Union. Against the dictates of Radical Republicans and many members of his Democratic Party. Like Lincoln, Johnson wanted to be lenient to the Southerners and reunite the Union as quickly as possible. In his Proclamation of Amnesty and Reconstruction, except for top Confederate military officers, government leaders, and wealthy Southern landowners. Johnson granted the Southerners full "amnesty and pardon" for their transgressions, rebellion, and killing of more than 400,000 Union soldiers.[20] With their pardon, Johnson returned their property, except for former slaves, and only asked that they affirm their support for the Constitution. The top Confederates and landowners were required to humble themselves and request a personal presidential pardon. The Confederate states were only required to formally repeal their ordinances of secession and ratify the Thirteenth Amendment, which abolished slavery, to rejoin the Union.[21] However, a Southerner and former enslaver, Johnson was not a man "after God's own heart" loving all men as himself, nor was he a man of moral integrity. Johnson denigrated African Americans and was one of, if not the most racist of US Presidents.[22] He refused to support congressional efforts of protection, voting rights, and citizenship by birth to formerly enslaved people.

Lincoln and Johnson went against strong Union opposition and pushback in their determined desires to completely forgive the South, without penalty, punishment, or retribution for the pain, misery, and cost of lives and resources they put the country through. As a result, the Southern Whites walked away from the Civil War with full pardons, their property returned, and freedom to rebuild their lives, owing nothing for their rebellion.

But to the shame of man and, I'm sure, the anger of God (Ps. 7:11), that was not true with the South's treatment of former slaves and Black people after the Civil War, as foreseen and feared by the Radical Republicans. The South, the Southern

White (Bible Belt) professed Christians, not all of them, but enough of them set the rules and actions of the South. Just like the wicked, ungrateful servant of Matthew 18:21–35 did after he was forgiven an enormous amount of debt. Once the restraints of Reconstruction were removed, the forgiven South went viciously after the freed slaves. They did not make amends or ask forgiveness of Blacks for the years of enslavement, poverty, denigration, killing, rape, and abuse they had inflicted. Instead, the South initiated, over the next hundred years, more vicious hatred, segregation, Protestant Ku Klux Klan (KKK), and other White mob murders and barbaric lynchings and mutilations of Blacks. Their highly destructive, debasing segregation and Jim Crow laws, besides their White supremacist attitudes with the aggressive support of the Southern White Christian church, have done enormous damage and cruelty to the individual Black African male, female, and African American families in general.

Like abuse in so many other areas of life, the negative mental, self-esteem, and adverse emotional effects of racism have been devastating and opened the door to Satan's evil suggestions, influence, and life paths. As such, many African American families have been incredibly damaged. Some affected are still passing down the impact of racial abuse, denigration, and low self-esteem from societal White American treatment from generation to generation. It's displayed daily in "Black on Black" crime in our cities, the disproportionate Black male prison population, the significant number of babies born to unwed Black mothers, and the lack of motivation and underachievement in schools. Suppose the ethos "Hope in the American dream" is used as a comparison. In that case, the difference in self-esteem, mental and emotional confidence, aspirations, and accomplishments between the ancestral slavery-born African American and post-Jim Crow Era African American immigrants, like those from Ghana (Ghanaian American) and

Nigeria (Nigerian American), is very significant. From a family income comparison over 2018 and 2019, median incomes for American Ghanaian, Nigerian, White, and Black families were $69,021, $68,658, $65,902, and $43,892, respectively.[23] Because modern-day American income is positively correlated with educational achievement,[24] the comparative college and professional degree relationships are also indicated in the ethnic income grouping. Observation of these simplistic ethnic-cultural family income and educational differences indicates that systematic racism, loveless treatment, denigration, and abuse have severely and negatively impacted many African Americans at the soul, mental, and emotional levels down to their basic survival level.

From what I learned from my dad regarding the principle of the "head." Suppose the "head," a strong leader, is of sound thinking, high moral values, and integrity and consistently executes those traits in their leadership. In that case, the body will likewise conform and move in that direction. The "head" determines where the body goes!

Racism would not have started, survived, and still be a living force in our country if the "head," namely, the leadership of our families, churches, and government (federal, state, and local), were "for real" committed biblical believers and practitioners. Or persons of high moral character and integrity accepting that all people are of one blood and created equal. None better or worse than another! Publicly rebuking and reprimanding those who attempted to preach, teach, legislate, live, and think contrarily.

For me, the following has confirmed the realization that, as the church of Jesus Christ, we have not lived according to God's will. Ever since I was saved by accepting Jesus as my Savior and Lord in the early 1970s, the US church has made a concerted effort to believe that God will heal and continue to prosper America according to the conditional promise of 2 Chronicles 7:14.

> If My people who are called by My name will humble themselves, and pray and seek My face, and turn from their wicked ways, then I will hear from heaven, and will forgive their sin and heal their land. (2 Chron. 7:14)

Looking back at our nation's progress from the early seventies, it is clear that our land (our country) is far from being healed! It has, in fact, continuously degraded ethically along with increased family weakness and moral division, with magnitudes of increased sexual immorality and gender confusion. The list continues with increased illegal and legal drug misuse, mass violence with murder and abortions, increased poverty, political division and divisiveness, unrestrained federal indebtedness, etc. From knowing biblically and personally that God is faithful to His Word. My blunt understanding is that God's people have not met the condition of "turning from our wicked ways." That is the most probable explanation for why America today is "sick and broken" and on a steep downward decline away from God, with sin and immorality increasing and our influence on the world decreasing.

Some people, however, believe that per its contextual setting, 2 Chronicles 7:14 doesn't apply to us, that is, to America. It was to Israel only in the stated context, as part of Solomon's temple dedication. However, I believe that 2 Chronicles 7:14, because of its consistency with other Old Testament and New Testament scripture verses, does apply to us.

> Seek the LORD while He may be found, call upon Him while He is near. Let the wicked

forsake his way, and the unrighteous man his thoughts; let him return to the Lord, and He will have mercy on him; and to our God, for He will abundantly pardon. (Isa. 55:6–7)

Let us search out and examine our ways, and turn back to the Lord; let us lift our hearts and hands to God in heaven. (Lam. 3:40–41)

Lament and mourn and weep! Let your laughter be turned to mourning and your joy to gloom. Humble yourselves in the sight of the Lord, and He will lift you up. (James 4:9–10)

Concerning 2 Chronicles 7:14, suppose I single out the "wicked way" of racism. In that case, it's apparent that many contemporary White Christians, as did their ancestors, are still walking, talking, and living in this wickedness. Or minimally, they are not correcting their families and church congregates' racist thinking and misconceptions as we continue to witness racism's effects on America.

Please make no mistake about it! White Christians, including White Christian Evangelicals, Fundamentalists, Pentecostals, etc., who harbor racism, White supremacy, and hatred in their hearts and minds, play a dangerous game with their souls and place of eternal residence! "God says what He means and means what He says." He is not duplicitous or double-minded. He will not, per His Word, let White Christian hate, detestation, and treatment of Blacks, Native Americans, or any of their descendant brothers and sisters from Noah go without judgment.

However, it must be highly emphasized that the same is equally valid for those of us who are non-White. God is no respecter of people; we're all held to the same standard. It's a crude and simplistic expression, but the truth for all of us is we do it God's way, or it's the path to hell for us!

Jesus told the Jews, "Therefore I said to you that you will die in your sins; for if you do not believe that I am He, you will die in your sins" (John 8:24). Who is He? He is Jesus. Who is Jesus? He is the Word of God (John 1:1). If you do not believe His Word, you do not believe Him, nor do you believe and accept the fact that He and His Word are *one* and inseparable. He is God! He honors His Word above His name. Thus, you will die in your sins if you do not accept and obey His Word! The Word is extremely clear and explicit about the judgment of unbelievers. It is also clear regarding the judgment of those who don't love and treat their brothers and sisters as God directed. Specifically regarding racism in America, unrepentant White supremacist Christians fall into the category of not loving their brothers and sisters, as demonstrated in the historical attitudes and treatment of Black people. Jesus says in Matthew (Matt. 5:21–24) that the abusive insult and treatment of one's brother or sister, like murder, place them "in danger of the judgment." Speaking to the multitudes in His Sermon on the Mount, Jesus says,

> You have heard that it was said to those of old, "You shall not murder," and whoever murders will be in danger of the judgment. But I say to you that whoever is angry with his brother without a cause shall be in danger of the judgment. And whoever says to his brother, "Raca!" [You're "empty-headed," insinuating that his brother is mindless and inferior to him] shall

be in danger of the council. But whoever says,
"You fool!" [You moron!] shall be in danger of
hell fire. Therefore, if you bring your gift to
the altar, and there remember that your brother
has something against you, leave your gift
there before the altar, and go your way. First
be reconciled to your brother, and then come
and offer your gift. (Matt. 5:21–24)

God knows that many White Christians, through no fault
of their own, have had their racist bigotry, hate, and White
superiority poured into them from their parents, grandparents,
and ancestors over generations. Over their lifetimes, their
racism and White supremacist beliefs have been continuously
reinforced by the devil's whispers and possibly supported by the
ungodly behavior they have witnessed in many Black people.
Thus, as it is for any of us with deep-seated spiritual issues
or embedded sin, the Lord's way of escape, as He says in
Matthew 17:21, is through a committed and determined period
of fasting and fervent prayer until our hearts have changed.

The Southern Baptist Church/Convention, which broke off
from the National Baptist church over slavery, was the most
aggressive, hateful, and vicious proponent of racial wickedness
in the American White Christian church. It is also the largest
Protestant denomination in America. Thank God that new heads
and leadership of the Southern Baptist Convention have risen
over the last forty years and have made some inroads toward
conformity to God's ways. In 1982, they publicly went on record
as "strongly opposing the activities of the Ku Klux Klan." [25]
In 1995, they formally apologized to African Americans for
supporting slavery and segregation. In 2017, they condemned
White supremacists in their continuing efforts to eliminate their
racial wickedness.[9, 26] Finally, the Southern Baptist Theological

Seminary in 2018, under the direction of its president, R. Albert Mohler Jr., fully exposed itself, confessing its history and support of White supremacy, racial hatred, and wickedness. They released a "Report on Slavery and Racism in the History of the Southern Baptist Theological Seminary." [27] The report illuminates their historical support of slavery, segregation, the confederacy, White supremacy, and Jim Crow. It additionally exposes the headship and leadership who propelled them along their historical racial, human injustice, and cruelty paths. The following are summary excerpts of the report's findings:

- The history of the Southern Baptist Theological Seminary is intertwined with the history of American slavery and the commitment to White supremacy which supported it. Slavery left its mark on the seminary, just as it did upon the American nation as a whole. The denomination that established it spoke distinctly in support of the morality of slaveholding and the justness of the Confederate effort to preserve it. The seminary's donors and trustees advanced the interests of slavery from positions of leadership in society and in the church.

- The seminary's leaders held to the different commitments enshrined in the nation's foundational commitments. In 1776 Americans declared that all men were created equal and were endowed by their creator with certain inalienable rights. In the United States Constitution, however, Americans effectively consigned black slaves to inequality as non-persons whose inalienable rights to life and liberty were indeed alienated.

- The contradiction went far deeper. As Christians, the seminary's leaders regarded blacks as equal in human nature and dignity because God created all humanity from one person. They therefore labored to save the eternal souls of blacks no less than of Whites. They urged them to repent of their sins and entrust themselves to

God's mercy through faith in Jesus Christ, who suffered for the sins of blacks and Whites alike, and rose again from the dead to give eternal life to all who believed in him, to both blacks and Whites, in order to make them one body.

o They contradicted these commitments however by asserting White superiority and defending racial inequality. The racism that was fundamental to the defense of slavery in America endured long after the end of legal slavery. The belief in White supremacy that undergirded slavery also undergirded new forms of racial oppression. The seminary's leaders long shared that belief and therefore failed to combat effectively the injustices stemming from it.

If the enemy can get to the "head," he will likewise get to those sheep with "ears to hear." American White Christians, not all, but enough who had "ears to hear," heard and believed that they were superior to Black Africans. As a man thinketh in his heart, so is he! As a result, they caused our history's extensive, horrendously destructive, and cruel treatment of African Americans. The following portion of the report's summary bears repeating:

The racism that was fundamental to the defense of slavery in America endured long after the end of legal slavery. The belief in White supremacy that undergirded slavery also undergirded new forms of racial oppression. The seminary's leaders long shared that belief and therefore failed to combat effectively the injustices stemming from it.

We must remember God says what He means, and He means what He says. He has said,

> Many will say to Me in that day, "Lord, Lord, have we not prophesied in Your name, cast out demons in Your name, and done many wonders in Your name?" And then I will declare to them, "I never knew you; depart from Me, you who practice lawlessness!" (Matt. 7:22-23)

Not everyone who calls themselves "Christian" will be saved! It's those who love God and keep His word.

> If anyone loves Me, he will keep My word; and My Father will love him, and We will come to him and make Our home with him. "He who does not love Me does not keep My words; and the word which you hear is not Mine but the Father's who sent Me. (John 14:23-24)

In another place, the Lord says through Paul,

> Examine yourselves as to whether you are in the faith. Prove yourselves. Do you not know yourselves, that Jesus Christ is in you?— unless indeed you are disqualified. (2 Cor. 13:5)

It's evident that the racist, segregationist, and supremacist, upon examination of themselves and finding hate for their African American brothers, sisters, and anyone else, are not in the faith and are disqualified, as Paul puts it. As a repeat, the apostle John makes this distinctively clear in 1 John 4:20–21.

> If someone says, "I love God," and hates his brother, he is a liar; for he who does not

love his brother whom he has seen, how can he love God whom he has not seen? And this commandment we have from Him: that he who loves God must love his brother also." (1 John 4:20–21)

Thus, White Christians, as well as Asian, Black, Brown, Red, or whatever Christians, who have hatred in their hearts and don't love their brothers and sisters as themselves, will find that Matthew 7:22–23 applies to them. Namely, those who have not walked in faith and obedience to God's Word, the Bible, when they stand before Him, the Lord will speak to them those verses. I assume He will additionally say to them, probably with extreme hurt in His heart and tears flowing from His eyes,

- I told you to love your brother as yourself! (Mark 12:31)
- I told you whatever you do to the least of my brothers. You do to me! (Matt. 25:40)
- I told you it would be better for you if a millstone were hung around your neck and you were thrown into the sea rather than you offend one of my little ones! (Luke 17:2)
- Why didn't you believe my Word and Me? (1 John 3:10).
- Why didn't you love Me with all your heart, soul, mind, and strength (effort and might)? (Mark 12:30)
- Why didn't you obey me (John 14:15)? Because you didn't, I have no pleasure in you! You are not in me, nor am I in you!"
- Now depart from me, you cursed, into the everlasting fire prepared for the devil and his angels! (Matt. 25:41)

Then those in that category will walk away weeping and gnashing their teeth (Matt. 25:30).

I pray that all clean their hearts and minds of racial superiority, hatred, and any other sin and unforgiveness and conform entirely to the will of God!

My Takeaway

- **It's my responsibility to love my brother as myself.**
- **I am not to lean on my understanding or take my parents', ancestors', or anyone else's understanding, thinking, or direction over God's Word, the Bible.**
- **It is my responsibility to lay myself out before God to cleanse and renew my heart if I have issues, unforgiveness, or malignant thoughts against or about my brother or sister.**
- **God says what He means and means what He says.**
- **I must examine myself and make sure I'm in the faith so that I don't become disqualified or a castaway from the kingdom of God (2 Cor. 13:5; 1 Cor. 9:27).**

Vignette 8

Choosing My Friends

As a significant part of my upbringing, Dad strongly emphasized that I was not to choose my friends based on their race, popularity, what I thought they could do for me, or the social group I would be accepted into if I were their friend. Nor was I to choose my friends based on their gifts and talents, including how smart or athletic they were. Instead, I was to choose my friends based on their character and values. If their character and morals did not coincide with those he and Mom had instilled in me, that person was not to be my friend or close acquaintance. I was not to play with that person or stay closely associated with them. My friends and close acquaintances were to have the same morals and values as I did, including obedience to their parents and respect for authority. If I didn't find someone with a similar character to mine, I was to go it alone until I did. During that time, he, Mom, my siblings, and cousins were to be my friends. He meant that, and I later found out what a solid forcing function his instructions had on me in my selection of friends and associates and how I related to people, especially boys, who wanted me to join their group. Throughout it all, from elementary to high school, there were only five guys I called "close friends," and they also had a relationship with my father. In truth, however, Dad was my most trusted friend and who I mimicked my character and values after. In fact, when Dad died the year I turned forty, he had been my best friend for years.

Observing my father and structuring my character and values after him, I found it interesting to see and hear Dad relate to kids and teens. Pop would go the extra mile and more to help a kid he saw in need. Or a young person who came to him sincerely requesting his help. He was incredibly open to providing a "hearing ear" and counsel to those who respected authority and others. However, Dad had little tolerance and patience for a rebellious and disrespectful kid. My siblings also noticed that trait in Dad, and we occasionally talked about it. My friends seemed to know Pop's nature instinctively and took great advantage of his desire to help and counsel them when they desired it. When one of my friends or an acquaintance came to visit me at our home, it was common for me to look around when I didn't hear a response from them and find them talking and joking with Dad or getting counsel from him. Pop had extraordinary practical life wisdom and knowledge or what people called "mother wit" or common sense. When they left me to talk to him, I would continue what I was doing and let them spend one-on-one time with Pop. Teenagers wanting time with my dad also happened daily at my high school.

Because of my younger brother Daryl's climate health issues, our family moved from Richmond, California, to Fresno, California, when I was in the eighth grade. In doing so, Dad left his exciting but dangerous and challenging, good-paying munitions stevedore job at the navy's Port Chicago, California, munitions base. Being primarily an agribusiness and service industry economy, Fresno caused Dad to adapt. He started a janitorial service and additionally worked as a custodian at the high school my siblings and I later attended. Fascinatingly, every day after school, a group of kids, sophomores, juniors, and some seniors lined up in a single file, waiting their turn to talk to and get counsel from Dad as he went from classroom to classroom, cleaning them. I learned this from my sisters and some fellow students who witnessed it. One day, I didn't have baseball practice and needed to talk to Pop, so I went to see him right after school let out. However, I had forgotten about the kids and the line that followed Dad daily.

When I got there, there was that line. In my selfishness, I got angry. I was angry that I had to wait in the back of the line to talk to my father. My fury increased as I lingered a few minutes, and nobody in front recognized me or seemed to know that Mr. Auten, who they were waiting to see, was my father. Pop didn't see me since I was at the end of the line in the hall, and he was inside the classroom. My anger had just about peaked when my sanity kicked in and prevented me from angrily shouting at my peers, "I want to talk to my father! Get out of here and go home!" With my sanity calmly taken back over, my thoughts changed. I thought, *Robert, these kids probably need to talk to Dad more than you. Let them have their time with Pop. Your issue is not so urgent that you can't wait to talk to him at home. Also, they probably have a home or other issue they can't speak to their parents about.*

It's interesting how you get insight when thinking of others above yourself. By that, I mean I learned the value of deferring to those kids, their problems, and their need to talk to Dad. One day at school, Pop saw me and pulled me aside to point out a girl to me. I was an outstanding varsity football and baseball player with schoolwide recognition and influence. Dad asked me to look out for her. He didn't ask me to seek or befriend her. Nor to go out of my way to find her. But to pleasantly acknowledge her when I saw her and to make sure no one was teasing or harassing her when I did. He wanted me to exert my leadership and stop them, going to her aid and support if they were. He never told me what issues she had or what others were saying about or doing to her. However, I could see his deep-felt concern for her as he instructed me to look out for the girl. From that day on, whenever I saw the girl at lunch or walking to class, I would always pleasantly acknowledge her, check out who was around her, and ensure she was not being harassed or put down. That simple lesson helped me to be more sensitive to others around me. It helped prevent me from looking at people, but not seeing them. More importantly, Pop's trust in me amplified the importance of my friends and close associates being boys of character and moral values.

I assume many other people also commonly overlook it. But brought to my brother's attention was how we took for granted the value of our dad's involvement in our lives and the overall quality of parenting, guidance, and love we received from our parents. My siblings and I all graduated from the same high school in Fresno. A few years ago Daryl, who has returned to nearly all his ten-year high school reunions, commented on his last reunion attendance. He said one of his female classmates very purposefully mentioned that she remembered Dad and his interaction with him. Daryl wasn't even aware that she or anyone else at school paid attention to how he interacted with Dad, let alone the little interaction they could have observed with Mom. In sincerity, his classmate said she wished she had parents as good as he had.

An enlightening consideration entered my mind as I thought about what Daryl's classmate said. What occurred to me was Daryl received many brownie points, not only for his character, kindness, consideration, athleticism, and good looks but also for his classmates' respect for Dad and Mom and their involvement in his life and upbringing. The truth of that played itself out in his high school senior year. In his senior year, a highly respected girls club on campus asked him to be their "True Gent." He was their lone male member as they conferred an honorary membership with invitations to their functions on him.

It's true that even when you think you're not being noticed, nothing out of the ordinary occurs to you or your life. Irrespective, however, there still is someone you are influencing and others watching and observing you!

My Takeaway

- I was not to choose my friends based on their race, their popularity, or what they could do for me.
- I was to choose my friends based on their character and values similar to mine.
- There is a time to stop being selfish and self-centered. A time to value others and their needs more highly than my own. A time to share what I have with others.
- You are always being watched, noticed, and influencing someone else for good, for bad, or for indifference based on your personality, character, actions, and interaction with others.

Vignette 9

Thou Shall Not Hit a Girl or Woman

My younger brother and I could not hit our sisters with our fists or hands. To do so was a "capital punishment crime." There was no excuse. No "No, I'm sorry," "No, she drove me to do it," "She pushed me to my limit," or "She hit me with her fist, and I hit her back." There was no excuse! If I hit one of my sisters or girl cousins, my only help was getting out of the house before my father got home and running forever! Dad thought one of the most cowardly things a man could do was hit a woman, knowing he had a distinct physical advantage. There were other ways to handle issues between a man and a woman, including physically getting away from her and quickly leaving her presence if her attitude, anger, words, or offense were too difficult to bear. The message laid on me was that a man must maintain his composure and proper disposition with all restraint, not allowing himself to be provoked to anger with retaliation of derogatory or abusive language or physical violence. This was another stern message from Dad. "You do as I say, not as I do or did!" Early in Dad and Mom's marriage, they would go clubbing, drinking, and dancing on a Friday or Saturday night. After drinking hard liquor, a mean streak would surface in Dad. On one occasion, after leaving a club, Mom said something to Dad that he found offensive and angrily slapped her across the face. It nearly ended their marriage and woke Dad up to hard liquor's effect on him. Dad stopped drinking distilled spirits then, confining himself to a beer or two on some weekends.

Dad and Mom were a couplet in their parenting, teaching, and raising my siblings and me. Mom added to Dad's lesson of maintaining composure and restraint when pressed by a female. She warned me that a woman's tongue, painted with anger-colored language, could be fierce, poisonous, vindictive, and demeaning. Mom informed me that my future wife could knowingly use her tongue like a sword with the utmost precision, purposely thrusting it where I'm the most vulnerable emotionally and intellectually, cutting me to ribbons. She could deliberately humiliate and strike me right through my manhood. But I was not to retaliate, engage, or allow her to pull me into her conflict. Instead, I was to know with certainty who I was and who I was not, maintaining my composure.

The tragic thing about what Mom told me was that I observed two elder female relatives tear into their husbands with extreme anger, firing the most vicious, vile, and caustic word bombs at them I've ever heard. But thank God, just as my parents instructed me, my male relatives, surprisingly to me, passively took the abuse calmly, without retaliation, purposely giving their wives separation space to ensure they did not engage physically. I was horrified at what I saw and heard the first time I observed it. When it occurred, I was in elementary school and prayed after the altercation ended, "Lord, please, please don't let me marry anyone like ..."

Another time I observed it, I was grown and married. One evening, I suddenly received a call from an older cousin to hurry and get to the apartment of one of our married relatives. Husband and wife were in a fierce argument that had been going on for hours. My cousin desperately needed help to mediate and bring a peaceful closure to their disagreement and issues. Upon my arrival, oh my! The female was in a verbal and body language attack state that I don't even have words to describe. There was no physical assault on her husband. It was all verbal. He was on the defense, maintaining a separation distance between them. But given little opportunity to say or respond to the vilest, most odious, and harsh words I've ever heard levied on anybody. When I attempted to intervene, my female relative pungently told me to stay out of their business.

I sat down and silently prayed fervently in the spirit, that is, in "tongues." It took a while, but things finally settled, and peace was restored. I later drove away, heading back home. As I did, I thought, *If my wife ever talked to me like that, it would be "Hasta la vista, baby! You have no place in my life!"*

The essence of Dad's teaching and commands was that I could not violently attack, retaliate, or hit a girl or woman. Or emotionally abuse her, curse her, or demean her in any way. Although a woman can surely do it, I cannot allow her to provoke me to violence, uncontrolled anger, or lose my composure. In concepts I better understood later in life. As the man, I was to treat and respect women as the "weaker vessel," always taking the higher ground, pulling it together, and keeping it together. I was the "captain of the ship." It was my responsibility to control myself and never allow a situation or a woman's "bad day" attitude to control or get the best of me. If necessary, I had to find other ways and methods to defend myself, including the ultimate defense, if I'm married, of leaving our domain temporarily or permanently by legal separation or divorce. Per Dad's teaching, regardless of the situation, it was my responsibility to assess whether I could positively verbally, attitudinally, and emotionally contend and reason with a cantankerous and fussy woman for the betterment of our relationship. If not, I was to extract myself promptly.

I found out later, as an adult, after I was saved and started reading the Bible. Extraction was also the Lord's method of escape from a potentially violent marriage relationship. The Lord prescribed through King Solomon. "It is better to dwell in the wilderness than with a contentious and angry woman" (Prov. 21:19). Solomon also said in alternate phrasing, "It is better to dwell in a corner of a housetop, than in a house shared with a contentious woman" (Prov. 25:24).

Women can say things to you, especially those closest to you, your sisters, cousins, girlfriends, and your wife, which can cut you to the bone. In summary, the lesson and message I received from Dad, simple in words but complex in execution, were as a man, even more so as a husband and head of my household, I cannot counterattack in violence or be combative physically with my wife. Nor can I, with verbal viciousness, in retaliation or revenge, attack her in response to her verbal strife, false accusations, and anger spewed out on me.

Based on the message "You don't hit a woman!" drilled into me by my dad, I remember when I first saw James Bond, Agent 007, smack a woman.[28] I was so shocked I almost fell out of my theater seat. Since then, in other episodes, I've seen James repeat his physical encounter where he popped or smacked a woman as he would a man to the acceptance of the audience. In recognition of the fiction in cinema, our society glorifies violence, except when it occurs in real life. Thus, it is taken very seriously if a man hits or physically abuses a woman, irrespective of what she did to him.

To that end, it's disturbing to me that the trend in movies today more and more readily shows female characters, in a glorified manner, hauling off and hitting men as if they could go toe-to-toe with them rather than depicting women using their cunning and wit. I believe it is because women don't have superior physical strength to men. They, instead, have a keener sense of cunning, cleverness, and a higher survival nature than men. These are some of the most valued gifts women bring as "helpmates" to their boyfriends and husbands. These and other specific man-women complementary differences open up many of life's problem-solving options for couples who do work together. My apologies to cat lovers, but the complementary skills, gifts, and talents of men and women working cooperatively together produce a plethora of optional ways for them, as a team, to solve problems or "skin the cats of life." If women strive to be more and more like men and vice versa, that highly favorable, God-given, male-female team-play will be compromised.

I remember being incredibly embarrassed one day by my mother. I was helping Dad move a large, weighty sofa from upstairs to downstairs at my parents' home. Mom had been watching us. Because of the couch's configuration, maneuvering wasn't at all straightforward. Mom was downstairs looking up, watching us toil and use our strength first and foremost to steer and align the sofa. We were making no progress, and sweat was pouring out of us. Finally, after watching for about five minutes, Mom, very calmly in a curious, questioning tone, said, "Why don't you do this ...?" Mom said it as if she wondered whether she was missing something because what she proposed, to her, was obviously apparent. However, Pop and I never considered the maneuver Mom suggested. We were moving the sofa in the way that came naturally to us, which was by brute force, and we were exerting much energy and effort doing it our way, but getting nowhere. I don't remember what "this ..." was that Mom suggested, but we instantaneously considered her suggestion. As we did, it was like "Duh! Why didn't I think of that?"

Within seconds of executing Mom's suggestion, we walked the sofa safely down the stairs without the enormous effort we were expending. Because I held an engineering degree, my embarrassment was magnified for missing something simple but highly clever. I humbled myself, and Pop and I both graciously thanked Mom for her suggestion. I also silently thanked the Lord that Dad and I didn't hurt or strain our backs and bodies doing it our way. After the experience, I thought, *Why didn't I think of that? It was so evident to me after Mom's suggestion.* I concluded Pop and I undertook the task without thinking about it. We acted using our physical strength, which came most naturally to us. I've seen this happen several times where women stand back and have the answers as we men attempt to simplistically brute force our way through life until we stop and listen to them, our helpmates! Be they our wives, mothers, sisters, relatives, girlfriends, or female friends.

However, getting back to TV and movies, when I see those "almighty women" scenes, my knee-jerk response is to react in repulsion to them emotionally, very negatively. My thoughts to the screenwriters' producers, and directors are *You don't want to do that! You don't want to put a violent and glorified fight impulse of "Dude! I'll knock you out"* thinking into girls' and women's minds. You don't want boys and men to become callous and disrespectful of girls and women, treating them as if they were men. In real life, if a girl hauls off and hits a guy like the movies depict, and he retaliates in like fashion, it will, in most cases, not be a pretty or healthy outcome for the woman. For the man, supposing there is a serious injury to the female. Even if she initiated the assault, from the cases that I'm aware of, he is the one the police and DA will go after because it's known that he has, by far, the greater strength, power, and physical advantage. Society commonly expects the man to use minimal physical restraint and "not excessive force" against a woman unless his life is in imminent danger. Even then, his actions may be questioned and challenged. An obvious comparison of relative fighting gender inequality is the following. What if MMA great Ronda Rousey (five feet, seven inches, 134 pounds [29A]) fought her male MMA great counterpart, Conor McGregor (five feet, nine inches, 136 to 155 pounds [29B])? Or if she fought boxing greats Manny Pacquiao (five feet, six inches, 118 to 146 pounds [29C]) or undefeated Floyd Mayweather Jr. (five feet, eight inches, 126 to 154 pounds [29D]), who has defeated both McGregor and Pacquiao? In an all-out blitz, if Ronda went after either of them, providing them no options other than protecting themselves. She, with little doubt, would be dead or severely maimed within the milliseconds of their reaction time. On second thought, that may not be true with Floyd. He is such a defensive master. He would likely have a matador's move to avert her. However, the message is clear. Being the world champion she is, she is no match for her male world champion counterparts.

It's clear why movies are trending in their display of violent and glorified, female-to-male "I'll knock you out dude" scenes. In this age of feminism and promotion of female greatness, producers attempt to draw into the theater females hungry to see the woman "on top" of her male counterpart in every aspect of life. They are trying to show that she is better or, at the least, his equal, even in fighting ability. My personal assumption is that many women rejoice, vicariously identify with, and implant themselves into the character of the "superwoman" beating the mess out of some man on the screen. They possibly receive what they view as a vicarious makeup for all the times men have beaten, abused, and mistreated them or other women.

Because I have a daughter and am very much aware of the world she lives in, I recognize the fundamental importance and value of teaching boys and girls self-defense and martial arts to defend and protect themselves if needed. Similarly, I'm aware that those who master self-defense skills are trained and disciplined to walk in humility and use their self-defense and fighting skills only when necessary. I have a cousin, Sifu Bill Owens, a martial arts grandmaster with a tenth-degree plus black belt and the kung fu "Blossom Fists" fighting style developer. Bill is the founder and owner of Cascos Martial Arts Academy in Oakland, California. His wife, Mary, is a ninth-degree black belt and instructor in their studio. She is mellow and as sweet as pie. She doesn't exhibit any aggressive "I'll kick your you-know-what" attitudes that are starting to appear in some female characters in cinema and TV series. Sifu has trained several female relatives and other women up and into black belt levels. Nor have I seen that attitude in any of those women I know.

In summary, if one looks at domestic violence statistics, it's apparent that fathers and mothers are not teaching and training their boys in the restraint and methods to nonviolently verbally and physically subdue and avoid heated confrontations with their female counterparts. Nor are they teaching them how to deal with their internal conflicts, failures, and insecurities to resolve their frustration and anger nonviolently and correctly. Nor how to handle the provoking poison that can come from a girl's or woman's mouth so that her word darts and attitude do not provoke them to violence.

I am thrilled my father taught me early in life not to hit a girl or woman. My mom reinforced his message with instructions on how to avoid a female provoking me to anger and violent retaliation with her mouthful of piercing and poisonous words.

My Takeaway

- **Except for imminent self-defense, there is no reason for a man to hit or physically manhandle a girl or woman!**

Vignette 10

Dad and Mom Loved My Siblings and Me the Same, but Our Obedience Is What Rewarded Us!

One crucial lesson my siblings and I received from my father was "Your mother and I love you all the same, but we will not treat you the same. You all have different personalities, and we will treat you with respect to your differences." I recall Dad doing this on two separate occasions. Once when I was about ten years old and again in my early teens. I don't remember any of us saying much in response to what Pop said because we understood on both occasions what he meant. We were very secure in Dad and Mom's love for us; they demonstrated it daily with the personal and individual attention they gave us. They provided adequately for us and made themselves available together or one-on-one to help us solve our problems. As a kid growing up, living in an environment where I saw my parents work cooperatively and hearing them talk pleasantly to each other notably added to my sense of family security and protection.

Daily, before Dad worked at night and always on the weekend, we ate dinner as a family nightly. After saying grace, during the passing of the food around the table, Dad would start with my older sister, Beverly, asking her how her day went and what she did. After hearing Beverly's response and her answers to any comments and questions from him, Mom, and the rest of us, Pop continued around the table individually, asking my siblings and me about our day. Dad would insist that we talk and share, and we all did except my younger brother. Daryl never said much for some reason, and Dad and Mom never overly forced or pressured him. He was the "baby" of the family and always had it easier than our sisters and me. Daryl continuously passed on, providing any input or his take on nearly all of our family discussions. He did so, even up to when I left home and went to college.

After delivering our contributions, it was common for Dad or Mom to introduce some subject, current event, or news item they were interested in discussing and wanted our input on. This request from my parents to think about what they presented to us, and for me specifically to give my opinion, was one of the most valuable learning and confidence-building practices I remember.

Dinner was always an enjoyable and beneficial time for us individually and as a family unless we disobeyed or did something wrong. Then for whoever the offender was, it was confronting and painful. At the dinner table and during the carry-on conversations after dinner, we learned about ourselves, social issues, politics, and my parents' plans for us, such as their educational and obedience expectations, our family vacation plans, etc. When it came to our education, their expectations were high but reasonable. Their goal was for us to get As and Bs in school and to have given our very best if we got a "C," in addition to being excellent "student citizens" with no deficiency reports. They backed up their expectations with active involvement in our schools, knowing our teachers and principals well, and actively participating in our school's Parent-Teacher Association (PTA).

From as early as I can remember, their simple requirements, with Dad in the lead, were for us to obey them and do our chores willingly without resentment or laziness. Dad hated laziness as well as a lazy disposition or attitude. Pop may not have hated laziness as much as he did lying and stealing. But oh, did he hate it and let us know loud and definitively if he detected it in us! Regarding education, in addition to doing well through high school, we were to complete college. It was never "If you go to college ..." It was always "After you graduate from high school, what college or university do you want to attend?"

In speaking for myself, when I operated in obedience and compliance to my parents' commands, principles, values, and expectations. I brought immense satisfaction to myself. When my siblings or I didn't, there were always the consequences of paying the price. It seems like the dinner table was often where the accusation against us surfaced, the trial held, and the judgment for any transgression was right then, and there meted out or applied. That sequence was likely to occur at the dinner table because that is where my tattletale younger sister, Karen, would pompously take that opportunity to blabbermouth everything she saw or heard Beverly or I do against my parents' directives or expectations. If we did anything wrong or violated my parents' teaching and training, that's when it would come out. That is also when dinner would be most painful for the offender. Karen would always start the same way, saying very slowly, dragging it out, "Dad ... dy," "Mom ... my," and then her explosive pronouncement, such as, "Beverly was smoking in the park!" This pronouncement of Karen's happened at dinner one Monday evening when Beverly was about thirteen years old. On Sunday, the previous day, our family was in Oakland, visiting my uncle, aunt, and cousins. We went to their neighborhood park with our cousins, and Beverly was hanging out with one of my older cousins and her friends, and they were experimenting with smoking. Karen and I came upon them unexpectedly. I rebuked and verbally chastised Beverly on the spot, demanding that she throw the cigarette away. That wasn't good enough for Karen, and she let it out at the dinner table the next day. Needless to say, when Karen finished, my father took over. That was not an enjoyable dinner for Beverly. She didn't pick up a cigarette again until after graduating high school, in college, away from home. Fortunately, I only had one notable dinner table experience Karen called me on. One day, I didn't go directly home after school as instructed but instead went to the park and played ball with my friends.

That evening, I learned very vividly and soundly from Dad that obedience to his and Mom's direction exceeded my will and wants and anything my friends wanted me to do. That painful personal correction and the many disciplinary examples I witnessed levied on Beverly. All fused within me that obedience to our parents with full conformance to their rules and guidelines preceded everything else. Compliance with my parents' will and instructions made my life much more comfortable and enjoyable. Namely, what flowed into my life was determined by my submission and compliance to Dad's and Mom's commands and rules! Beverly continually pushed the limits of rebellion and disobedience much more than my other siblings and I did combined, three times over. She was on punishment and limited in freedom for an overwhelming amount of time compared to us.

One day, as teenagers, while Dad and Mom were not home, Beverly fussed, ranted, and complained about her predicament. I remember telling her, "Beverly, Beverly, Dad and Mom are easy! They are easy! They are simple, incredibly simple to please! All you have to do is obey and act responsibly! Then you will get more and more freedom and everything else you want. Of course, you won't always get it as soon as you want, but you will." I learned by experience what I told her: Obedience made my life more pleasant and substantially more peaceful and rewarding. However, Beverly never seemed to get it. Even into college, she often pushed the envelope or out and out disobeyed, receiving the consequences of her nonconformance.

My Takeaway

- My parents loved my siblings and me all the same. However, they treated and disciplined us based on what they felt was best for each of us according to our differences, personalities, and needs.
- As with my parents, so it is with God. The path to peace, freedom, and rewards is through obedience!

Vignette 11

The Lesson of Fallbrook

During WWII, my dad enlisted in the US Navy. Sometime after his enlistment, he was stationed at the Fallbrook Naval Ammunition Depot in northern San Diego County, California, east of Camp Pendleton Marine Base. Dad and Mom met in their early twenties while he was on leave in Los Angeles, and she was working as a "Rosie the Riveter" at Lockheed Aircraft Corp. They fell in love after a period of dating during Dad's weekend leaves. Their dating included nightclubbing in Los Angeles and visiting the Pike Amusement Park in Long Beach, California. Pike amusement park had a famous roller coaster called the Cyclone Racer, which extended out over the Pacific Ocean. After discussion, they set a day in April 1945 as the date for their marriage. Pop requested leave to get married and some additional days off for a short honeymoon as the time approached. However, his request was flatly denied by his commanding officer.

When the time came for his and Mom's scheduled marriage, he left the base anyway. He went away without leave (AWOL). In war, going AWOL is very serious, incredibly dangerous, and as foolish a thing as a military person could do. Being AWOL when, as a country, we were at war could be regarded by the military as an act of desertion. The consequences could be death if the shore patrol (SPs) or military police (MPs) caught him and he resisted arrest or if his court martial so ordered. After they married and were enjoying their honeymoon, Mom noticed that Dad was amazingly relaxed about his time off, and she asked him how much time off he had. Dad let her know that he was AWOL. Mom knew the seriousness of the matter and the vast trouble Dad would face if caught. She urged and pushed him to return to the base immediately. Dad returned, and his court martial dictated that he do some time in the brig or naval base prison, and he did. Love makes you do some mindless and foolish things, and my dad, in his youth, got caught in its web.

During his time in the brig, Dad and the other African American imprisoned sailors were grouped separately (i.e., segregated from the White detained sailors). They were also poorly treated and physically abused in some cases. They were treated significantly worse than their White imprisoned sailor counterparts and in overtly derogatory and denigrating ways. On separate occasions, Dad and Mom explained that in the US Navy during WWII, segregation, inequality, prejudice, racism, and harsh and unfair treatment of Black sailors were prevalent. Dad described a situation that occurred while he was in the brig.

He said the Black sailors in the brig with him came to a point where they had enough of the ill and negative treatment they were receiving. They decided to stand up for themselves in protest and refuse to obey demeaning orders. They wanted immediate and just consideration of their complaints, accompanied by respect owed them as men and sailors. They all agreed to stick together, no matter what until their conditions were met. Soon after, the inmates made their cooperative agreement and commitment. A situation occurred on the drill field. The brig guards and drill officers said and did something to them that he and the other African American sailors took immense umbrage to. It triggered their enough-is-enough reflex, and the sailors stood side-by-side in their resistance, just as they had planned.

As a collective, Dad and his fellow sailors refused to respond to the commands and instructions and demanded that base officers hear their complaints and grievances. He said the officers in charge went right into their "Who in *Hades* do you

you-know-whats think you are?" Then called in a truckload of heavily armed, locked and loaded naval military police ready to shoot and kill all dissident prisoners. When the SPs arrived, the officer in charge, with his armed backup, defiantly challenged them, calling out those Black sailors who defied the status quo and their treatment to step forward. Pop stepped forward. After a few seconds, he felt strange and looked around, finding himself standing alone with no one beside him. No one else stepped forward, not even the leaders who initiated and organized their civil resistance effort. Pop was all by himself. When the "mess hit the fan," so did those sailors' commitment and "guts" go with it.

After Dad's fellow inmates' cowardly inaction left him standing alone, they all weakly submitted back under the authority of their racist, biased, and abusive White guards and then dismissed. Dad was taken into custody, treated harshly, and received additional time in the brig. Fortunately, the event didn't affect his later honorable discharge. Still, it did teach him a valuable lesson about people, groups, the power of fear, and group psychology; all of what he learned from that incident he instilled in me. He taught and trained me, no matter how just the cause, to reject the alluring and enticement of the "crowd" and its dominant vocal leaders. I was never to join a group or make "an all-out" commitment to any group, person, idea, or philosophy without understanding the ramifications and potential worst-case scenario risks to myself and others. Pop's message was that if there was an issue, I felt strongly about and felt the need to take a stand, I was to take that stand based on my decision and willingness to commit, knowing and fully considering the risks. I was by no means to expect or assume backup and support from anyone else, including a crowd or group! Thus, Dad's overall message to me was not to place myself in a position where I was trusting in the dedication and loyalty of others. However, if confronted with something worth taking a stand for or against that could jeopardize my life, health, career, or freedom due to beatings, death, blackballing, jail time, or imprisonment. He emphasized that my stand was to be solely my decision and choice after thoroughly weighing the potential consequences to myself and others.

Pop's sobering message of wisdom has hung over my mind and heart like a watchful cloud ever since Dad gave it to me in my preteens. It has been a warning and a heads-up to consider all implications and consequences before making any commitments. It was one of, if not the main reason, that I did not join a fraternity or political action group in college. I wholeheartedly determined that I would not give my will up or my unmitigated alliance to any person, dogma, or group!

Years later, after receiving Jesus Christ as my Lord and Savior, I understood what God wanted from me. With that understanding, Dad's message became far more real to me than before. I now knew, with certainty, that it was to God and Him only that I was to make an absolute commitment to with an unmitigated alliance. God's reason and purpose for creating me and His requirement were for me to love Him with all my heart, soul, mind, and strength (effort and might). Which encloses my whole being, including my desires, wants, and ambitions. The Lord's requirement and command leave no room for any other unalterable obligation. His expectations of me were vividly pointed out as I read and accepted the following verses of scripture:

> And great multitudes went with Him. And He turned and said to them, "If anyone comes to Me and does not hate **(that is, loves more than Me)** his father and mother, wife and children, brothers and sisters, yes, and his

own life also, he cannot be My disciple. And whoever does not bear his cross and come after Me cannot be My disciple." (Luke 14:25–27)

Additionally, the Lord confirmed and clarified what He said and meant by repeating,

He who loves father or mother more than Me is not worthy of Me. And he who loves son or daughter more than Me is not worthy of Me. (Matt. 14:37)

He who loves his life will lose it, and he who hates his life in this world will keep it for eternal life. (John 12:25)

And they overcame him by the blood of the Lamb and by the word of their testimony, and they did not love their lives to the death. (Rev. 12:11)

The reality of my commitment to the Lord and the depth of the love He requires of me was soberly and poignantly pointed out when I first read *Foxe's Book of Martyrs*.[30] I learned of the true love and commitment to the Lord made by men, women, boys, and girls. I read of their courage and steadfastness in the Lord as they stood firmly, boldly, and unwavering in their refusal to deny their faith and love of Jesus in the face of imminent torture and the unimaginable, painful death that confronted them. It was very sobering and emotional to visualize them standing in faith while threatened, undergoing cruel and savage torture and beatings. Some had their brains bashed out with clubs. Some were mauled and eaten by wild animals. Some were burned at the stake; some were beheaded; others were crucified and then covered in wax and set on fire as night candles. Others were pulled asunder by horses. I saw that love for the Lord, courage, resistance to fear, and suffering through unimaginable pain was not a "gender or age thing" but a "heart thing." In the book, I saw men as old as Polycarp at eighty-six years old and a teenage girl who did not give an inch to fear or to their tormentors' threats and demands that they deny Jesus and accept their gods. Through Foxe's words, I witnessed their lives snatched from them as they stood steadfast, unwavering in their faith and love of Jesus, their God, Lord, and Savior. Their lives were violently taken from them through some of the most brutal acts of cruelty the world has known. Because of the trauma and emotional responses I experienced as I read each martyr's story, it took me more than five years to get through my first reading of the book.

In conclusion, Dad told me, "If there was something worth taking a stand for, or against, that could jeopardize my career, my health, or possibly lead to my death. If I felt a strong sense to commit and involve myself, I was to take my stand based on no expectation of getting any backup, help, or support from anyone else, including any leaders, the crowd, or any group supporting the cause. It was to be my sole decision after weighing the potential consequences of my decision to myself and others." Therefore, after accepting the Lord and reading *Foxe's Book of Martyrs,* I know where my convictions lay. The simplest way to state my stance then and now is "I've opened my mouth to the Lord, and I won't take it back!"

Saying it another way, as my father instructed me, I have carefully considered the consequences of my choice and commitment. I have made the choice my Creator put before me! I chose Him, Jesus, the Christ, my Lord, and Savior! I have no expectation of getting any backup, help, or support from anyone other than the Lord Himself, regardless of any circumstance I find myself in.

My Takeaway

- **Do not make any commitment without seriously and soberly thinking through all the potential consequences of my decision.**
- **Do not make a potentially life-threatening health, career, or possible jail time commitment, and expect backup or support from vocal leaders, supporting crowds, or groups.**
  - **My decision to stand for an issue must be mine alone based on sound principles after weighing the potential consequences to my family, myself, and others.**
- **My love, conviction, and commitment to the Lord are with all my heart, mind, soul, and strength. It supersedes any and all my other obligations and commitments. Even unto death if need be!**

Vignette 12

Financial Lessons from My Parents

I learned from observation that my parents' financial personalities differed significantly and distinguishingly. In the early years of our family, while my siblings and I were in elementary school, Dad managed the family budget. It seemed like we never had anything good. It was always the necessities of life: no frills, special outings, or good vacations. There were no cookies, pies, or cakes on the shopping list, just the essentials. Then one late August, just before returning to school, we had noticeably grown over the summer, and Mom needed to buy us new school clothes, shoes, and school supplies. As I was listening to Dad go over the budget with Mom, when he concluded, Mom gently asked, "Bob, where is the money for the kids' back-to-school clothes and supplies?"

Dad was stumped. There was a brief pause as he considered it for the first time. It was clear from Dad's silence that no money was allocated or set aside for our back-to-school expenses. Mom asked to work with the budget to see what she could do. He gave it to her. She put her glasses on, and I watched her work diligently for the next few hours with our bills, due dates, and amounts. When she finished, she and Dad reviewed her revised proposed budget, which included allocations for our school clothes and supplies. She also got some other goodies in for us. However, the best thing was that she asked Dad to let her take over the budget, and he gave it to her. I can't tell you how happy we were. No! "Happy" is not the word. How ecstatic we were with Mom taking over the budget.

Suddenly, one Sunday a month, we would go to a sit-down restaurant and have dinner. On many Friday nights, Mom would fry chicken, make Kool-Aid, have us put on our pajamas, and we would go to a drive-in movie for $1 a carload. We started taking vacations, mainly to visit Mom's family in LA. Those vacations were great. We visited Disneyland, Knotts Berry Farm, Hollywood, Santa Monica, and Pacific Ocean Park (POP). We even got maps to movie stars' homes and drove to them, slowly cruising by their houses, hoping to see at least one or two stars. We went to Beverly Hills, Rodeo Drive, and the upper-end department stores of the day, like Saks Fifth Avenue, Joseph Magnin, and I. Magnin. These were the stores of the rich and famous.

My aunts in Los Angeles did an excellent job planning, helping us with our vacations, and taking us to some recreation and great eating places. We did all this after Mom took over the budget and incorporated her thorough, informed planning and balancing process. Mom came from Texas and was a stickler and an excellent example for keeping your word to everyone you gave it to, including your creditors. This virtue was deeply drilled into her by her mother, my grandmother, Betty. We heard the constant mantra "Your word is your bond, and your bond is your word." Mom firmly trained us that when you owe a debtor or have a bill you have made and committed to, you pay the bill on time when it's due. If you don't have the money, call the lender or merchant before it's due and make revised arrangements. No exceptions! Dad and Mom were stern and firm about keeping your word, doing what you say, and meaning what you say. Daddy regarded not keeping your word as lying. As I mentioned, he forged into my siblings and me, and I say "forged with an iron of steel," "I hate a liar. If you lie, you'll steal, and if you steal, you'll lie. I hate a thief, and I hate a liar." Thus, as a couplet, my parents instilled in my siblings and me the message to pay our bills on time and keep our word to our creditors and all others.

There was a considerable difference between Mom and Dad's financial personalities and management styles. Under Dad's budget and management plan, we endured life. While under Mom's management style, we enjoyed life. Dad intensely disliked borrowing and owing anyone anything. Therefore, he paid as much as he could monthly to pay off our debts and bills. One day, Mom told one of her sisters on the phone that Dad would be thrilled with all the bills paid and having only money for coffee in his pocket.

Mom's fiscal management style viewed life, and our family's physical and material needs as a whole. Mom initiated her revised expense plan after getting Dad's agreement to take over the budget. Recognizing they had insufficient money to pay their loans, bills, and other family and household needs and desires, including our back-to-school clothes and supplies. Mom called their creditors to execute her strategy. She let them know they would be late making that month's payment and, as necessary, renegotiated future installment amounts and dates.

She renegotiated the monthly payment amounts to incorporate and balance all our family's financial needs. Including setting aside some money for emergencies and what she called "play money." Of course, in the long run, Mom's method required them to pay more interest as they extended their repayment periods, but we could now live! We could finally live! Thank You, Lord, for Mom taking over the budget. Thank You! Wow, what a difference and relief! Under Dad's management, I once had to put a piece of cardboard in one of my shoes because of a hole and wait for the next paycheck to get new shoes.

When Mom took over the budget, my siblings and I were happy, and Dad also liked Mom taking over the bills. The pressure to pay everything off as soon as possible and the fear and dislike of debt were off him. It was at least no longer his day-to-day concern, and he liked gathering his kids and eating a good meal out sometimes, as well as going to the drive-in theater on Friday nights. I also think he liked just being able to concentrate on work. Mom was creative in managing the money she budgeted for family needs. For instance, every so often, for our casual and school clothes, we went to San Francisco to Willys. When we went, we usually went early on a Saturday morning with two of my cousins and their mom, my aunt Mae, who had turned Mom onto the store. Willys was a rather large department store with multiple floors. We didn't get our underwear and other personal items from there. Mom strictly prohibited that; it was an absolute no-no! As I found out some years later, the reason was they were used clothes. Nor did we buy what we called our "good clothes" from there.

We got our underwear and other personal items from JCPenney or Macy's. Willys, as I found out in my teens from my older sister who, when we were younger, always seemed to be a step or two ahead of me, was the Goodwill store in San Francisco. Mom and my aunt Mae always referred to it as Willys. Thus, when I heard some kids in our elementary school made reference to thrift or Goodwill stores as "Poor people's stores," I had no idea Willys was one of them they were referring to. Therefore, I never associated us with being anything less than middle-class financially. In a nutshell, Mom did a great job of budgeting, financial planning, and stretching our family dollars.

In my early teens, when our family budget was not as financially stretched. Or as Mom liked to put it, "financially strapped." Dad and Mom taught my older sister, Beverly, and me how to budget and implement our family's financial plan—from listening, learning, and the experience of monthly, performing our budget, and writing checks. I gleaned that I was more inclined to Dad's budgeting approach than Mom's. Like father, like son, Dad's process gave me greater mental peace, less anxiety, and far less work and effort. However, as I learned, Dad's way required a monthly cash flow significantly above the total necessary monthly expenditures, such as food, home mortgage, car payments, insurance, utilities, and other obligations and bills. It also required having adequate savings for emergencies like car repairs, plumbing, a new refrigerator, a new roof, vacations, and "play money." Not having the necessary cash flow to meet all of those family needs and desires meant all the frills and nonessential items of life were done away with, and you would additionally have to take out loans to survive, as we had experienced firsthand. I viewed and studied the details as I understood our family's budget. In doing so, I recognized that Mom's budget implementation incorporated several line items Dad willingly sacrificed to apply more money to pay loans and bills off. Instead, Mom stretched out their financial obligations as far as she could to free up and reallocate as much money as possible to cover all our family needs she deemed valuable. This upbringing and the knowledge I gained were instrumental in helping me understand the value of money, the importance of budgeting and monetary planning, and the development of the financial path I wanted to walk.

The financial path I saw for myself required me to strive, commit, and place myself in a position to obtain a high-paying job or develop a profitable business that provided me an income much, much better than the average family. From my vantage point, my income needed to be notably more significant than the average family's. The reason was that the price of things, including houses, cars, and clothes, was based on what most families could afford. I would struggle like them if I didn't make significantly more than the average family. We were middle-class; thus, I reasoned that we were middle-of-the-road or lived off an average family income. I noted that Dad and Mom had middle-class jobs and were doing everything they could to keep our family's financial nose above water, and we sure didn't live and spend money wastefully or extravagantly. Yet as practical as life is, we felt the effects of sudden car repairs, a burned-out refrigerator, or a worn-out washing machine. I sure didn't want those experiences when I grew up.

When my parents gave my sister Beverly and me the family budget to learn about financial realities, it was a tremendous educational blessing and an accompanying set of outstanding lessons. We quickly discovered that there were no fancy gimmicks or methods; you either had the money or didn't, which dictated your financial plan, budget, and spending.

Managing our family's budget and writing the checks for bills gave my sister and me a sense of responsibility and perked our consciences to monitor our monetary requests to our parents. As big sister and brother, it helped us to defer some of what we wanted to help our younger sister and brother get some of the things they needed or wanted, and at times, to likewise request that they also delay or push out their demands for some of the things they desired. In short, Dad and Mom's teaching in finance was enlightening, practical, and applicable for insertion into our lives "bucket of lessons and experiences." The financial lessons we learned were very, very good for us! Some years later, as part of my financial path, those lessons quickly helped me decide to be an engineer rather than a physicist or mathematician when I saw the salary differences between the average engineer, physicist, and mathematician before I chose my college major.

I also received a financial independence lesson from my family budgeting experience. I was excited one day to realize that I didn't need to ask Mom for money anymore. We lived in Fresno, California, seemingly the agricultural capital of the world. Farm and harvest work in the fields was abundantly available to me in the summertime. On my initiative, with my older sister

Beverly's help, I got my social security number and work permit. I learned to cut, turn, and roll grapes, chop (hoe) cotton, and pitch watermelons. I made exceptional money from pitching watermelons and also enhanced my arm, forearm, and hand muscle strength for baseball and football, which I played. Later, as I aged, I worked for Dad in his janitorial service before going to college. The financial lessons and experience significantly helped me grow in responsibility and maturity.

As I started working, right at my first payday, as part of my financial responsibilities, Dad trained and instructed me to give Mom half of all I made right from the top of my earnings. Dad had two reasons for this. One was for me to respect Mom and show her appreciation for all she had done and was doing for me. His second reason was to train me for marriage. His training and teaching regarding the financial aspects of marriage were "When you get married, you and your wife don't have separate lives or funds. You are one! Your money is not your money! Don't call it your money; don't consider it yours! Everything you have is hers also, including your money! It is joint, 50/50, as much hers as it is yours. So don't claim it as yours! She has as much right and say as you do about how family money is spent! When it is spent, and what it is spent on. Don't resent it! You are one! You are one family!"

-

My Takeaway

- **My preferred financial and budgeting approach was closer to my dad's than my mom's. I would rather sacrifice, be frugal, and give up nearly all frills, having no debts and owing no one anything rather than taking on debt or extending indebtedness.**
  - **Like father, like son, Dad's approach gave me greater mental peace and less anxiety.**
- **My path to financial success required me to strive, commit, and place myself in the position to get a great-paying job or start a profitable business that would provide me an income much better than the average family's income.**
- **When I got married, everything was to be joint with my wife. It was not my money or her money. It was to be 50/50 our money. It's the family's money!**
- **When I married, my wife would have the same rights as me regarding spending our money. When it is spent, and what it is spent on!**

Vignette 13

The Lesson of the Dance

When I was fifteen, a big dance was approaching in September. It was the end of summer, "Back to School Dance." My friend Tommy and I excitedly looked forward and started planning for the dance in the middle of the summer. We coordinated our dress, cologne, and dance moves. My goal and plans were to "catch" the prettiest girl at the dance. At the time, I was reasonably good-looking, a good student, a recognized and accomplished athlete excelling in baseball and football, with good manners, and showed courtesy and respect to all. Also, my dad had taught me how to fistfight and protect myself and my sisters. Therefore, with all things considered, I had the respect of friends and acquaintances in all my peer group social circles, including the hoods or hoodlums (we didn't have any "gangs"). My parents and family were well respected, and they taught me to respect myself and others. Never put anyone down, make fun of them, or laugh at derogatory jokes about anyone. In reverse, my parents taught me not to let others bully or put me down and what to do if it occurred. My social skills were enhanced and matured from my three years of debutante balls participation and etiquette training and my membership and involvement in the Sophisticates young men's gentlemen's club. This helped me be confident, well-known, and accepted by all my peer social groups. I was keenly aware of my confidence and comfort around all people, whether boys and girls or men and women.

As the dance date grew eminent and my interest and enthusiasm grew, Tommy was at our house one day, and he and I were discussing the dance in the living room. I told him how I would conquer the prettiest girl at the dance, boasting in a very confident braggadocio manner. The dance was two weeks off, and I was already primed, locked, and loaded. My purpose and directives were clear to me. My sight and focus were primed on the prettiest, most gorgeous, vivacious girl there. I was "going in for the kill." As I was talking to Tommy, suddenly I looked to my side and saw my dad looking at us. He had this very attentive, earnest look on his face. I hadn't noticed him earlier, but from the look on his face, our conversation caught his attention and drew him in to hear more. When I saw him, I wondered if he wanted something or needed me to do something for him. So I paused and looked at him, expecting a command or a question. I couldn't imagine anything in our conversation that would have grabbed his interest or scrutiny. I paused and waited for him to speak, but he said nothing. So I assumed that he didn't want anything or needed me to do anything. Therefore, I placed my attention back on Tommy and continued talking. Pop left shortly after without saying anything to me, and I didn't think about it anymore.

On the day of the dance, all my plans came together. I had gotten permission to ride with some of my older Sophisticates Club brothers. Tommy was at the house and going to the dance with my club brothers and me. We were dressed perfectly, with our cologne properly applied and ready to conquer. As we left the house and went out the back door, my dad called me, saying, "Robert, come here." I told Tommy to go on, and I would join him and the guys at the car in a minute. My dad was in the living room by himself. As I met him in the middle of the room, he approached me face-to-face. He looked me square in my eyes about three inches away and said, "When you get to the dance, there will be some girls there who no one will have asked to dance for some reason or another. They may be ugly, fat, have acne, or just be unattractive. They may be known for having a bad attitude, being unpopular for some reason, or being strange or different. However, they will not have been asked to dance for whatever reason. We used to call them wallflowers. They, however, are there to enjoy themselves and have fun, just like you and the others. I want you to ask one of them to dance!"

When I heard Dad say that, I thought, *I know I didn't hear what I think I just heard.* Then I seriously looked at my father and saw his eyes focused sternly on me. I thought, *He did say what I heard. Dad has gone mad! This man is mad and out of his mind.* I didn't even see Pop as my dad anymore for those seconds. I in no way said it, but in my mind, the description of what he had just said to me brought up a bold, manly thought from deep inside me. What came to me was "From where in Hades did this come? I can't even imagine a thought like this. From where in Hades did it come? Pop has got to know who I am and that what he is asking me to do is social suicide. He can't be that ignorant of who I am. He's been around me long enough and interfaced with my friends long enough to know who I am. This man is insane. What has happened to him?"

Then Dad spoke again. "You only have to dance with her once. But when the dance is over, don't leave her on the floor and walk away from her. Instead, escort her back to her chair, help her sit down, and thank her for the dance." As I heard Dad's last words, I continued thinking, *He is mad and insane! How did this happen?* He then asked if I understood what he said. I replied that I did and walked away with a giant piano on my back. A few minutes ago, I was happy, elated, and full of joy, hope, expectation, and enthusiasm. In less than five minutes, all of that was now gone. It was completely gone. I was now carrying a hefty weight. All my thoughts and accompanying emotions were *What will my friends think of me? What are the pretty girls going to think of me? They'll all see me as weird, strange, a loser, and I will lose their respect. It's social suicide what Dad's asked me to do.* Then feeling sympathetic for myself, my final thoughts as I turned and walked away from Dad were *Man! Why is Pop doing me like this?*

When I got to the car, my friends were exuberant, laughing, playing, and full of excitement, joy, and anticipation like I was five minutes earlier. I sat far away from them in the backseat, mentally and emotionally. All I felt was the weight my father had just placed on my back. The joy of the dance was all gone from me, and my night was now ruined.

When we got to the dance, I tried to enjoy it as best as I could, but I was miserable knowing that at some time, I would have to do what Dad said to do. With my parents, everything was for a reason and an intended purpose. When I was younger, every spanking I received from Dad was preceded by a description of what I did wrong—followed by his request and demand for feedback and acknowledgment of what I did and why my action (or inaction) was wrong. Then finally, my explanation of why I wouldn't do it again before he spanked my rear to seal the deal. With Dad, everything was a lesson—a "teaching," an intended experience with a purpose. I never got out of a teachable moment, and if I didn't get out of a lesson what Pop expected, I could be sure another lesson was coming down the pike with the same intended purpose. But as I had painfully learned from personal experience, that second time around was very likely to be a far worse or more difficult challenge than the first time. Therefore, I learned quickly, without question, to obey the first time. The same principles applied to a chore or job I was directed to do. I knew to do it right the first time, or my life would stop, including my time to play with friends, sports, recreation, TV, and nap time until the job was done right to Dad's satisfaction.

Whatever the case, I learned quickly not to play games with commands, instructions, or assignments given to me. The loud and simplistic message to me was "Robert, do it right! Do it right the first time, for your sake and benefit!" Thus, there was no question in my mind that I would obey my Pop's command. I was going to comply with no additional queries in my mind. I would not return home, face my father, and say I didn't do it. No way would I allow myself to see an expression for my disobedience on Dad's face or hear the "roar of his words" that would follow and penetrate my ears. "No way!"

However, as the dance went on and approached the halfway point, the piano on my back got heavier and heavier, and it was getting harder and harder for me to get my will up to do what Pop told me to do. Therefore, I stopped procrastinating and scanned the dance floor to find the girls Pop had described. The girls that no one had asked to dance for whatever reason. I noticed those girls were gradually collecting or forced to one perimeter corner of the dance floor. They were on the other side of the dance floor from where my friends and I were. As I continued watching, my fear, that is, my fear of rejection by the pretty girls and my fear of being put down and mocked by my friends and other boys, continued to grow. It was becoming increasingly difficult for me to get over the hump and act on what I knew I had to do. Before it became impossible for me to move, I stopped thinking about what would happen to me and my reputation. I pushed past my emotions, mentally ate, and accepted the inevitable consequences of my task at hand.

To help me, I scanned my mind for experiences similar to what I was about to do. As I did, I thought of my baseball and football experiences. I compared my dance situation with the pressure of being at bat, with the game on the line, at the bottom of the ninth inning. Or similarly being given the football, with time running out and our need to score a touchdown to win. Thinking of those experiences and how I performed was monumental in getting me "off the dime."

I selected the girl who I was going to ask for a dance. When the music started, I walked across the floor to her position. Even today, that was the longest walk I've ever taken. I felt like every eye, especially the pretty girl's eyes and the eyes of those who very much respected me, was on me. My heart was pounding thump-thump, and I was sweating profusely all over my body as I very self-consciously walked to the girl I selected. As I approached her, I noticed a couple of other girls out of the corner of my eye, hoping that I was coming to them. I remember being very careful not to make eye contact with them because I didn't want to give them a false expectation. I had decided who I was going to ask. As I approached the girl of my choice, she helped me a lot because her face lit up as she noticed my approach. She gave me a beautiful smile and appeared very pleased that I chose her for a dance when I walked up and pleasantly asked for her hand.

On the dance floor, I still felt that everyone's eyes were on me and that they had now gotten bigger, fully dilated, with their mouths widely opened in surprise and unbelief. My sweat and fear were pouring out of me. My mind was working a thousand miles an hour. I wondered again why my father did me like this. I struggled immensely from the fear of peer pressure and rejection that I had placed on myself—besides my self-inflicted thoughts of being highly embarrassed in front of the pretty girls I wanted to attract, take my pick of, and swoop up.

I could feel the fear and its incredible intensity as we danced on the floor. However, into that dance, I noticed something at about the halfway point. My thinking started to change. I thought, *Since I had already embarrassed myself and my reputation was blown, I might as well conquer this fear and get out of this experience whatever Dad wanted me to get out of it.* So I pushed aside my fear and embarrassment and immediately settled down emotionally; my thoughts began to sober as I did. I then realized what initiated Dad's instructions to me. He heard me, his son enormously puffed up with pride, talking about the prettiest of the pretty girls that I was going after and would conquer.

My self-aggrandizement proclamation that "I'm going in for the kill." That expression and the tone in which I said it implied that I was not the "lion," but I was, first and foremost, "the lion king, king of the jungle." I am the king of lions on the prowl for the choicest "game" of the land. As I considered what I said to Tommy, I perceived Dad's assignment motive in those few moments on the dance floor. On no uncertain terms, after hearing me, would Dad allow me to be cloaked in my own selfish and self-centered world, being unaware and uncaring about the needs of others. His concern was that in whatever state I come across people, like at the dance, I was to give them proper consideration and respect, whoever they were. Society's rejection and devaluation of people were not to be mine.

I started seeing the lesson in Dad's instructions. I could not ignore people or look past them, seeing only my goal and what I wanted, which I boastfully described to Tommy as my purpose. As I settled down emotionally, what Dad's lesson was about and his intended message became more and more apparent. Pop was saying to me, "You're not as great as you think you are. Nor are you as smart as you think you are. Nor are you as important, suave, sophisticated, and debonair as you think you are. Nor are you all that, whatever all that is, you think you are!"

I got it! I finally got the meaning of the lesson and what Pop intended. Maybe he didn't go temporarily insane after all. Perhaps the thought of what he told me to do was not from the pit of Hades. Maybe Pop saw more than I saw. After thinking those thoughts, my attitude changed. I pleasantly felt some joy, hope, and excitement come over me when it did. I then asked my partner for a second dance when the current song ended. I thought, *The first dance was for Pop; the second is for me. I've already been embarrassed, and my reputation has been shattered. I now need to face and conquer all my fears of peer pressure, acceptance, and rejection. I need to get all I am supposed to get out of this lesson so that I don't have to go through it again.* After our second dance, I did just as Pop said. I politely walked my partner back to her seat, helped her sit, and thanked her. As I turned and walked back across the dance floor to where my friends were, I felt again that it was an incredibly long walk and that every eye was still on me. When I got to where my friends were and walked up to them, they didn't then or ever mention what I did. But instead, Tommy and the rest of my friends didn't look me in the face; they just turned their backs and quietly walked away from me.

Interestingly, however, as they walked away, their body language was "Wow! I respect you, man! I wish I had the courage and guts to do what you just did!" After they walked away, I felt no rejection and no embarrassment whatsoever. Instead, I felt an enormous release of pressure and joy. I felt like a "real man," a conqueror. It was a high I had never experienced before. It was better than scoring a winning touchdown or scoring the winning run in a baseball playoff game. I did what my father told me to do. I obeyed him even when I didn't want to. I felt like I had conquered my fear of people and what people thought of me. I did the right thing. I did the absolute right deed. I didn't reject that girl because of what other people thought of her. Instead, I placed the same value on her as I put on myself. Regardless of what others thought of her or viewed her, I asked her for a dance. Daddy was right to make me get out of my self-centeredness and take notice of someone else.

The piano was off my back. My joy and exuberance were now ten times greater than before my dad called me to himself in our living room. I was *happy,* and I thoroughly enjoyed the rest of the dance and evening. When I got home, I purposed to act like what I did was no big deal. First, I talked to my mom and sister, Karen, in the kitchen. Then just as I heard my dad call me earlier from the living room, he called me again. I went in to see him as if I were cool, calm, and collected, as if what he had asked me to do was no big thing.

When I got to the middle of the living room, Pop came up to me face-to-face, just like before. Then he looked me eye-to-eye. This time, however, I saw doubt in his eyes and face. Clearly, he was uncertain about whether I had obeyed him. Finally, he said, "Did you do what I told you to do?" I couldn't contain my joy from submitting to Pop's will. My pleasure and the explosive satisfaction of acting like a "real man" of character. A man of courage. All forced a bright booming smile to come over my face as I looked Pop in his eyes and said, "Yes, I did!" Then I found out that nothing, I mean absolutely nothing, is like pleasing your father, satisfying your dad. When I saw my father's pleasure and affirmation of me, I knew what joy was! I had never known or felt joy and happiness like that before. Nothing I experienced in sports, on my birthday, or at Christmas, opening a gift compared to it. It was like I've heard people say, "It was joy, unspeakable." I'll never forget it!

My Takeaway

- **I'm not as great as I think I am!**
- **Life is not all about me. I am to take notice that there are people with needs that I can help fulfill.**
- **I am not to disregard or overlook others who have been or are being mistreated or rejected.**
- **Obedience to your parents truly does bring absolute joy and appreciation to your life.**

Vignette 14

The Lesson of the Dance

Sequel: I Never Learned My Father's Intended Message from the Lesson of the Dance

About six years ago, I taught an "Introduction to Space" class to boys twelve to fifteen years old enrolled in our church's Rites of Passage (ROP) Program. Unfortunately, unexpected audiovisual changes to my assigned classroom required me and others, for the entire class period, to quietly work on resolving the issues before the next class was to start. To fill my time slot, another ROP village elder (VE) provided an impromptu but timely and appropriate topic message to the boys as we resolved the audiovisual issues. Toward the end of my scheduled class time, Irving Tolbert, ROP program chairman, and Jack Lightsy, program director, suddenly, surprisingly, and enthusiastically rushed into our classroom to close out the class by offering a $1 reward for each correct answer given by a boy on that day's lesson. However, after being informed that my planned class did not occur, Irving immediately asked me to share a story with the boys. After hearing my story, he would give $1 to each boy who first correctly answered a question I would ask from the story. Quickly, off the top of my head, or more likely from the Lord. The "Lesson of the Dance" I received from my father when I was the boys' age came to mind. After sharing my story and completing Irving's following question and answer reward session, suddenly and very loudly, Jack shouted a question I had never considered. He asked me, "What happened to the girl?" Namely, the girl I had walked across the floor and asked for a dance.

Although Jack didn't know it, his question totally caught me off guard. I sensed my deer-in-the-headlights look, which he couldn't see because of the distance between us. But he could see my dumbfounded, open-mouth, loss-of-words response. Thus, he asked me again, "What happened to the girl?" I still didn't have a reply, so my mouth remained silently open. To be sure, his question blew me away, placing me in la-la land. I was in the mental state of plainly understanding his question but could not articulate or release an audible response.

After what appeared to me to be a long, quiet pause while Jack and others waited for me to answer. Irving then shouted, also from the back of the room, "Did you marry her?" My mouth became operational again, and I could answer his question with a clear, affirmative no! I very much appreciated Irving getting me off the hook. But it didn't get me out of the hot water.

The Lord did a poker "call" on me with Jack's question. He metaphorically "called" me on the poker hand I was holding. Jack had no idea what was happening in the spirit realm or that God had used him to "expose" me. God, my Heavenly Father, decided to take that moment and expose an aspect of my blindness. He made the "call," now it was time for me to "show my hand." That is, for my heart to be brought to light as God saw it. Jack's question was a "CAT scan" of my heart that provided a clear image. I saw clearly how deceptively subtle and unbeneficial to others my selfishness was. I then recognized that I never got the "Lesson of the Dance" my dad attempted to get into me.

I don't know what happened to the girl! After our dance, she never crossed my mind again!

She wasn't a concern to me. All that was important to me was my fear, embarrassment, and thoughts of what the pretty girls and my peers would think of me. Not about the person, the girl, my father told me to ask for a dance. Dad wanted me to see her! To see her as a living person who also desired attention and consideration even though she was not the prettiest, shapeliest, most popular, or whatever else. He wanted me to learn to be attentive and sensitive to others' needs and desires. To recognize that not everybody is pretty, socially acceptable, or a part of the "norm" and I was not to overlook or be blind to anyone, including those who were not. Instead, I was to pay attention to those on the outside looking in and give them proper and just recognition, treatment, and respect, even if it meant going out of my way. Irrespective of what others thought or the inconvenience to me.

The Lord's conviction brightly pointed out my self-centeredness through Jack's question. Not since the end of that dance had I thought about that girl. I took my dad's lesson as being all about me, about my obedience to him, and my resistance to peer pressure, embarrassment, and rejection. Pop, however, wanted me to see others besides myself. To recognize that others might need a helping hand from me, and I should not be blind to that nor look away and ignore them or their need for me.

As I thought, I remembered seeing the uneasiness on Dad's face when I returned home, and he called me back into our living room. His concern had switched to whether I had obeyed him. I believe Pop realized after he gave me my predance instructions, and I left his presence, heading to the dance. My challenge was going to be whether I obeyed him. That is why his first words to me after I returned home were "Did you do what I told you to do?" Dad had come down to my level and accepted my obedience as my lesson learned. However, my compliance was not his initial concern or his intended purpose. From my history of obeying him, that was a given. But it appears Dad adapted to what he perceived in me and accepted what I could give him then. It was similar to how Jesus took what Peter could give him when the Lord wanted Peter to love Him unconditionally (agape). But Peter could only brotherly (phileo) love Him (Ref: John 21:15–17 TPW).

My Takeaway

- I never learned the lesson Dad intended me to learn from "the Lesson of the Dance." My heart was just not there yet.
- It took more than five decades of growth and God using someone to point out my blindness and selfishness for me to finally see and understand that life is not all about me!
- Although I didn't get it when I was fifteen years old, I've grown to be more sensitive and observant of others.

Vignette 15

Speaking to Dad, Mom, and Authority Figures

Dad told my siblings and me, "You can say anything you want to your mother and me as long as you approach us properly and speak in the proper attitude, tone, and manner." Implied in this was we also had to speak to them at the proper time. For example, attempting to speak or question them when they told us to do something was inappropriate. This permission to approach them was huge for me because it took away all my pent-up frustration and anger over any decision they made that I didn't like. For example, my sisters and I had a party at home when we were teenagers. I was driving then, and just before the party started, some of my Sophisticates Club brothers called me and asked me to pick them up and bring them back to the party. They were older than me, and I felt they were using me a little. But simultaneously, I felt somewhat honored that they asked me. I was now at their level. I told them I would leave to pick them up after getting permission from my dad to use the car. With no doubt in my mind, I told Dad of my friends' request and asked if I could use the car to pick them up and return to the party. Pop said no! I responded in shock. He said again no! I explained what it would look like if I couldn't pick them up. His answer still was no!

At sixteen years old, I went to my bedroom and cried like a baby in frustration at the thought of my embarrassment and the idea of my friends thinking that I was still a little boy needing his daddy's permission. As I cried, I knelt and prayed, explaining to the Lord what had happened. He brought what Dad had repeatedly told us to my mind, but I had never exercised before. "You can say anything you want to your mother and me as long as you do it in the proper attitude, tone, and manner." I don't remember thanking the Lord for reminding me of what

Dad had so often told us. However, with the answer to my dilemma, in hope, I got up off my knees and started thinking about what I would say to Pop. I began deeply thinking and walking back and forth in my bedroom, pondering the words I wanted to say to Dad. As I did, I came out of my frustration. I also stopped thinking about the embarrassment I would feel if I gave my friends and club brothers a negative answer to their request. I additionally took the time to release my anger. I kept thinking, *My words have to be right! My attitude has to be right! My tone and mannerisms have to be right!* Finally, I came up with my words and spoke them to myself repeatedly until I felt comfortable with them. I then rehearsed them in a low voice until I could hear my attitude, tone, and manner were OK. When I reached the proper state, I bolted out of my bedroom to find Dad. He was in our family room.

Then I said to him, "Dad, did you mean what you said when you said that *we can say anything we want to you and Mom as long as we do it in the proper attitude, tone, and manner?"* He looked me in my eyes, walked right up to me, nose-to-nose, and said yes! I told him how unfair his decision was and why I thought it was unfair. I then asked him to rethink his answer and consider my reasons for borrowing the car to pick up my friends. After speaking my mind to him clearly and distinctly, I stopped talking. After a short pause, Pop said, "Are you finished?" I said that I was. Pop said without justification or rationalization, "My answer is still no! You can't go and pick them up!"

To my amazement, I said, "OK," without any ill feelings or anger. Then I respectfully thanked Dad and dismissed myself from his presence to call my friends and give them my answer. What amazed me was how I took Pop's no! There was no rebellion, anger, frustration, or concern about embarrassment as I turned and walked to the phone. On the phone call, I did not dis my father, throw him under the bus, put the blame on him, curse him, or say or imply anything disrespectful of him. Instead, in a responsible, grown-up way, I let them know that I could not pick them up and that they would have to get another ride to the party. They acknowledged my answer and said that they would find another way.

I felt OK about Dad's final decision because I got a fair "trial." Dad, as the judge, patiently heard me. He gave me his full and undivided attention as I explained my case. He considered my reasons, and they still fell short of convincing him of their superiority to his first consideration for saying no to my request. Dad, my father, had responsibility for me. From the time I could understand, throughout my youth and teenage years, it was clear that he and Mom made the final decisions for my life until I was out of the house and on my own. Therefore, I had no problem accepting his conclusive no!

In examining my response, I felt that my anger and frustration after Dad's first series of no's was due to me thinking my request was reasonable. Although I felt I was being used a bit by my friends, I still felt there was no reason to deny or reject their request. When the Lord brought to my attention what Dad had told us repeatedly for years, it gave me a way out of my frustration and "dead end." It did the trick. It allowed me to state my case to the "judge" respectfully. After I did, all my negative emotions and thoughts were gone. I could and did accept Pop's no in peace.

My Sophisticates Club brothers did arrive at the party shortly after I turned down their request to pick them up. Sometime after they had integrated into the party, Pop was observant and came to me, pulling me aside and pointing out several things I had also noticed. One was that my friends did successfully find another way to the party. Two was that they had no ill feelings or issues with me, and three, they had fully acclimated and were enjoying themselves and their interaction with me with no resentful feelings. As we briefly talked, he told me why he said no to me leaving the house to pick them up. His reason was they were using me and putting something on me that was their responsibility. They were grown and mature enough to find another way to the party. I was cohost of the party with my sisters. My duty and responsibility were to greet our guests and support my sisters. I appreciated Dad pulling me off to the side and talking to me. It was good to hear his no was not him being harsh, mean, or inflexible, but his way of caring for me. He was helping me understand that I needed to say no to people who attempted to use or take advantage of me. That is, people who would try to pull me away from my responsibilities to take on theirs or take on a care or burden of theirs, as in this specific instance.

It was an outstanding lesson and experience, and I've always remembered it. It has helped me on more than one occasion to say no to someone's unreasonable or irrational request that is not in wisdom, common sense, my ability to supply, or in my family's best interest. It has also caused me to think and ask myself before supporting someone's requests. Whether fulfilling it will negatively impact my commitments or jeopardize my budget, provisions, time, or other necessary resources dedicated to my family or me. It was a simple but excellent life tutorial.

Additively, it was a lesson that alerted me to my responsibility to respectfully challenge those in authority who deny a reasonable request from me or levy what I consider a questionable demand on me or others.

My Takeaway

- I can say anything I want to my parents and any authority as long as I do it with respect at an appropriate time, with the proper attitude, tone, and manner.
- Think before I commit to supporting someone's requests of me.
  - Are they using me as a tool to do something they should do for themselves?
  - Will their request negatively impact or put at risk my current responsibilities and commitments?
  - Does their request place a significant imposition on my family or me?
- It's my responsibility to respectfully approach those in authority regarding any questionable request they make of me, an issue I have with them, their leadership, or an assignment given to me.

Conclusion

What I have written in this book is my recall of the Lord's sovereign claim on me as my Creator, Redeemer, and Father and the process He used through my parents to bring me to Himself. In reviewing my life as recorded in this book, I readily accept the Jewish sages' precept that there are three partners in every human being's life: God, their father, and their mother. Through this triune partnership, God established how I was raised, taught, trained, instructed, and corrected throughout my upbringing. His purpose was to bring me to Himself for my edification and the fulfillment of His glory, purpose, and will in creating me. God's triune partnership with my parents brought about my conception, birth, teaching, training, instruction, and correction. All of which have resulted in the man and person I am today.

As my firsthand recollection, description, and account of God's triune partnership with my parents, this book described how He worked His unique plan for me through my father and mother. All while behind the scenes, He quietly shepherded and directed my paths in life from birth. A process He worked to bring me to obedience and love for Him with all my heart, soul, mind, and strength (effort and might).

God's direction and interaction with me through my parents was the same method He instructed the Old Testament Israelite parents to use in Deuteronomy 11:19 and 21. In paraphrase, God instructed the Israelite parents "to teach His Words to their children, speaking of them when they sat in their houses, walked by the way, laid down, and arose. So that their days and their children's days would be multiplied in the land of which the LORD swore to Abraham, Issac, and Jacob to give them."

In that very same manner, my parents, as a couplet, taught me life's lessons and God's principles *by teaching, instructing, and talking about them when we sat at home, when we walked or rode in the car together, before we laid down and went to sleep at night, and when we arose from sleep and got up.* They taught me as an aspect of the normal flow of life when an opportunistic situation presented itself. From this book's panoramic view of my life from childhood to my adulthood threshold, it is crystal clear that the Lord was and is, in fact, my Shepherd. He continuously directed my paths through my parents, uncles and aunts, teachers, life experiences, and circumstances.

Like my brother Daryl's female high school classmate told him at their latest high school reunion (part 2, vignette 8). I recognize that some who read this book will say, *Robert, I didn't come from a balanced, loving, couplet father/mother nuclear family like you did. I wish I did have the upbringing and parentage you had. I wish my parents had been like the parents God gave you, but they weren't.* I came from:

- a non-father matrifocal single working mother family, or
- a physical and verbally abusive father or mother family, or
- a sexually assaulting, immoral, incestuous, pedophilia parental family, or
- a father/mother drug/alcoholic, unbalanced and dysfunctional family, or
- a poor, highly needful, full of lack, poverty-dominated family, or
- a self-absorbed work, career, money-first, family-second parentage or
- a non-family: I was an orphan or foster child raised without any relationship with my birth parents, or
- a . . . family

I therefore knowing that these parent-child dysfunctional relationships are unfortunately true for so many people. And no one knows why God allows such bad and evil things, out of one's control, to happen to them. However, that being the case, I'd like to say to those who have come from such relationships, who don't know God and have not received His love and healing, nor have they not been able to forgive their parents. I'm encouraged to tell you that God, your Creator, exceedingly loves you and wants to heal you of your wounds and trauma. He saw and knows everything you've gone through and every emotional, traumatic, and physical need you have. He wants to bring you to Himself as your heavenly Father. In His abundant love for you, He greatly desires to comfort and heal you of your hurt, emotional, and personal lack; and supply your every need according to His riches. Recognize, therefore, that God, through His Son Jesus, wants to and is able to do exceedingly abundantly above all that you ask and allow Him to do for you.

Because of what you have gone through and endured, if you have doubts about God's love and concern for you. Or whether or not He is a good God. Or you are holding a grudge against God, angry with Him, and holding Him accountable for what has occurred to you with the selection of your parents, life's circumstances, your upbringing, or anything else in your life. Or for something of high importance that you asked Him for but you didn't get. Consider that Christianity is not a religion but a very personal Father-son-and-daughter relationship with God through Jesus Christ. As such, I strongly suggest that with respect and sincerity, in the proper attitude and tone, you talk to God at length honestly about your feelings and thoughts of Him. In your call to God, recognize that He hears you as you speak to Him openly, candidly, and prayerfully. After you have said all that you desire to say, be patient and take the time to listen and hear His response and any leading He gives you through His Word, the Bible.

In addition, if you have not accepted Jesus as your Savior, acknowledge that per the Biblical description of you as a sinner, "lost," and in need of a Savior. Accept what John 3:16 and 4:6 say: Jesus is the Savior of all who believe in Him. He is the only way to God, the only One who can forgive your sin and give you eternal life. He is the only One who can heal your heart and your wounds of life. If you call on God sincerely, Scripture guarantees your salvation and healing as you trust and submit to Him. For Scripture says,

> For "whoever calls upon the name of the Lord shall be saved." (Rom. 10:13)

How do you effectively call on the Lord for salvation? Scripture tells us how.

> That if you confess with your mouth the Lord Jesus and believe in your heart that God has raised Him from the dead, you will be saved. For with the heart one believes to righteousness, and with the mouth confession is made to salvation. (Rom. 10:9-10)

For your salvation, healing, and restoration, accept Jesus into your heart by faith and confess to yourself and others that Jesus is alive and who the Bible says He is. Namely, He is God "Incarnate" (the Son of God in the flesh) sent by God to die on the cross for you, whom God later raised from the dead.

In short, confess with your mouth what God has told you to believe in your heart, and you shall be saved and your hurts and wounds of life healed as you, through God's grace, forgive those who offended you!

Your brother,
Robert
October 22, 2024

Notes

Preface

1   The Stone Edition, the Chumash, p. 411, Exodus 20:12, 12. "Fifth Commandment: Honoring Parents," Rabbi Nosson Scherman/Rabbi Meir Zlotowitz, ArtScroll Mesorah Publications, Ltd, 11th ed., March 2000–December 2014.

2   "Testament of Noah," Dead Sea Scrolls, 1Q20, column 6, "Ancient Testaments of the Patriarchs," by Ken Johnson, ThD, 2017.

Introduction

1   The Stone Edition, the Chumash, p. 411, Exodus 20:12, 12. "Fifth Commandment: Honoring Parents," Rabbi Nosson Scherman/Rabbi Meir Zlotowitz, ArtScroll Mesorah Publications, Ltd, 11th ed., March 2000–December 2014.

Part 1: Lessons from My Mother

Vignette 4
1   *Little Shop of Horrors,* "Feed Me, Seymour," movie clip, https://www.youtube.com/watch?v=L7SkrYF8lCU.

Vignette 7
2   "The Sad Story of Ahithophel: Wisdom Destroyed by Bitterness," https://www.calvarychapeljonesboro.org/articles/the-sad-story-of-ahithophel-wisdom-destroyed-by-bitterness.

3   "Judgement of the Nephilim," chapter 3, pp. 35–47, Ryan Patterson, Days of Noah Publishing, NY, NY, 2017.

4   The Stone Edition, the Chumash, p. 27, Genesis 6:1–2, 2, "The Sons of the Rulers," Rabbi Nosson Scherman/Rabbi Meir Zlotowitz, ArtScroll Mesorah Publications, Ltd, 11th ed., March 2000–December 2014.

5   Donald Trump *Access Hollywood* video, https://www.youtube.com/watch?v=NcZcTnykYbw.

Vignette 8

6   October 2012, "Brazilian Auction of Virginity for $780,000; Man for $3,000," http://www.nydailynews.com/news/world/brazil-woman-sells-virginity-780k-online-article-1.1190958.

7   American Institute for Economic Research (AIER) Cost of Living Calculator, https://www.aier.org/cost-of-living-calculator/.

8A   Havocscope Global Black Market Information, "Prostitution Revenue Worldwide," https://www.havocscope.com/prostitution-revenue-by-country/3809085/.

8B   "A Havocscope Report: Black Market Crime, "Prostitution: Prices and Statistics of the Global Sex Trade," Havocscope E-Book, 2015, Amazon.com.

9   List of Global 2022 Largest Companies by Revenue (Note: Data updated on link annually), https://en.wikipedia.org/wiki/List_of_largest_companies_by_revenue.

10   "Strange but True," February 19, 2017, "How Big Is the Porn Industry?" https://medium.com/@Strange_bt_True/how-big-is-the-porn-industry-fbc1ac78091b.

11   "Aileen Wuornos Biography," https://www.thefamouspeople.com/profiles/aileen-wuornos-4113.php.

Vignette 9

12   *Woman Thou Art Loosed,* chapter 6, Bishop TD Jakes, Treasure House Publisher, 1993.

Vignette 10

13   *Ken and Bob Radio Show,* KABC, LA, CA, https://www.latimes.com/archives/la-xpm-1997-04-05-mn-45640-story.html.

Vignette 12

14   African Methodist Episcopal Church (AME), "Sticks and Stones" adage, https://en.wikipedia.org/wiki/Sticks_and_Stones.

Vignette 14

15   Television Series, Card: *Have Gun–Will Travel,* starring Richard Boone, https://en.wikipedia.org/wiki/Have_Gun_%E2%80%93_Will_Travel.

16   1875 to 2023 Inflation Calculator, https://www.in2013dollars.com/us/inflation/1875?amount=1000.

Vignette 15

17 Jake Abbott (Frank J.) Dodgers minor league player; Roosevelt High School baseball coach, https://www.baseball-reference.com/register/player.fcgi?id=abbott001fra.

Vignette 20

18 The Stone Edition, the Chumash, p. 411, Exodus 20:12, 12. "Fifth Commandment: Honoring Parents," Rabbi Nosson Scherman/Rabbi Meir Zlotowitz, ArtScroll Mesorah Publications, Ltd, 11th ed., March 2000–December 2014.

Vignette 21

19 Jesus's Crucifixion Described in Graphic Detail by Physician in Lee Strobel's book *The Case for Christ,* by Kevin Porter, *Christian Post Reporter,* October 31, 2016, https://www.christianpost.com/news/jesus-crucifixion-described-graphic-detail-physician-lee-strobels-book-the-case-for-christ.html.

Part 2: Lessons from My Father

Vignette 2

1 Caryl Chessman, https://www.britannica.com/biography/Chessman-Caryl.

Vignette 5

2 Vikings' Adrian Peterson Accused of Child Abuse https://www.usatoday.com/story/sports/nfl/2014/09/13/vikings-adrian-peterson-accused-of-child-abuse/15537665/.

Vignette 6

3 "Jefferson's Attitudes toward Slavery," Thomas Jefferson, Monticello, https://www.monticello.org/thomas-jefferson/jefferson-slavery/jefferson-s-attitudes-toward-slavery/.

4 "Washington's Changing Views on Slavery," https://www.mountvernon.org/george-washington/slavery/washingtons-changing-views-on-slavery/.

5A George Washington's Decision to Free His Slaves, https://www.mountvernon.org/george-washington/slavery/washingtons-1799-will/.

5B George Washington's Last Will and Testament, July 9, 1799, https://www.mountvernon.org/education/primary-sources-2/article/george-washingtons-last-will-and-testament-july-9-1799/.

6 Strom Thurmond, 1948 Presidential Candidacy Speech, https://www.quotetab.com/quote/by-strom-thurmond/i-wanna-tell-you-ladies-and-gentlemen-that-theres-not-enough-troops-in-the-arm.

7 "Monticello Affirms Thomas Jefferson Fathered Children with Sally Hemings," https://www.monticello.org/thomas-jefferson/jefferson-slavery/thomas-jefferson-and-sally-hemings-a-brief-account/monticello-affirms-thomas-jefferson-fathered-children-with-sally-hemings/.

7 "Strom Thurmond's Black Daughter: A Symbol of America's Complicated Racial History," Mary C. Curtis, February 5, 2013, the *Washington Post.* https://www.washingtonpost.com/blogs/she-the-people/wp/2013/02/05/strom-thurmonds-black-daughter-a-flesh-and-blood-symbol-of-americas-complicated-racial-history/.

9 "Oldest Institution of Southern Baptist Convention Reveals Past Ties to Slavery," Adeel Hassan, December 12, 2018, the *New York Times,* https://www.nytimes.com/2018/12/12/us/southern-baptist-slavery.html.

10 "11 A.M. Sunday Is Our Most Segregated Hour," Kyle Haselden, *New York Times,* August 2, 1964 https://www.nytimes.com/1964/08/02/archives/11-a-m-sunday-is-our-most-segregated-hour-in-the-light-of-the.html.

11A From the "Princeton & Slavery" project. Princeton and Slavery: Holding the Center, Martha A. Sandweiss and Craig Hollander, https://slavery.princeton.edu/stories/princeton-and-slavery-holding-the-center.

11B PBS, *The Underground Railroad,* https://www.pbs.org/wgbh/aia/part4/4p2944.html.

11C History Channel, *The Underground Railroad,* https://www.history.com/topics/black-history/underground-railroad.

12 John Rankin (Abolitionist) https://en.wikipedia.org/wiki/John_Rankin_(abolitionist).

13 Moses and the Kushite Woman: Classic Interpretations and Philo's Allegory, TheTorah.com, https://www.thetorah.com/article/moses-and-the-kushite-woman-classic-interpretations-and-philos-allegory.

14 Septuagint Quotes in the New Testament, Scripture Catholic https://www.scripturecatholic.com/septuagint-quotes-new-testament/.

15A Google Books: Moses' Ethiopian Wife: Josephus, the Complete Works, book 2, chapter 10, https://books.google.com/books?id=kyaolb6k2ccC&pg=PA145&lpg=PA145&dq=Josephus+miriam+rebellion&source=bl&ots=HSVyGSCCUa&sig=ACf

U3U2OZ-BPmUOcxQf77wK4-27G9QYT3Q&hl=en&sa=X&-ved=2ahUKEwjigoHL8rznAhVkNn0KHSrvB-4Q6AEwDnoECAoQAQ#v=onepage&q=Josephus%20miriam%20rebellion&f=false.

15B Book: Moses' Ethiopian Wife: Josephus, the Complete Works, book 2, chapter 10, translated by William Whiston, AM, Thomas Nelson Publishers, 1998.

16 Systematic Theology, 2nd ed., part 3: The Doctrine of Man in the Image of God, chapter 21, The Creation of Man, p. 575, Zondervan Academic, 2020.

Vignette 7

17 "Rude Awakening on Racism Gave Minister New Mission," Teresa Watanabe, Los Angeles Times, July 25, 1999, https://www.latimes.com/archives/la-xpm-1999-jul-25-mn-59449-story.html.

18 Book Series: Race Religion and Racism, Fredrick K. C. Price, DD, Faith One Publishing, Los Angeles.

19 Death Toll from the Slave Trade, the African Holocaust, 60 Million Dead at the Hands of White Christian Imperialism, World Future Fund, http://www.worldfuturefund.org/Reports/Slavedeathtoll/slavery deathtoll.html.

20 New Estimate Raises Civil War Death Toll, Guy Gugliotta, April 2, 2012, the New York Times, https://www.nytimes.com/2012/04/03/science/civil-war-toll-up-by-20-percent-in-new-estimate.html.

21 Restoring the Union, US History II (OS Collection), ER Services, https://courses.lumenlearning.com/suny-ushistory2os2xmaster/chapter/restoring-the-union/.

22 "The 11 Most Racist US Presidents," Ibram X. Kendi, contributor, updated May 28, 2017, HuffPost, https://www.huffpost.com/entry/would-a-president-trump-m_b_10135836.

23 "List of Ethnic Groups in the United States by Household Income," https://en.wikipedia.org/wiki/List_of_ethnic_groups_in_the_United_States_by_household_income.

24 Educational Attainment in the United States, https://en.wikipedia.org/wiki/Educational_attainment_in_the_United_States.

25 Southern Baptist Convention. Resolution Strongly Opposing KKK Activities, New Orleans, Louisiana, 1982, https://www.sbc.net/resource-library/resolutions/resolution-on-ku-klux-klan/.

26 In Quick Reversal, Southern Baptists Denounce White Nationalists, Jacey Fortin, June 15, 2017, the New York Times, https://www.

nytimes.com/2017/06/15/us/southern-baptist-convention-alt-right-resolution.html.

27   Report on Slavery and Racism in the History of the Southern Baptist Theological Seminary, December 12, 2018, The Southern Baptist Theological Seminary, https://sbts-wordpress-uploads.s3.amazonaws.com/sbts/uploads/2018/12/Racism-and-the-Legacy-of-Slavery-Report-v4.pdf.

Vignette 9

28   James Bond (Agent 007) Hitting Women, https://www.youtube.com/watch?v=YJWfObq2cFk.

29A Wikipedia: Female MMA Champion Ronda Rousey's physical statistics, https://www.google.com/search?biw=1920&bih=1089&ei=iiWhXcemAs7J-gSz2JCICA&q=ronda+rousey+&oq=ronda+rousey+&gs_l=psy-ab.3..0i67i70i251j0i131j0l8.35764.38806..41161 ... 0.0..0.113.1501.16j1 ... 3..0 ... 1..gws-wiz ... ... 0i67j0i22i30.of2W8GwsIGE&ved=0ahUKEwjHk7a4wpXlAhXOpJ4KHTMsBIEQ4dUDCAs&uact=5.

29B Wikipedia: Male MMA Champion Conor McGregor's physical statistics, https://en.wikipedia.org/wiki/Conor_McGregor.

29C Wikipedia: Male boxing Champion Manny Pacquiao's physical statistics, https://en.wikipedia.org/wiki/Boxing_career_of_Manny_Pacquiao.

29D Wikipedia: Male boxing Champion Floyd Mayweather Jr. physical statistics, https://www.google.com/search?q=What+weight+does+Floyd+fight+at%3F&sa=X&ved=2ahUKEwiXutPMipXlAhVDrZ4KHWUABbEQzmd6BAgOEAs&biw=1920&bih=1089.

Vignette 11

30   PDF, *Foxe's Book of Martyrs,* Tufts University Digital Library, https://dl.tufts.edu/pdfviewer/sn00b904s/t435gr109.